Adventures of Garibaldi

Anthony Di Perno

Full Court Press
Englewood Cliffs, New Jersey

First Edition

Copyright © 2006 by Anthony Di Perno

Published in the United States of America
by Full Court Press, 601 Palisade Avenue,
Englewood Cliffs, NJ 07632.
www.fcpress.com

ISBN 0-9772681-0-1

Editing and book design by Barry Sheinkopf

Colophon by Liz Sedlack

Author photo by Mark Dian

*Cover: hand-tinted albumin print by John Clarck, 1861, courtesy
National Portrait Gallery, London*

DEDICATION

*To all Americans of Italian descent
who nurture a great pride in their
Italian cultural heritage*

Garibaldi, engraved from a photograph presented by him to T. White

Author's Note

Of the great men of the 19th century, none was more colorful than the swashbuckling revolutionary Giuseppe Garibaldi. His heroics in the cause of freedom both in Europe and South America made him "the hero of two worlds"—the Old World and the New.

Known mainly as a soldier and adventurer, Garibaldi was also a sea captain and, as such, was sometimes cast in the role of a swashbuckling corsair with a price on his head. His incredible exploits on land and sea captured the imagination of the people and made him appear invincible to a world hungry for romantic heroes. Journalists hailed him as a "great liberator" and the "champion of the oppressed" in the struggle against tyranny.

Coming from humble beginnings, Garibaldi had an understanding of ordinary people that goes far toward explaining his great following among the masses. His victories on the battlefields of South America made him and his "Red Shirts" legendary, and his conquest of southern Italy prompted an American diplomat to describe him as "Hercules, George Washington, and Robin Hood all rolled up into one."

During his lifetime, Garibaldi attracted an almost fanatical devotion that knew no national boundaries. Virtually everywhere he went, he created euphoria. The tumultuous welcome accorded him by the people of England during his visit there in 1864 shocked Queen Victoria and sent tremors throughout the European royal establishment.

Adversity also contributed to Garibaldi's popularity by helping to create an aura of invincibility about him. In 1834, his involvement in revolutionary activity led a Piedmontese court to sentence him to death in absentia. Branded an "enemy of the state," he was forced to flee from his homeland under an assumed name. He wandered the world for nearly eighteen years, journeying to North Africa, South America, New York, and the Far East. He was imprisoned three times and once brutally tortured. He was wounded many times and endured severe physical hardship. He was snubbed by royalty and betrayed by politicians. Still, he remained a determined foe of tyranny and oppression.

As a youth, Garibaldi envisioned a united Italy with Rome as its capital. He then spent a lifetime striving to make that vision a reality. He proved that exemplary courage and determination could overcome all obstacles in the struggle to create a united Italy. He accomplished his goal in 1860 when he liberated southern Italy from the Bourbons and handed the conquered territories over to King Victor Emmanuel of Savoy. Taking nothing for himself, he then retired to his farm on the desolate island of Caprera.

Even in retirement, Garibaldi was a force to be reckoned with. Twice he returned to lead expeditions for the liberation of Rome, and once for the liberation of Venetia. In the Franco-Prussian War, he was given command of a French army and, once again, distinguished himself in battle. During the U.S. Civil War, President Abraham Lincoln offered him a command in the federal army with the rank of major general. Garibaldi was told that, if he accepted the position, the name of LaFayette would not surpass his in the annals of American history. Garibaldi politely refused the offer, citing other impending duties.

Today, more than 120 years after his death, Garibaldi remains a greater-than-life figure, his heroics forever enshrined in legend and folklore. He is recognized as a national hero in Italy as well as in Uruguay. The Catholic Church has even forgiven his attacks on the Papacy. Literally thousands of streets, plazas, and buildings have been named for him in countless municipalities around the world. Elite army units bear his name, and the so-called "Garibaldi sign" with only the forefinger extended upward has become synonymous with being "number one." And it has been recorded more than once that Garibaldi actually gave a needy person "the shirt off his back."

Garibaldi's legacy is one of unselfish devotion to the cause of Italian unification. He was the driving force behind the *Risorgimento*, and his was the sword that unified Italy. However, it must be said of Garibaldi that, in the course of modern history, no other person did more for his country and received so little in return.

—Anthony Di Perno
February 2006

ACKNOWLEDGEMENTS

This book owes a great deal to those who have helped me see it through. First and foremost, I want to thank my wife Mary. Without her efforts, it would have been impossible for me to have finished this manuscript in the time period that it took to complete.

I also wish to thank Carol Lutchen, self-publishing consultant at Tech-Repro, Inc., in Hackensack, New Jersey, whose advice and guidance proved invaluable in preparing the book for print.

I want to acknowledge the fine work of Barry Sheinkopf, Director of The Writing Center in Englewood Cliffs, New Jersey, and publisher of Full Court Press, who meticulously edited and designed the book. Barry was also instrumental in the selection of many of the photographs and illustrations.

Special thanks goes to my dear friends Joseph and Diane Jesuele for the use of their photos of Garibaldi's house and of the Church of San Francisco de Asis in Montevideo, Uruguay.

My thanks as well for the assistance of John Dabbene, Chairperson, and Emily Gear, Curator/Director, of the Garibaldi-Meucci Museum in Staten Island, New York, where I was able to gain access to some rare copies of documents, letters, and publications on the Italian *Risorgimento*. The Museum's library contains a valuable collection of books on Garibaldi, including early biographies by Theodore Dwight, Alexandre Dumas, Elpis Melena, Jessie White Mario, and George Trevelyan. Also on hand is an assortment of books and other publications that provide insight into virtually every aspect of Garibaldi's life. The availability of this great reservoir of information enabled me to gather and piece together the intricate details of my subject's tumultuous life.

This book includes a chronological series of discourses and narrations dealing with various aspects of Garibaldi's life, including family relations, capricious escapades, political entanglements, and military undertakings, all of it embellished with a collection of love stories and folk tales about the flamboyant hero.

I want to thank Italo Ciampoli for his translation of the book into the Italian language.

And finally, I wish to extend my gratitude to all those dear friends whose encouragement gave me the impetus to see this monumental work through to its completion.

All photographs not otherwise identified are by the author, who wishes as well to gratefully acknowledge the following for permission to include various pictures and illustrations:

- National Portrait Gallery, London, for the hand-tinted albumin print by John Clarck (1861) which appears on the cover.

- New York Public Library Digital Gallery, for "Engraving of Garibaldi from a photograph presented by him to T. White," following dedication page; "Garibaldi after the Battle of Salto (by Gaetano Gallino), p. 128; the portrait of Sarah Margaret Fuller, p. 162; "Garibaldi disembarks with Anita at Magnavacca" (by Emilio Paggioaro), p. 193; "General Garibaldi," from a portrait by Orsini, p. 262; "Count Cavour," p. 273; "Departure of Garibaldi and his followers on the night of May 5, 1860," p. 283; "General Giuseppe Garibaldi on the cover of Harper's Weekly, June 9, 1860," p. 292; "Garibaldi welcoming Victor Emmanuel II as King of Italy," p. 343; "King Victor Emmanuel visits the dying Cavour," p. 364; "Garibaldi lands in Southampton," p. 380; "Garibaldi greeted by Alfred, Lord Tennyson at Farringford Hall" (from the *Illustrated London News*, April 23, 1864), p. 380; and "King Victor Emmanuel II," p. 418.

- cronologia@cronologia.it (Franco Gonzato), "Giuseppe Mazzini," p. 13.

- promobrasil@ciliberti.191.it (Attilio Ciliberti), "Statue of Anita in front of the Old Town Hall in Laguna," p. 48; "Salon where La Republica Juliana was proclaimed on July 29, 1839," p. 48; "Anita's cottage in Laguna," p. 56.

- info@pmnews.it (Giuseppe and Claudia Campana), "The Royal Palace at Caserta," p. 344.

- Wikipedia, the free encyclopedia, "Bento Gonçalves," p. 36; "Juan Manuel de Rosas," p. 84; "Napoleon III of France," p. 249; "Pope Pius IX," p. 396.

❧

LIST OF MAPS

Contents

1

Young Peppino

GIUSEPPE GARIBALDI WAS BORN July 4, 1807, in Nice, which at that time was part of the empire of Napoleon Bonaparte. Records of his birth show that he was originally given his Christian name in the French form, Joseph Marie Garibaldi. However, after Napoleon's defeat in 1814, Nice reverted to the Kingdom of Sardinia, and the youngster officially became Giuseppe Garibaldi. The language that Giuseppe grew up with was a local Ligurian dialect called *Nizzard*. French was his second language. It wasn't until he was in his teens that he learned the Italian language, but his accent revealed that it was not his natural tongue.

Nice, or *Nizza* as it is called in Italian, is located on the Mediterranean coast, and Garibaldi was born in the old port section of the city. His father, Domenico Garibaldi, was a sailor who came from the town of Chiavari in what used to be the Republic of Genoa. In 1794, Domenico married Rosa Raimondi, a girl whose family had also moved from Genoese territory to Nice. The couple had six children: Maria Elizabetta, who died at the age of two, Angelo, Giuseppe, Michele, Felice, and Teresa. The Garibaldi family lived in a house facing on the harbor front at the north side of the old port. All of the Garibaldi children except for Teresa were born in this house, which is no longer there. When the harbor was enlarged in 1897, the house was demolished, and the area is today covered with water.

In 1816, the Garibaldi family moved to a larger house on Quai Lunel, the street which runs along the west side of the harbor front. This is where Teresa was born, and where Giuseppe and his brothers spent their childhood. The modest, three-story house at No. 3 Quai Lunel is still there today. However, it sits somewhat inconspicuously and would go unnoticed if it were not for the small marble plaque beneath one of the window sills. The plaque commemorating Giuseppe Garibaldi, was placed there by the Italian Society of Charity on the fiftieth anniversary of his death. Aside from this simple plaque, the site has nothing to commemorate the legendary hero who once lived there—there is no museum, no souvenir shop, and no information office. But then, we must remember, this is France and not Italy.

Today, the house faces out on a harbor filled with luxurious yachts and pleasure craft—it is, after all, the Riviera. In the time of Garibaldi, the same harbor was crowded with sailboats and fishing craft. This was the waterfront where young Giuseppe, or "Peppino" as he was called, would hang out and talk to the sailors and fishermen. He listened to their stories of the sea while he learned to tie knots, trim sails, and mend nets. Sometimes, the fishermen even allowed him to come along when they went trawling for shellfish.

The harbor in Nice

The Garibaldi family home, No. 3 Quai Lunel, Nice

As a youngster, Peppino exhibited the reckless courage so char-acteristic of him in later years. When he was only eight years old, he saved a woman from drowning. The story goes that she was washing clothes when she lost her balance and fell head first into deep water. Without hesitating, Peppino dove into the water and pulled her to safety! This daring rescue cast him in the role of a hero, one he was destined to play for the rest of his life. Again at age twelve, he saved three boys from drowning when their boat capsized. There are at least a dozen more recorded incidents in which Peppino Garibaldi saved someone from drowning.[1] Garibaldi himself never remembered learning how to swim but seemed to have been born a natural swimmer.

On days when he didn't frequent the waterfront, Peppino would go hiking in the hills above Nice. He would hike alone for hours, enjoying the solitude and acquiring a love for nature. He also enjoyed hunting game in the woods, and as he grew older, he became an excellent marksman. As a youngster, he attended church regularly, and for a while, his parents wanted him to become a priest. However, his love of the sea convinced them that the priesthood was not his vocation. As it turned out, he later acquired a dislike for priests and considered the Church an obstacle to the unification of Italy.

For the most part, Peppino's childhood was a happy one. His parents were kind and loving, and though he expressed his desire to become a sailor, they insisted that he receive a good education. They hired a private tutor to teach him proper Italian as well as mathematics, geography, and astronomy. Afterwards, he was sent to a school in Genoa, but his lack of interest in the academics caused him to drop out. So he got his way and became a sailor like his father and three brothers. When he was sixteen, he sailed to

Odessa, in Russia, as a cabin boy on a ship named the *Costanza*. The following year, he sailed on his father's ship, the *Santa Reparata*, to Rome with a load of wine. The year was 1825, and it was Peppino's first visit to the Eternal City.[2]

Rome is called the Eternal City because it is one of the oldest continuously inhabited municipalities in the world. According to legend, the city was founded in 753 B.C. by the twin Latin princes, Romulus and Remus. It grew in size and power to become the capital of the mighty Roman Empire. Although the Empire eventually fell, the city remained as an undying symbol of past Roman glory. Rome was also the seat of the Papacy and the spiritual center of most of the Christian world. Whereas Domenico Garibaldi saw Rome as a holy city, young Peppino began to envision it as the capital of a united Italy. It was a vision which would become a reality forty-six years later.

2

The Merchant Seaman:
1825—1833

THE FORMATIVE PERIOD IN GARIBALDI'S LIFE occurred during his tenure as a merchant seaman. It was then that he gained the knowledge and the expertise that would prove invaluable in his later endeavors. From 1825 to 1833, he pursued a career that led him to distant lands and introduced him to different cultures. These voyages across the dangerous waters of the Mediterranean exposed him to many perils and sometimes caused him to endure severe hardships.

Garibaldi was to get his first taste of battle when his ship, the *Cortese*, came under attack by pirates. Pirate attacks were a frequent occurrence in that part of the world, and more than once did

Garibaldi barely escape with his life. After one such attack, in which the *Cortese* was forced to surrender, the pirates plundered the ship, taking everything of value—including the crew's shoes and clothing! Garibaldi and the others had to make new clothes for themselves out of the material used for sails. Then at the next stop, they had to go ashore barefoot in search of supplies. In another attack, the pirates seized the ship's navigation equipment, leaving the crew to sail onward without any instruments to keep the ship on its course. These encounters with pirates later prompted Garibaldi to comment: "It is always better to fight when one is attacked than to yield without a struggle."[1]

During a voyage to Istanbul, Garibaldi became very ill and had to be left behind. He remained in Istanbul for many months, sustaining himself by tutoring youngsters in that city's small Italian community. He taught Italian, French, and mathematics, thus making good use of the academic education he had received as a youngster in Nice. Members of the Italian community came to his aid, and eventually he was able to book passage on a sailing ship and return to Nice in Spring 1831.[2]

All of these experiences served to instill in Garibaldi a sense of self-reliance that enabled him to persevere under the most adverse conditions. From these sea voyages, he had also developed a love for travel and adventure that was to remain with him for the rest of his life. And finally, he had become a skillful sailor, respected by both the officers and the other crewmen.

Upon returning to Nice from Istanbul in 1831, Garibaldi rushed to the house of his girlfriend, Francesca Roux, only to learn that she had married another man during his long absence. After more than two years of waiting, the girl had come to believe that her Peppino would never return. Without much to say, Garibaldi wished her happiness and left.[3] It was a sad ending to a true love story, and although Garibaldi was able to get over the initial heartache, he could never really forget her.

Garibaldi fared much better with his other love—the love of the sea. In 1832, he was granted his master's certificate as sea captain and was given his first command as captain of a ship named *Our Lady of Grace*. With her, he completed several short voyages in the Mediterranean. Then, for reasons unknown, he signed on as first mate of the *Clorinda*, a ship bound for the Russian port of Tagonrog on the Black Sea.

On this voyage, he met an exiled French revolutionary named Emile Barrault, a Saint Simonian Socialist who believed in universal brotherhood and the elimination of social classes. This would be achieved through the redistribution of wealth and the ownership of goods in common, concepts which were first put forth by the Count de Saint Simon, a French nobleman who had barely escaped the guillotine during the French Revolution of 1789. Like his mentor, Barrault was an idealist who envisioned a society of equals living peacefully in a communal environment. Garibaldi was impressed by his sincerity, and he did accept Saint Simon's doctrine of universal brotherhood. However, he rejected Saint Simon's socialistic economic theories, and throughout his life he remained a firm believer in private enterprise.

In the meantime, while Garibaldi was sailing the Mediterranean in search of a worthy cause, the rising tide of nationalism was sweeping across the region of Italy. The Italian national identity had begun to manifest itself after centuries of remaining dormant. This upsurge of Italian nationalistic fervor was called the *Risorgimento*, or "Resurgence," and it would eventually result in the formation of a united Italy. Garibaldi was not fully aware of the movement until his arrival in Tagonrog during his voyage on the *Clorinda* in 1833.

There he first met Giovanni Cuneo, an Italian sailor who talked about the Risorgimento and the doctrines of a secret society called *Young Italy*, the principal goal of which was the formation of a united Italian republic. The impetuous Garibaldi quickly expressed his desire to join the society, and in return, Cuneo gave him the names and addresses of contacts in Marseilles, France. These contacts were to introduce Garibaldi to the founder of Young Italy—Giuseppe Mazzini. Unknowingly, Cuneo had just recruited "the sword" that would eventually unify Italy.

3

The Revolutionary

Since the Renaissance, scholars had believed that there was some sort of bond between the people of the various states of the Italian Peninsula. They all spoke related dialects derived from Latin, and in ancient times this region had been at the very core of the Roman Empire. Could it be that these people were the descendants of the Ancient Romans? The sixteenth-century Florentine diplomat, Niccolo Machiavelli, thought so. In 1523, he published *The Prince*, a book on power politics. In it, Machiavelli called for the expulsion of foreign invaders from Italian soil and the unification of the nation under a strong leader, whom he goes on to describe in his book. Today Machiavelli ranks high on the list of early Italian nationalists.

The actual unification of Italy would prove to be a very difficult and almost impossible task to accomplish. People there did not think of themselves as Italians, but rather as Piedmontese, Lombards, Venetians, Genoese, Tuscans, Romans, Neapolitans, etc. A story dating back to 1764 recounts how a stranger entered a café in Milano and was asked whether he was a Milanese or a foreigner. The stranger replied that he was neither a Milanese nor a foreigner. He said that he was an Italian, and that an Italian was not a foreigner anywhere in Italy![1] The movement to establish Italian national identity got a jump start when the armies of Napoleon Bonaparte invaded Italy in 1802. He liberated northern Italy from the Austrians and ousted the Bourbons from Naples. Napoleon, whose parents were Italian, established his brother, Joseph Bonaparte, as King of Naples and declared himself King of Italy. The creation of the Kingdom of Italy marked the first time in modern times that a state had the name *Italy*.

Napoleon's brief rule over Italy was not unpopular. He abolished many of the outdated laws of the Old Regime, and he encouraged popular education and religious toleration. He built roads and bridges, and streamlined the old system of measurements. But more importantly, he did give the Italian people a sense of national identity.

Napoleon's rule became less popular when he suppressed republican and radical movements, and taxed the Italian people for the benefit of France. Nevertheless, the Italians never turned against Napoleon. The Italian regiments in his army fought with such valor that he was moved to design a special banner for them—a tricolor of red, white, and green. It was similar to the French tricolor, except that Napoleon substituted his favorite color, green, for the blue. Today, that banner is the flag of the Republic of Italy.

After Napoleon's defeat at Waterloo in 1815, the Congress of

Vienna redrew the map of Europe and reestablished the old regimes. Reactionary monarchs were returned to power, and radical revolutionaries were imprisoned. Most of Napoleon's reform measures were rescinded. The press was censored, and an elaborate spy network was created to inform the authorities of all subversive activities. A powerful multinational military force stood in readiness to crush any uprising that threatened the *status quo*. A period of severe repression followed.

During this period, the region of Italy remained divided into numerous small states—some of them independent, some ruled by the Papal authority, and some controlled by Austria. The Kingdom of Sardinia, in the north, was the strongest of the independent states. The so-called Papal States of central Italy were ruled by the Pope in Rome, and the rest of southern Italy was under the rule of the Bourbon dynasty of Naples. Almost all of the remaining states were controlled by Austria, either directly or through puppet rulers. A map of the region looked like a jigsaw puzzle. Yet this was the Italy that Italian nationalists would have to piece together in order to form a unified nation.

The victorious monarchs who attended the Congress of Vienna in 1815 believed that the ideals of the French Revolution had died with Napoleon's defeat. However, a new and more sinister form of opposition arose to carry on the struggle against oppression. The new revolutionaries would resort to clandestine warfare. They formed secret societies that organized revolts and carried out political assassinations. Unlike the Sicilian *Mafia* and the Neapolitan *Camorra*, these secret societies had political objectives.

The first of these secret societies was the *Carbonari*, or "charcoal burners." Centered in northern Italy, it also had branches in France and Spain. Its principal aim was the overthrow of autocratic governments and the establishment of egalitarian republics. One of its members was a young idealist from Genoa named Giuseppe Mazzini.

Giuseppe Mazzini

Mazzini was a brilliant political thinker and writer. However, he was also incapable of belonging to any group he did not dominate. He soon left the Carbonari but was betrayed to the police and arrested for engaging in subversive activity. He was imprisoned for three months and, upon his release, forced into exile. He went to live in Marseilles, France, where in 1832, he formed his own secret society, Young Italy. He also published a propaganda journal of the same name and had it smuggled across the border into Italy. The journal called upon Italians to overthrow foreign rule and unify Italy as a republic. Many Italian patriots were attracted to the cause of unification and joined Mazzini's Young Italy Society.

Garibaldi, who had heard of him and been given the name of someone to contact in Marseilles for a personal meeting with Mazzini, was one of them. Upon his return to Marseilles late in 1833, Garibaldi did meet the contact, who then led him to the house of a French radical named Demosthenes Oliver. Oliver introduced him to Mazzini. Garibaldi was so impressed by Mazzini that he decided to join Young Italy. He took an oath "in the name of God and the Martyrs of Italy to fight against injustice and tyranny, and for a free and unified Italy."[2] He was given the code name *Borel*, through which he could make contact with other members of the Society. It was the beginning of his career as a revolutionary.

As a member of Young Italy, Garibaldi received the dangerous assignment of enrolling in the Sardinian Royal Navy for the purpose of instigating a mutiny. He was assigned to the frigate *Euridice* and listed in the ship's register as a seaman, third class. The register also contained one of the few authentic descriptions of Garibaldi's physical appearance. He was described as being five feet, seven inches tall and having reddish hair, an aquiline nose, and chestnut-colored eyes.

Garibaldi and a fellow crewman named Edoardo Mutru began agitating for a mutiny, which was planned to coincide with an armed uprising in Genoa. The revolt took place as planned on February 4, 1834, but it was quickly crushed by the authorities. Garibaldi, who had left his ship to join the uprising in town, soon learned that the revolt had failed to materialize and that the perpetrators had been arrested. Although he was implicated in the attempted mutiny, he was able to dodge the police with the help of a pretty shopkeeper named Teresina Forzano. She hid him in the back of her store and then gave him one of her husband's suits. The next day, dressed as a civilian, he made his way to the house of a woman whom he knew by the name of Caterina. She gave him food and drink and allowed him to remain there until nightfall. Under cover of darkness, he set out again, following a series of narrow, winding alleyways which eventually led him out of the city.[3] Accounts of Garibaldi's escape from Genoa are somewhat confusing, but it appears that he was sheltered in the homes of several different women, including Teresina, Caterina, and Natalie, before he departed from the city. Garibaldi later commented that "women are angels in that kind of situation," and when he retired to Caprera, he received letters from these women who had helped him escape. In response, he wrote letters of thanks to each of these "angels."

Garibaldi spent the next ten days hiking through the mountains along lonely footpaths. He travelled by night and slept in the brush during the day. After an exhaustive journey of almost two hundred miles, he finally reached Nice. There, he recounted the story of the attempted mutiny to his parents. They were shocked by what he had done. This was the son they'd hoped would become a priest! They decided that it would be best for him if he escaped to France. He was accompanied by two of his friends to the frontier, where he entered France by swimming across the Var River. From the other side, he waved goodbye and then disappeared into the brush. He would not return for fourteen years, and he would never see his father again.

Upon his arrival, Garibaldi was detained by the police in the town of Draguignan, but he escaped by jumping out of a window and hiding in the nearby fields. Stopping at an inn, he narrowly avoided being apprehended by speaking fluent French and singing popular Provencal songs in a songfest held in the inn. His fine tenor voice so impressed the guests that the innkeeper didn't even bother asking for his identification papers. He stayed the night and then left for Marseilles in the morning.[4]

After reaching Marseilles, Garibaldi made contact with the members of Young Italy, who found him a place to stay near the old harbor. As an illegal immigrant, he needed a new identity. Luckily, he found an English seaman named Joseph Pane who willingly sold him his identification papers. This enabled Garibaldi to resume his career as a merchant seaman under the assumed name. It turned out to be a scary existence, living in constant fear of being apprehended by the authorities and sent back to Genoa. By now, Garibaldi had learned that he had been found guilty of high treason by a naval court in Genoa and sentenced to death in absentia.[5] His friend, Mutru, had been arrested and charged with insurrection. He was found guilty and sentenced to prison.

During his stay in Marseilles, Garibaldi saved a French schoolboy from drowning in the harbor. The youngster, Joseph Ramboud, was playfully jumping from one boat to another when he suddenly slipped and fell into the water. Garibaldi, who saw the mishap, alertly dove in and, after three attempts, managed to pull the boy from beneath one of the boats and to the safety of the dock. The daring rescue was witnessed by an applauding crowd of spectators and by an anxious Madame Ramboud.[6] The boy and his mother warmly thanked their hero, who identified himself as Joseph Pane, seaman. Neither of them knew who he really was.

At that time it was unwise for Garibaldi to reveal his true identity, because every government in Europe was clamping down on the revolutionary activity of political exiles. France was no exception. As police surveillance increased, life in Marseilles became more difficult for these illegal refugees. Garibaldi now made the decision to go to South America. In September 1835, he secured passage on a French ship called the *Nautounier*, which was bound for Rio de Janeiro, Brazil. He signed on as Giuseppe Pane and served as a crewman during the long voyage across the Atlantic. He would not return to Europe until 1848.

4

The Exile

FROM THE TIME OF THE CONQUISTADORES until the early 1800s, nearly all of South America was part of the Spanish and Portuguese colonial empires. Only three small enclaves on the northeast coast of the continent, and some of the islands in the Caribbean, belonged to the British, the Dutch, and the French. The vast territory on the east coast of South America known as Brazil belonged to the Kingdom of Portugal. The remainder of the continent was part of the Spanish Empire.

Napoleon's defeat of Spain sparked a series of revolutions in South America that led to the establishment of nine independent republics by 1821—Venezuela, Colombia, Equador, Peru, Bolivia, Chile, Paraguay, Argentina, and Uruguay. The leading figure in the revolution against Spanish rule was Simon Bolivar, who came to be known in the Americas as *the Great Liberator*.

While the Spanish colonies were gaining their independence, events in the Portuguese colony of Brazil took a somewhat different twist. During the Napoleonic Wars, King John VI of Portugal had moved the royal court from Lisbon in Portugal to Rio de Janeiro, where he remained until after the conflict in Europe was over. The king eventually returned to Portugal in 1821, leaving his son, Dom Pedro, to rule over Brazil as regent. However, when a liberal revolt broke out a year later, Dom Pedro unexpectedly joined with the revolutionaries and issued a proclamation declaring Brazil's independence. Three months later, he was crowned Emperor Pedro I of Brazil. Pedro's liberal policies eventually brought him into conflict with conservative elements in the country and he was forced to abdicate in 1832. He was succeeded by his five-year-old son, Pedro II, who ruled through a regent named Antonio de Feijo.

The regent's ultra-conservative policies pleased the wealthy classes, but his high-handed manner of dealing with the Brazilian parliament caused much resentment among the liberal elements around the country. Few Brazilians were surprised when the southernmost province of Rio Grande do Sul revolted in 1835. The revolt was led by General Bento Gonçalves, a wealthy rancher who believed that his province would fare better as an independent republic. The Brazilian government refused recognition, and civil war ensued. It was against this backdrop of events that Garibaldi arrived in Rio de Janeiro late in 1835.

Sugar Loaf Mountain was the first site to catch Garibaldi's eye as he sailed into Rio harbor and was rowed ashore by Black African slaves. At that time, the city had a population of slightly less than 200,000, over half of whom were slaves. Rio was a classic

Portuguese colonial city with bright-colored houses and bright sandy beaches. The city was dotted with spacious plazas where fountains spouted water into the balmy air. Palm trees and lush tropical vegetation added to the city's exotic dreamlike appearance. The pace of life was slow and somewhat laid back.

During the early 1800s, many foreigners had come to live in Rio de Janeiro. Some of these were Italians who had come in the hope of starting a new life in the New World. Coming to a foreign land and unable to speak the language, Garibaldi experienced loneliness and despair, and the urge to return home. Nevertheless, he persevered and sought to make new friends. One day, while walking in the city's main square, he met a young Italian journalist named Luigi Rossetti. It was the beginning of a great friendship.

Garibaldi and Rossetti became partners in the business of selling provisions, mainly pasta, to the many Italian restaurants that had sprung up in Rio and at the nearby coastal town of Cabo Frio. They borrowed money and purchased a sailing ship, which they renamed the *Mazzini*. Using his experience as a sea captain, Garibaldi sailed the *Mazzini* back and forth between Rio and Cabo Frio, delivering supplies to restaurants. The ship flew the red, white, and green tricolor which Young Italy had adopted as its banner. This greatly annoyed the Sardinian consul in Rio, who reported to his government that a wanted fugitive named Garibaldi had been sailing his ship in and out of Rio harbor flying the Italian tricolor.[1] The consul also complained about this to the local authorities, but nothing was done about it.

When their joint business venture failed to show a profit, Rossetti and Garibaldi decided to give it up. But though he had failed in business, Garibaldi had succeeded in gaining the friendship of other Italian expatriates in Rio. Some of these belonged to

Young Italy. He also joined a Freemasons' lodge in Rio.[2] Freemasonry in South America was associated with revolutionary movements, whereas in Europe it had become an organization mainly of wealthy businessmen. The Catholic Church denounced Freemasonry as an anti-Catholic society, because its members sub-scribed to a ritual and doctrine that seemed to conflict with church dogma. Other critics accused the Freemasons of being a front organization for revolutionary groups. Consequently, many European monarchs looked upon Freemasonry as a seditious and revolutionary organization.

While in Rio, Garibaldi also gained attention by saving a man from drowning, this time a Black. One Sunday while he was on the waterfront, an African slave fell into the harbor. While onlookers stood and watched, Garibaldi, who was dressed in a suit and tie, dove into the water and pulled him to safety.[3] The rescue created a sensation, because such bravado for the life of a slave was rare in the Brazil of 1836. For Garibaldi, it was just another way of manifest-ing his desire to help his fellow man.

5

The Corsair

AFTER LIVING IN RIO DE JANEIRO for more than a year, Garibaldi began to feel restless and sought to engage in some sort of revolutionary activity to help the cause of Italian unification. He even entertained the thought of becoming a corsair and attacking Sardinian and Austrian merchant ships off the coast of Brazil. However, he soon discarded the idea in favor of joining the fight for the independence of Brazil's break-away province of Rio Grande do Sul.

When the insurrection broke out there early in 1835, the Brazilian government had dispatched military and naval forces to put down the revolt. The revolutionary leaders, including Bento Gonçalves and his secretary, Tito Zambecarri, had been captured and imprisoned, but the rest of the Riograndense rebels had withdrawn into the interior to continue the struggle for independence. Shortly after his imprisonment, Gonçalves escaped by swimming out to a waiting boat, which then took him down the coast to Rio Grande do Sul. Zambecarri, however, did not escape, and remained in prison in Rio de Janeiro.

Garibaldi's friend, Rossetti, had known Zambecarri back in Italy, and the two now got permission to visit the latter in prison. During their visit, Zambecarri suggested that they use their schooner to help the war effort against the Brazilian imperial forces. Garibaldi, who had come to sympathize with the Riograndense cause, then offered to fight as a privateer under the banner of Rio Grande do Sul. The offer was secretly relayed to officials in the rebel government of the break-away state.

At that time, the practice of privateering was permitted under international law, although some governments considered it nothing more than legalized piracy. The system permitted a private citizen to attack and pillage the ships of nations at war with his own country. For this venture, certain letters of marque had to be issued by the established government of a nation at war, which in this case was Rio Grande do Sul. The letters would authorize a private citizen such as Garibaldi to arm and outfit his ship for the purpose of raiding enemy shipping. These letters of authorization were duly signed by General Lima of the Riograndense Army on November 14, 1836.[1] It would be another six months before the documents reached Garibaldi in Rio de Janeiro.

While awaiting them, Garibaldi was arming and equipping his schooner for war. The work was done near the fish market in Rio harbor, right under the noses of the port officials. He enlisted a crew of about eight men, most of whom were Italian.

Among them were Luigi Carniglia, Maurizio Garibaldi (no relation to Giuseppe), and his former co-conspirator, Edoardo Mutru, who had recently been released from a Genoese prison. The journalist, Luigi Rossetti, was to go along as a passenger. The ship was stocked with fish, dried meat, and flour. Beneath these provisions were hidden guns and ammunition.

Garibaldi received the letters of marque from Rio Grande do Sul on May 4, 1837. Three days later, the *Mazzini* sailed out of Rio harbor, having received clearance from the port officials. Garibaldi had applied for port clearance under the assumed name of Cipriano Alves and had falsely stated that he was transporting a cargo of meat up the coast to the town of Campos.[2] Thus he began his career as a corsair and adventurer. As he sailed southward toward the rebellious state of Rio Grande do Sul, he experienced an intense feeling of freedom. He was now the master of his own destiny, and he was in his own element—the sea.

Shortly after leaving Rio de Janeiro, Garibaldi attacked and captured a large ship. She was the *Louisa*, a sixty-ton Brazilian schooner bound for Europe. She was carrying a few passengers and a large cargo of coffee. Although the *Louisa* was much larger than Garibaldi's ship, she was unarmed and offered no resistance. He took possession of the ship and its cargo in the name of the government of Rio Grande. At the sight of Garibaldi's villainous-looking crew, one frightened passenger offered him a box containing three diamonds as the price for his life. Garibaldi, who did not wish to rob the passengers of their valuables, gave the box back, assuring the man that his life was not in danger. He told him "to keep the diamonds for an occasion when they might be more useful."[3] He did, however, seize some jewels that belonged to the ship's owner.

As the *Louisa* was the larger and better ship, Garibaldi transferred his armaments and equipment to it, and then scuttled his own ship. Although there is some disagreement among writers as to whether he renamed the captured ship the *Mazzini* or the *Farroupilha*, evidence indicates that it was rechristened the *Mazzini*.[4]

Sailing further south along the Brazilian coast, Garibaldi allowed the captured crew and passengers to take their personal belongings and row ashore in the ship's long-boat. This kind act deprived his crew of a lifeboat. He also set free several African slaves who were on board the *Louisa*.[5] In doing so, he demonstrated his opposition to slavery or human bondage of any kind. The released captives immediately reported what had happened to the Brazilian authorities, who labeled the seizure of the *Louisa* as "an act of piracy." Thus, Garibaldi acquired the reputation of being a "pirate," a reputation that stayed with him for the duration of his stay in South America.

Although Garibaldi loved the role of a swashbuckling privateer, he was not a pirate in the purest sense of the term. He was too much of an idealist to be a soldier of fortune seeking personal reward. He sincerely believed that he was fighting for a cause—the cause of freedom. Although he attacked ships indiscriminately, he treated his captives humanely, even providing them with safe passage to shore. Under international law at that time, his seizure of ships in South American waters were lawful acts of privateering against a belligerent foe.

Continuing on his southward course, Garibaldi found it too risky to put into any port along the coast of Rio Grande do Sul. He knew that Brazilian imperial forces controlled most of the coastal towns, and that a Brazilian naval squadron under Captain John

Grenfell was patrolling the coastal waters.*

Garibaldi decided to sail farther down the coast to Uruguay in search of supplies: He understood that the government of Uruguay was neutral in the Brazilian civil war and would allow ships from both sides to dock in its ports. Having rounded the southern tip of Uruguay, he then sailed his ship into the port of Maldonado. Maldonado is now known as Punta del Este and is a popular seaside resort town.

Garibaldi's stay in Maldonado was an eventful one. He purchased some supplies for his ship and sold the cargo of coffee and a few jewels, which he claimed belonged to the ship's former owner, to a local merchant. The merchant promised to pay him later. Since Garibaldi and his crew didn't conceal their identity, it wasn't long before the Brazilian consul in Maldonado learned that the privateers were in town. He promptly asked the Uruguayan government to arrest them and seize the *Louisa*, which Garibaldi had renamed the *Mazzini*. President Manuel Oribe of Uruguay then ordered their arrest.

However, before the order could be carried out, Garibaldi learned of the government's decision and ordered his crew to prepare to sail. One last-minute matter remained—he had not yet received payment for the coffee and jewels! The merchant who purchased them was hoping that Garibaldi would be arrested, and that he wouldn't have to pay him. But Garibaldi was in dire need of money and decided to pay the merchant a last-minute visit. He went to the merchant's house armed with two pistols and, at gun point, forced the conniver to pay him for the coffee and jewels.[6]

---

*Captain John Grenfell was an Englishman in the service of Brazil who became Commander-in-Chief of the Royal Brazilian Navy.

Money in hand, he rushed to his ship and sailed out to sea. Shortly afterward a Brazilian warship arrived at Maldonado—too late to capture "the pirates."

A storm prevented Garibaldi from sailing eastward into the Atlantic Ocean, so he turned to the west, up the estuary of the La Plata River. His hurried departure had prevented him from taking on adequate food supplies, thus making it necessary for the ship to make another stop. Unable to put into any other Uruguayan port, Garibaldi sailed along the desolate coast in search of a safe place to land. Eventually, he spotted a lonely farmhouse in the distance and decided to go ashore in search of food. But getting ashore posed a problem, because the ship's only lifeboat had been used to put ashore the original crew of the *Louisa*. Garibaldi had not replaced the boat in Maldonado and he was now forced to improvise. Using a makeshift raft comprised of a cabin table tied to a couple of casks, Garibaldi and a crewman named Maurizio made it to the shore, the raft being carried along by the waves. Once there, they reached the farmhouse, where they were kindly received by a gaucho and his wife. Several hours later, they were able to return to the ship through the heavy surf, hauling the carcass of a bullock on top of the table raft.[7] The bullock had been given to them by the generous gaucho, who you could say had literally put food on the table!

During the stop, Garibaldi's ship had been sighted from the shore, and the Uruguayan authorities quickly dispatched a gunboat to intercept it. It overtook the *Mazzini* and demanded its immediate surrender. When Garibaldi refused to obey, the gunboat opened fire, and a fierce struggle ensued. There was an exchange of volleys from the decks of both ships as the gunboat came alongside the *Mazzini* and her crew prepared to board it.

Garibaldi and his men beat back the boarding party, inflicting heavy losses. During the violent action, Garibaldi's helmsman was killed and he himself was shot in the neck, the bullet lodging behind his ear. He fell to the deck unconscious as his crew fought on bravely. The Uruguayan gunboat soon broke off the action, and the *Mazzini* was able to slip away to the west. With Garibaldi seriously wounded, Luigi Carniglia took the helm and piloted the *Mazzini* safely into the Argentine port of Gualeguay some twelve days after the sea-fight.[8] Uruguayan warships dared not pursue them, for they had now entered the forbidding domain of Juan Manuel de Rosas.

6

Gualeguay

ON JUNE 27, 1837, the *Mazzini* put into the port of Gualeguay, a small town of 2,000 people located in the Argentine province of Entre-Rios. There, Garibaldi and his crew asked for political asylum. However, at that time, diplomatic relations between Argentina and Brazil were already strained, so the question of granting asylum to these privateers had to be referred to the Argentine government in Buenos Aires. In the meantime, Garibaldi and his crew were to be dealt with as prisoners of war and ordered to remain in the town of Gualeguay until the government reached a decision on their petition for asylum.

Of greater urgency was the matter of obtaining medical treatment for Garibaldi, who was hovering between life and death. Governor Pascual Echaque of Entre-Rios now stepped in to help.

He brought in a doctor named Ramon del Arco to perform surgery on Garibaldi. The operation took place in the house of a Spanish merchant named Jacinto Abreu. Dr. del Arco removed the bullet from Garibaldi's neck, thus saving his life.[1] The operation was carried out without the use of anaesthesia and caused Garibaldi to suffer great pain. He would remain to convalesce in Abreu's house, where he was nursed by Señora Abreu and his friend, Luigi Carniglia.

The healing process was slow, but Garibaldi fully recovered after three months. He was placed on parole by Governor Echaque and allowed to remain at Abreu's homestead and to go about freely, on one condition—that he give his word of honor not to try to escape. Garibaldi agreed to the condition. What he didn't know was that Argentine dictator, Juan Manuel de Rosas, had reached a decision about the *Louisa* and the privateers. Rosas decided that the ship was to be returned to its Brazilian owners. The privateers were to be set free—except for Garibaldi. He was to remain detained indefinitely at Gualeguay. Thereupon, the freed crewmen boarded a ship sailing for Montevideo. They reached Montevideo without incident and then made plans to join the rebels in Rio Grande do Sul.

As for Garibaldi, he remained in Gualeguay living in Abreu's house. He developed a friendship with several of the families in town and came to know many of the local inhabitants. In those times, Gualeguay resembled a pioneer town in the western United States. It was located in the sparsely populated Province of Entre-Rios, where cattle raising was the principal occupation. Many of the ranchers were immigrants from Spain, France, Italy, and the British Isles. Occasionally, they would come in to Gualeguay to sell cattle and hides and to purchase supplies. Maintaining law and order was the responsibility of the local military commander, Major Leonardo Millan. Although they seldom saw each other, Millan scrutinized Garibaldi's every move. Millan had been instructed by Governor Echaque to show Garibaldi "every consideration"—as long as he didn't attempt to escape.[2]

During his time in Gualeguay, Garibaldi mastered two skills that would prove very valuable to him later: He learned to speak Spanish, and he learned to ride a horse. In the land of the gaucho, good horsemanship was an essential requirement. He also spent some of his time reading outdated newspapers in an attempt to learn what was happening in the rest of the world. Had Garibaldi not been a restless revolutionary, he might have been happy in the beautiful surroundings of Gualeguay. As it was, he resented being forcibly detained and longed to join the rebels in Rio Grande do Sul in their struggle for independence from the Empire of Brazil.

After being in Gualeguay for six months, Garibaldi learned from friends that the authorities were planning to send him to the district of Paraná, an isolated place from which he feared he would never return. He was told by friends that this would be his last chance to escape. So Garibaldi decided to break his parole and attempt to escape. However, he realized that he needed some help.

According to local folklore, he was aided in his escape by Jacinto Abreu, who provided him with a horse and pistol. Another friend provided Garibaldi with a professional a guide named Juan Pérez. Pérez was to take him to the ranch of an English settler located on the banks of the Paraná River, where he would be sheltered until he could be stowed away on a boat going to Montevideo in Uruguay.

The events that ensued are shrouded in mystery and suspense, and accounts of what happened are somewhat confusing.

However, according to a story recounted by the locals, Garibaldi and his guide set off from Gualeguay, on a rainy night, heading toward the Paraná River. After riding all night in the soaking rain, they arrived at an isolated ranch. The guide then told Garibaldi to wait in the woods while he went ahead to see if it was safe to enter the rancher's house. An exhausted Garibaldi dismounted, tied his horse to a tree, lay down to rest, and fell asleep. He awoke three hours later to discover that the guide had not returned!

When he crept to the edge of the woods to see if he could sight him, he was suddenly set upon by soldiers on horseback with drawn swords. As the soldiers were between him and the place where he had left his horse, escape was impossible. Garibaldi was forced to surrender to the soldiers.[3]

These events leave many unanswered questions. What happened to Garibaldi's guide? Where did the soldiers come from, and how did they know where to find Garibaldi? Was Garibaldi set up by the authorities in Gualeguay, or was he betrayed by a friend? Garibaldi could not provide these answers himself, but he never accused the guide of having betrayed him. Nevertheless, the circumstances of his capture seemed very suspicious, thus causing much speculation about what really happened that fateful morning.

This is where local folklore attempts to provide some of the answers. It says that the guide, instead of taking Garibaldi to the banks of the Paraná, had actually led him around in a large circle to the vicinity of an army camp. Then, under guise of going to investigate the ranch house, he had gone to the camp and informed the soldiers of Garibaldi's whereabouts.

Garibaldi was taken back to Gualeguay. The soldiers made him ride on his horse with his hands and feet tied while the mosquitos attacked him mercilessly. Virtually his entire body was covered with bites. When they reached their destination, he was whipped and brutally tortured by the military commander, Major Millan. In an attempt to make him reveal the names of his accomplices, he was hung by the wrists to a beam in the roof. With the whole of his weight on his wrists, and with his feet about five feet off the ground, he was asked by Millan to reveal the names of his accomplices. As Millan was standing almost directly beneath him, Garibaldi was able to spit in his face. Millan abruptly left, leaving Garibaldi hanging there in intense pain. After two hours, he lost consciousness; and when he awoke, he found himself in a prison cell chained to another prisoner.[4]

Millan's brutal treatment of Garibaldi did not go unnoticed in Gualeguay. Many of the townspeople expressed their indignation publically, and one brave lady, Señora Rosa Sanabria de Alemán, even brought food and other necessities to Garibaldi in the prison. This outpouring of sympathy for a prisoner who had broken parole angered Millan, causing him to become more repressive. Abreu and several others were arrested on suspicion of having aided Garibaldi in his escape attempt. However, because of a lack of evidence, they were soon released.

Shortly afterward, Garibaldi was transferred to a prison in Paraná, where he recovered from the effects of the torture. However, he continued to experience occasional pain in his wrists for the rest of his life. After spending another two months in a dark, dungeon-like cell, Garibaldi was released from prison on orders of Governor Echaque.[5] He then made his way by boat to Montevideo, where he joined his good friends, Rossetti and Carniglia. A month later, the three of them journeyed on horseback to the frontier of Rio Grande do Sul, a distance of about three hundred miles. Upon entering Rio Grande, they went to the town of Piratini where they were to meet with the President of Rio Grande—General Bento Gonçalves.

7

Río Grande do Sul

AFTER THEIR LONG JOURNEY from Montevideo, Uruguay, to Río Grande do Sul, Garibaldi and his two companions, Rossetti and Carniglia, finally met President Bento Gonçalves at his headquarters at Piratini. The three were immediately impressed by the handsome president, who greeted them unpretentiously. He was well aware of the fact that they had fought as privateers under the red, yellow, and green banner of Río Grande do Sul.

Bento Gonçalves da Silva Pilho was descended from an aristocratic Portuguese family and had served with distinction in the Brazilian army. The people of Río Grande looked upon him as their leader and supported him in the struggle for independence from the Empire of Brazil. The son of a rancher, Gonçalves was a fine horseman and an excellent marksman. In appearance, he was tall of stature and picturesque in dress. As an army general, he was brave in battle and magnanimous in victory. He shared his soldiers' rations when on campaign, and he always treated people with courtesy and respect. His troops revered him, and the ladies loved him. To the people of Rio Grande do Sul, he stood for freedom and independence. Unquestionably, Gonçalves was the model leader whom Garibaldi admired and later copied. He was everything that Garibaldi wanted to be—and then some!

Bento Goncalves

At that time the Republican forces under Gonçalves' command totaled about 9,500 men, but over half of these were gaucho reservists who would be called up as cavalry during an emergency. The Imperial Brazilian Army numbered about 24,000 men, 7,000 of whom were reservists.* By European standards, these armies were small, and the size of the territory in which they operated vast. This translated into lower casualties and greater intervals between battles. However, when the hostile armies met, the battles were fierce. No quarter was given, and none asked for. In this remote wilderness, where conditions made it virtually impossible to guard prisoners, the rules of war were dictated by military expediency. Captured prisoners were summarily executed by their captors, and seriously wounded soldiers were often shot by their own comrades rather than left behind to be captured by the enemy.

During this period, much of South America was a wild and untamed wilderness, a land where immigrant peoples struggled for survival in an atmosphere of lawlessness and cruelty. Life was cheap and the stakes were high as rival groups battled for control of the vast riches the territory had to offer. The whole scene could be described as a *school of war*. It was in this environment that Garibaldi was to spend the next twelve years of his young life. This period would prove to have the greatest formative influence on his character.

With a land area of 100,150 square miles, Rio Grande do Sul was roughly the size of the American State of Colorado. A vast tropical grassland interspersed with forests covered the region, extending from the shores of the South Atlantic to the mountains of the interior. In the 1830s, Rio Grande do Sul had a population of about 150,000 people, most of whom were engaged in agricul-

---

*These figures are given in Jasper Ridley's *Garibaldi*, pp. 71–72.

ture or ranching. There were a few scattered towns, the most important of which were Porto Alegre, San José do Norte, and the port of Rio Grande. All of these towns were located on Lagoa dos Patos (Lagoon of the Ducks), a large lagoon separated from the Atlantic Ocean by a long, narrow strip of land. The only entrance to the lagoon was at the southern end, through a narrow strait less than a mile wide. At that time, the three above-mentioned ports were occupied by Imperial troops, and the strait was patrolled by the Brazilian navy. This effectively blockaded the rebels, who controlled most of the interior of the province and a narrow stretch of coastline on the lagoon near the town of Camagua.

The defeat of the Imperial Brazilian forces at the Battle of Rio Pardo had left Bento Gonçalves and the rebels in virtual control of most of the province. The Imperial forces continued to control the coastal areas but did not pose much of a threat to Gonçalves' rule. It was in his own backyard that he faced his greatest menace—a marauder named Moringue!

Moringue was a cunning guerilla leader who at the time was terrorizing the local population with his fierce band of horsemen. His deadly raids turned the countryside into a cauldron of fear—people were killed, livestock slaughtered, and *estancias* (ranches) burned down. Moringue was known as a ferocious warrior and a great horseman, the men under his command were mercenaries and adventurers who had little regard for human life. Moringue's real name was Francisco de Abreu, and he held the rank of colonel in the Brazilian army. Later, he was to be given the title of Baron de Jacuhy by the Imperial Brazilian government. He reputedly had inherited the nickname of "Moringue" from his father, who had been given it because he had large, pointed ears like a Martian.[1] It was inevitable that Moringue and Garibaldi would eventually cross swords.

8

The Rio Grande Navy

PRESIDENT GONÇALVES, who was eager to break the Brazilian naval blockade of Rio Grande, appointed Garibaldi Commander of the Rio Grande Navy, and ordered him to put a fleet together on Lagoa dos Patos (Patos Lagoon). There, at a small naval base near the town of Camagua, Captain John Grigg, an American, was already outfitting two warships for the new fleet. Grigg was a New Yorker, in line to inherit his family's vast fortune. In the meantime, he had decided to sail to South America in search of adventure. He'd found it in Rio Grande do Sul and volunteered to join the fight for independence. Now, he encountered another adventurer who had joined the cause—Garibaldi. The two immediately became friends.

Garibaldi was eager to attack Brazilian shipping as he had previously done when he was a privateer. Now, along with Grigg, he could operate from a base in friendly territory. The only problem was that the Brazilian fleet had blockaded the narrow strait which led from the Patos Lagoon to the Atlantic Ocean. Garibaldi and Grigg would deal with that problem later.

At that time, the Navy of Rio Grande consisted of about sixty men and two ships—the *Republicano* and the *Farroupilha* (whose name derived from a Brazilian term meaning "rag pickers"). Grigg was to command the *Republicano*, Garibaldi the slightly larger *Farroupilha*. Each ship mounted two cannon and carried a crew of thirty men. Garibaldi's crew included seven Italians—Carniglia, Mutru, and five others who had been with him on the *Mazzini*. As soon as the two ships were made ready, Garibaldi and Grigg engaged in a running war with the Brazilian fleet, the largest in South America. Both men displayed an uncommon boldness in attacking the bigger enemy ships. Grigg later was given command of a newer ship named the *Seival*, and Garibaldi's ship, the *Farroupilha*, was renamed the *Rio Pardo*.[1]

Operating from a naval base on the western shore of the Patos Lagoon, the two ships attacked Brazilian merchant ships sailing on the two-hundred-mile-long lagoon. Their aim was to disrupt the supply line to the Imperial garrison at Porto Alegre. The captured goods were handed over to the Republic of Rio Grande, with Garibaldi, Grigg, and their crews receiving a portion of the booty as their pay. Once again, Garibaldi was branded a "pirate," and a reward was offered for his capture. The Brazilian officer who captured or killed him would certainly be given a promotion. Garibaldi thus became prey for Moringue!

One morning in April 1839, Garibaldi and about fourteen of his men were eating breakfast near a fortified storehouse at their naval base on the western shore of the lagoon. They had left their weapons in the storehouse, unaware of the impending danger. Without warning, Moringue, with a force of 150 cavalrymen, emerged from the forest and attacked them.[2] Garibaldi and his men ran to the storehouse, with Garibaldi reaching it just as a horseman lunged at him with a lance and ripped his poncho. Once inside the storehouse, Garibaldi retrieved his carbine and proceeded to shoot down several of the raiders. Eleven of his men managed to reach the storehouse safely. A few others ran into the forest but were hunted down and shot. Only one of them escaped—Mutru. Garibaldi and his men held the storehouse, exchanging fire with the superior enemy force. Moringue himself attempted to set fire to the storehouse, but he was shot down by one of Garibaldi's men—a freed African slave named Procopio. Badly hurt, Moringue broke off the action, thus ending the first clash between the two swashbuckling adversaries.

In the meantime, President Gonçalves had appointed Luigi Rossetti as editor of a newspaper called O Povo (The People), the mouthpiece of the Republican forces in Rio Grande. Rossetti was now in his element—journalism. The objective of the publication was to drum up support for the war effort against the Empire of Brazil. As editor, Rossetti proved quite adept at exaggerating the scope of Republican successes and minimizing the effect of its setbacks.[3] Unsurprisingly, Rossetti gave very favorable news treatment to Garibaldi's action against Moringue.

There was a lull in the war during the summer of 1839, thus allowing the Riograndense upper class to enjoy some social life. President Gonçalves had two sisters, Doña Antonia and Doña Anna, both of whom owned large estancias near the western shore of the Patos Lagoon. Both sisters served the Republican cause by hosting gala parties for their brother's friends and fellow officers. Garibaldi was usually invited to these affairs, and he was totally charmed by the beautiful women in attendance. Evidently, Garibaldi felt quite at home in these aristocratic surroundings.

It was at a gathering hosted by Doña Anna that he met and fell in love with a beautiful girl named Manuela Ferreira. She was the daughter of a wealthy landowner who happened to be a close friend of President Gonçalves. Believing that she was in love with him, Garibaldi privately professed his love for her. As it turned out, Manuela was already engaged to Gonçalves' son! Putting his personal feelings aside, Garibaldi decided not to steal her away because of his devotion to the president. However, he always remembered those delightful outings—and the beautiful girl named Manuela.[4]

Late in 1839, President Gonçalves decided to take the offensive by invading the neighboring province of Santa Catarina. Along with Rio Grande do Sul, Santa Catarina is one of the two provinces that comprise what is known as the "Brazilian panhandle." In 1839, the province had a population of about 70,000 people, most of whom were engaged in herding cattle. Unlike the Riograndenses, most of the Catarinese had remained loyal to Emperor Dom Pedro II. However, there were revolutionary elements in the coastal towns of Laguna and Florianapolis who wanted to establish an independent Republic of Santa Catarina. Through secret contact with Bento Gonçalves, a plan was devised whereby the Riograndense invasion of Santa Catarina would coincide with Republican uprisings in the above-mentioned towns.

Upon learning of the ambitious invasion plan, Garibaldi realized that the Rio Grande Navy could play a key role in the invasion —provided that he could get his ships out of the Patos Lagoon and into the open sea. A long, sandy strip of land separated the lagoon from the Atlantic, and the lagoon's only entrance was blockaded by the Brazilian Navy. Unable to sail his ships out to the open sea, Garibaldi reverted to a method of transporting ships used back in 1453 by the Ottoman Turks during the siege of Constantinople. He would haul the ships overland!

Garibaldi proposed that he and Grigg sail their ships to the narrow peninsula on the eastern shore of the lagoon and then drag them overland to the Atlantic Ocean. He selected a route across the strip where the land was not so soft and sandy. The route across the peninsula covered a distance of about fifty miles.

Pursuing their bold plan, Garibaldi and Grigg sailed across the Patos Lagoon to the Bay of Capibari. There, they consulted a local engineer named Joachim de Abreu for advice on how to transport the two ships across the narrow peninsula. Abreu (not to be confused with Colonel Francisco de Abreu) advised that the ships could be hauled overland on huge wooden carts. With Garibaldi's okay, Abreu proceeded to construct two enormous wooden vehicles mounted on wheels measuring ten feet in diameter! Upon their completion a few weeks later, the huge vehicles were then lowered into the water under the ships. Each ship was mounted on a vehicle and then hauled ashore. Two hundred oxen assisted Garibaldi's men in dragging the vehicles with the ships on them for three days across the fifty-mile strip of land. Because of their ingenious design, which had all four wheels placed under the front part of the vehicle, the oxen were able to draw the ships without too much difficulty.[5]

On July 14, 1839, the mission was successfully completed as the two ships were refloated in the Atlantic Ocean. As it turned out, this monumental undertaking has become part of Brazilian folklore and is considered an important event in Brazilian history. It remains a credit to the boldness of Garibaldi's conception and to the ingenuity of an obscure engineer named Joachim de Abreu. The two vehicles that carted the ships probably rank as the most famous wooden structures since the Trojan Horse! Today, they are on display at a museum in the City of Porto Alegre.

9

Santa Catarina

AFTER HAULING THEIR SHIPS OVERLAND from the Patos Lagoon to the Atlantic Ocean, Garibaldi and Grigg sailed northward along the coast. The next day they ran into a violent storm, the kind that arises suddenly off the coast of South America. Garibaldi was up on the mast, scouting the shoreline for a safe haven to land, when the ship was slammed by a huge wave and suddenly capsized. Garibaldi, who was thrown clear from the ship, managed to swim to shore. However, most of his crew, including all seven of his Italian companions, perished in the turbulent sea. Also lost at sea was Procopio, the former slave who had wounded Moringue in a skirmish a few weeks earlier. Fate had thus deprived Garibaldi of his closest friends.[1] He and the other survivors then made their way inland and joined the Riograndense forces, which were advancing northward into Santa Catarina. Meanwhile, Captain Grigg had managed to bring his ship safely to land without losing a single man! This feat can only be attributed to his skill as a sea captain—and the will of God.

Despite the shipwreck, Garibaldi and the other survivors were able to participate in the attack on the coastal town of Laguna. Garibaldi was given command of a captured gunboat called the *Itaparica* and soon joined with John Grigg's *Seival* for the attack. On July 22, 1839, only one week after the shipwreck, Garibaldi and Grigg blasted their way into the harbor at Laguna as Riograndense troops under Colonel Davi Canabarro attacked the town from the land side. The Brazilian garrison put up a stiff resistance for much of the day but surrendered when their situation began to appear hopeless. The Riograndenses captured sixteen cannon and more than four hundred rifles, took seventy-seven prisoners, and seized eighteen ships in the harbor.* It was a great victory for the Republican cause. Most of the townspeople greeted their liberators and decorated their cottages with red, green, and yellow ribbons—the colors of the Riograndense flag. Church bells rang and a *Te Deum* was sung in the Church of Sant Antonio dos Anjos. A few days later, the Riograndense high command issued citations to five officers who partook in the battle. One of those receiving a citation was Captain José Garibaldi.[2]

A nineteenth-century writer described Laguna as a "romantically remote" place in a "dark and wild continent." This early portrayal of the place as an idyllic hideaway in an untamed part of the world reflected a tendency to romanticize the mysterious and forbidden. Until its capture by the Riograndenses in July 1839, Laguna's exis-

---

*These figures are given in Anthony Valerio's *Anita Garibaldi*, pp. 21–22.

tence was virtually unknown to the rest of the world, and ultimately, it was from its association with Garibaldi, and the woman whom he met there, that the town would get its main claim to fame.

Situated on a deep blue inlet and virtually surrounded by lush green mountains, Laguna's setting was nothing short of spectacular. The sailing ships in the harbor, the blue water lapping against white pebble beaches, and the brightly colored cottages set against a backdrop of tropical flora all helped create a strikingly beautiful vista. Adding to the dreamlike aura was the scent of wild flowers filtering through the balmy air. It was a perfect setting for a love story.

Though many of the people there yearned for independence, others were quite satisfied with their condition under the Emperor of Brazil. Of course, the liberating Riograndenses sought to encourage Catarinense independence. So on July 26, 1839, Colonel Canabarro issued a statement proclaiming the independence of the province of Santa Catarina, henceforth to be constituted as the Republica Juliana, because the revolt had taken place in July. The proclamation was signed on a large oak table in Laguna's town hall, and Garibaldi was present for the ceremony. A provisional government was formed, composed mainly of local politicians. The new government promoted Canabarro to the rank of general and appointed him Commander-in-Chief of the Army of Santa Catarina. Garibaldi's friend Luigi Rossetti was appointed secretary of state. To many of the Catarinese, the whole affair seemed more like a conquest by the army of Rio Grande than a liberation from the Empire of Brazil. They now began to look upon the Riograndenses as "invaders."[3]

In retrospect, the capture of Laguna marked the high point of the independence movement in southern Brazil. A Republican

Statue of Anita in front of the Old Town Hall in Laguna

Salon where La Republica Juliana was proclaimed on July 29, 1839

uprising in the town of Desterro, now called Florianapolis, was crushed by Imperial troops, thus stymying Canabarro's advance. Within a short time, the Riograndense forces were meeting opposition, and passive resistance in areas they controlled. It began to appear as if the tide of war was turning in favor of the Imperial forces. Determined to regain control of Santa Catarina and Rio Grande do Sul, the Brazilian Imperial government now sent an army under General Soares de Andréia to recapture the two lost provinces. De Andréia had recently crushed a rebellion of mulattos in the northern state of Pará. He now advanced southward, knowing that he would have the support of many of the Catarinese against the "invaders" from Rio Grande do Sul.

An uprising in support of the Imperial forces occurred in the coastal town of Imarui, located about ten miles north of Laguna. The provisional government of Santa Catarina considered the people of Imarui rebels and dispatched a naval force under Garibaldi to recapture the town. He was ordered to punish the rebels by sacking the town. What followed was one of the most regrettable incidents of Garibaldi's South American experience.

Even though the rebels had fortified the harbor area, Garibaldi was able to land his men down the coast and attack Imarui from the land side. He easily captured the town and then, obeying government orders, allowed his men to sack the place. The nightmarish scene that followed haunted him for the rest of his life. He was horrified at the sight of his men looting and killing. In angry desperation, he ordered them to return to the ships, but before this was achieved, the town was wrecked! Garibaldi later wrote that "his men behaved like unchained wild beasts," and that "the worry and fatigue experienced on that miserable day in trying to restrain them were unspeakable."[4] The news of the sacking of Imarui

shocked the Catarinese and served to re-enforce Garibaldi's image
as a "bloodthirsty pirate!"

During this period, Garibaldi experienced what the Portuguese
call *saudade*—the sadness that one feels at the departure of friends or
loved ones. He had lost his closest friends, Luigi Carniglia and
Edoardo Matru, at sea, and now, even though he had a brave new
crew, they were still strangers to him. Also weighing on his mind
was the sacking of Imarui. Everything began to seem meaningless
as he suffered loneliness and despair. Eventually, he came to the
realization that he needed a woman, a woman who could give him
the love and affection he needed. He decided to begin searching
for "the woman of his heart."[5]

The port of Laguna offered Garibaldi an excellent base for
raiding Brazilian shipping as far north as the coastal city of Santos.
He and Grigg made several successful raids during the late summer
of 1839, returning to Laguna with large quantities of booty. On his
return from one of these, he first saw "the woman of his heart."
Garibaldi was on the quarterdeck of his ship, scanning the shore
with his telescope, when he spotted a beautiful girl with long black
hair walking near the cottages on the *barra*, or hill, above the harbor.
As she moved along, she occasionally glanced out at his ship, almost
as though beckoning him to come ashore. Then she suddenly disappeared from view. Garibaldi continued to scan the hillside for
the girl but was unable to sight her again. He began to wonder if
she was real, or only an illusion. It all seemed like a dream to him—
the girl with the long black hair, the remarkably beautiful setting,
and a lonely sailor looking for love.

Feeling as though he were living a dream, he quickly put in to
shore in a longboat and climbed the hillside to search for her. But
the girl with the long black hair was nowhere to be found. She

seemed to have vanished! Garibaldi began to feel despondent. Then he happened to see a man he knew, standing in front of a cottage. The man greeted him and invited him in for a cup of coffee. The aroma of freshly brewed coffee soon filtered into the room where the two sat down to chat. When a girl emerged from the kitchen to serve them coffee, Garibaldi realized to his astonishment that she was the very one for whom he had been searching!

Virtually spellbound, Garibaldi greeted her, saying in Italian: "*Tu devi essere mia!*"[6] (You must be mine!). With these words began one of the great love stories of all time. The girl, who only spoke Portuguese, simply nodded, as though in acquiescence.

What happened next is shrouded in mystery, because Garibaldi never explained it in his memoirs. But one can surmise that the two rendezvoused secretly, because when Garibaldi's ship sailed from Laguna a few days later, she was with him.

Her name was Anna Maria Ribeiro de Jesus, but her friends knew her as "Anita." She was destined to become an integral part of the Garibaldi mystique.

He later wrote in his *Memoirs*: "I had come upon a forbidden treasure, but yet a treasure of great price! If there were guilt, it was mine alone. And there was guilt. Two hearts were joined in an infinite love, but an innocent existence was shattered . . . . I sinned greatly, but I sinned alone."[7] This is the most famous passage in the *Memoirs* — and probably one of the most intriguing.

There are several different editions of Garibaldi's *Memoirs*, each published by a different editor, and each describing Garibaldi's first meeting with Anita in a somewhat different light. Alexander Dumas, in his account, noted that Garibaldi's description of his original encounter with Anita was "wrapped in a veil of obscurity." Dumas reportedly asked Garibaldi to clarify his statements about that first meeting, whereupon Garibaldi replied: "It must stay as it is."[8]

Garibaldi never explained what he meant by the passage. In fact, the vagueness in his *Memoirs* about the first meeting with Anita left many unanswered questions: Who was the man who invited Garibaldi into his cottage that day in Laguna? Was he the "innocent existence" mentioned in the *Memoirs*? If so, what happened to him? And finally, who was Anita and what was her marital status? These unanswered questions, and his silence on the subject, eventually gave rise to the rumor that Anita was already married when she met him.

10

Anna Maria Ribeiro de Jesus

ANNA MARIA RIBEIRO DE JESUS was a dark-eyed beauty with long, flowing black hair and a freckled face. Her exotic looks, combined with a lively personality, made her one of the most desirable young ladies in the town of Laguna. Some writers have described her as a Creole, but indications are that she was of pure Portuguese stock, her people having emigrated to southern Brazil from the Azores. Her father, Bento Ribeiro da Silva, was a farmer from the province of Sao Paulo who, in 1815, moved to Santa Catarina. There, he settled in a little village named Morrinhos, near the town of Tubarão. Morrinhos has since been renamed Anita Garibaldi.

Bento and his wife, Maria Antonia de Jesus, had several children besides Anita, but there is some confusion about the exact number, and their names. In the frontier wilderness of Brazil, infant births often went unrecorded, and even if they were duly recorded, the registers were sometimes lost or destroyed. Local tradition has it that Anita had two sisters and two brothers. However, only the registers of baptism of her brother Manoel (1822) and her sister Sicilia (1824) have survived.[1] There is no record of Anita's birth, but indications are that she was born in 1821.

Anna María Ribeiro de Jesus (rendering by the author)

The wooden cottage where she was born in Morrinhos was built on piles alongside a stream called the Tubarão, or "Shark River." As a youngster, she played in the woods—running barefoot through the brush, climbing trees, and swimming in the stream.

Growing up, she worked with her father clearing away patches of jungle to be used for pasture, and, on occasion, he took her for rides along the clearings of banana trees on his favorite horse, Pinha. It could be said that Anita's childhood was somewhat similar to that of Tarzan's jungle girl Jane.

Anita's father was a cattle herdsman or *tropeiro*, and as such he rode out with other *tropeiros* on hunts for wild cattle and horses—the cattle for their meat, hides, and tallow; the horses for use in future drives. An excellent horseman himself, he taught young Anita how to gentle a colt, and by age ten she was able to saddle, mount, and ride it.[2]

When she was only twelve, her father died in a tragic accident. He had climbed onto the roof of a storehouse to do some repair work when a beam split underfoot, sending him crashing to his death. The family was devastated by the sudden loss of its bread-winner. Anita's widowed mother sold the livestock to pay off debts and then moved the family to the coastal town of Laguna, where the children would be near their godfather, João Braga.[3]

There, Anita grew up in a poor White community where most of the people earned a living by fishing and the most exciting event was the arrival in the harbor of a foreign sailing ship. Aside from the sailing ships, the only means of transportation in this tropical wilderness was by horseback. Consequently, most of the inhabitants were good horsemen. Anita was no exception. Like other girls in Laguna, she learned to ride a horse at an early age and was usually allowed to ride about unescorted. As time went on, she grew into a vivacious young woman who could attract suitors with her accomplished horsemanship as easily as with her looks. For this reason, her family was eager to get her married.

Laguna is a place where fact and fiction tend to merge into

Anita's cottage in Laguna

folklore, and folklore eventually becomes gospel truth. Many of the stories about Anita's early life and her subsequent elopement with Garibaldi cannot be substantiated but were nevertheless collected by the Brazilian novelist Virgilio Varzea and published in his *Garibaldi in America*. The book was translated into Italian by Clemente Pitti and published in 1902. It has since become a major source of information on Anita's early years.

Stories of Anita indicate that she had an adventurous disposition. Her closest friend, Maria Fortunata, once described an incident in which Anita was attacked in a wooded area by a rejected suitor. The suitor dismounted from his horse and attempted to rape her. According to the story, Anita seized the attacker's whip and whacked him across the face with it, jumped on his horse, and rode to the police station to file a complaint against him. Although the rejected suitor later pressed charges against her, Anita was absolved of any wrongdoing.[4]

After this incident, Anita's family reputedly pressured her into marrying a local fisherman named Manoel Duarte. Though Anita agreed to it, she confided to her girlfriend, Maria, that she had serious misgivings. What happened next was veiled in obscurity for the longest period, and many people rejected the notion that Anita was married before she first met Garibaldi. However, Church records discovered in 1932 by the Brazilian scholar José A. Boiteux, conclusively proved that she was indeed married. The records showed that Anna Maria de Jesus married Manoel Duarte di Aguiar on August 30, 1835.[5] She was fifteen years old, Duarte twenty-five. The wedding took place in the Church of Santo Antonio dos Anjos in Laguna and was duly recorded in the church register. Boiteux thus proved what people in Laguna had known for almost a century—that Anita was already married when she first met Garibaldi.

Adding to the wedding drama is an old legend describing an unlucky omen that occurred before the ceremony. According to the story, Anita tripped while entering the church and lost one of her satin slippers. This was taken as a sign that she was destined to abandon her husband.[6]

Anita was married to Duarte for four years before she met Garibaldi. The marriage produced no children. Duarte continued to earn a living as a fisherman until the time of the Riograndense invasion of Santa Catarina. He then supposedly joined the Brazilian Imperial army to fight against the Riograndenses. What happened next remains an unsolved mystery. Duarte seemed to fade out of the picture after Garibaldi and Anita eloped in October 1839, and no one has been able to determine what happened to him. It is not known whether he fought in the battle for Laguna or was sent elsewhere. Only the conflicting stories remain—that he died of wounds in a hospital in 1839; that he was killed either in the battle for Laguna or in a brawl with Garibaldi; or that he left Anita to join the Imperial army because she didn't love him. Of these theories, the last is the most credible, because it was the custom in South America for wives of soldiers to accompany their husbands as "camp followers" on military campaigns. As it happened, Anita remained living in Laguna.

The riddle would be solved if Duarte's death certificate were found. However, numerous searches undertaken to find the elusive document have failed to locate it. It remains unlikely that Duarte's death certificate will ever be found, or that the mystery surrounding his fate will ever be solved.

As for Anita, when she embarked from Laguna with Garibaldi, she did it willingly, and her only motive was to accompany the man she loved into battle. She actually participated in numerous engagements, and many stories attest to her personal courage and fortitude. On one occasion, she was captured by Imperial troops but promptly escaped into the wilderness, seeking to rejoin Garibaldi. For four days she wandered through the wilds, enduring every hardship—hunger and thirst, physical exhaustion, exposure to the elements, and the danger of being waylaid by the enemy. She finally managed to obtain food and a horse from a friendly farmer. Garibaldi himself later recounted how she continued on horseback, crossing the raging Canoas River by holding on to her horse's tail while encouraging it to swim across. Upon her reaching the other bank, the sight of a long-haired woman emerging from the dark waters of the river so frightened two armed waylayers that they fled in panic. They reported to the authorities that they were being pursued by a "supernatural being" from the depths.[7]

Showing incredible fortitude, Anita continued on in her search for Garibaldi, stopping in the town of Lages only long enough to drink a cup of coffee and obtain information of his whereabouts. She finally rejoined him at a place called Vacaria after a horrendous journey lasting eight days and nights. Such was her love for the man!

Love begets jealousy, and Anita was known to become extremely jealous when she thought Garibaldi was flirting with other women. One story from Montevideo recounts how she came to Garibaldi armed with two loaded pistols, telling him that one was meant for him and the other for her suspected rival. Needless to say, she knew how to get her point across. There were also times when she would make Garibaldi cut off his shoulder-length hair. She thought the long hair made him look more appealing to other women.[8]

On September 16, 1840, Anita gave birth to a son, whom they named Menotti. The baby was named after a young Italian revolutionary, Ciro Menotti, who had been executed by the Austrians for encouraging an uprising in the City of Modena ten years earlier. A few days after Menotti's birth, Brazilian raiders led by Colonel Moringue attacked the farm where Anita was staying. Garibaldi was away on a mission at the time. The attack occurred at night, and Anita, who was in her night clothes, fled on horseback, clutching the baby in her arms. Dashing into the forest, she eluded the cunning Moringue and remained in hiding until Garibaldi returned the next day.[9]

In 1841, Garibaldi and Anita were given permission by President Gonçalves of Rio Grande do Sul to emigrate to Montevideo in Uruguay. There, the couple were married in a Catholic ceremony on March 26, 1842, and lived in a one-room apartment, sharing a kitchen with three other families.[10] They remained in Montevideo for seven years, taking part in Uruguay's struggle to maintain its independence from Argentina. Garibaldi distinguished himself at sea as a fleet commander, and on land as Commander of the Italian Legion. During this period, the Garibaldi family was expanding. Anita had three more children—Rosita (1841), Teresita (1845), and Ricciotti (1847). (Rosita died of scarlet fever when she was four years old.)

Despite his legendary heroics in battle, Garibaldi's marital status remained a subject of controversy both in South America and in Europe. Rumors began to circulate that Anita had already been married to someone else when she eloped with Garibaldi. At first it was thought that Garibaldi and Anita had never been through a marriage ceremony, but when a copy of the marriage certificate was made public, many considered the marriage bigamous. Garibaldi himself did nothing to clarify the situation, so the controversy over his relationship with Anita continued.

Early in 1848, news of revolutions in Italy caused Garibaldi to decide to return to his homeland. Upon their arrival in Nice, Garibaldi left the children in the care of his mother. Then, he and Anita journeyed to Rome and joined in the struggle to defend the newly created Roman Republic, which was being attacked by a French expeditionary force. The ten-week battle for Rome resulted in a French victory, but Garibaldi and Anita led a spectacular retreat from Rome to San Marino, where he disbanded his army. During the long, difficult march, Anita fell seriously ill with fever. Garibaldi wanted to leave her in the safety of San Marino while he escaped to Venice, but she insisted on accompanying him. It was against his better judgment that he allowed her to come. During that escape, Anita died of fever at a lonely farmhouse in the marshes of the Po delta. She was only twenty-eight. With the enemy in hot pursuit, there was only time for a hasty burial in a shallow grave. Thus died the legendary Anita. A sorrowful Garibaldi made his way safely to Nice disguised as a peasant.

Years later, Garibaldi wrote a passage in his *Memoirs* in which he seemed to reproach himself for taking Anita away from her home in Brazil to a tragic death in Italy. In describing his first meeting with her, he implies that he committed a wrong against an innocent person. He ended the passage with these words: "She is dead! I am unhappy! And he is avenged, yes avenged!" [11]

This intriguing passage seems to indicate that Garibaldi did someone great harm by taking Anita away with him, and that her tragic death came as punishment for his wrongdoing. Although Garibaldi doesn't specifically name the injured person in the passage, one can conclude that it was Manoel Duarte.

11

Retreat from Paradise

By LATE NOVEMBER 1839, Brazilian Imperial forces were rapidly closing in on Laguna. Their objective was to destroy Garibaldi's base of operation. A fleet of twenty-three Brazilian warships sailed toward the port, while an army under General Andréia advanced on the town from the north. As the Army of Rio Grande prepared to evacuate Laguna, General Canabarro ordered Garibaldi to bring all of his supplies and equipment ashore in preparation for the retreat inland.

Garibaldi obeyed the order, but while his men were in the process of bringing the equipment ashore, the Brazilian warships entered the harbor and opened fire. Only a few of Garibaldi's crew were on board ship at the time. Anita, who also was on board, promptly fired a cannon at the enemy ships, starting a vicious exchange of cannonades. Realizing that his position was unten-able, Garibaldi ordered Anita and the others ashore while he remained on board to cover the evacuation. Then he set fire to his ship and rowed to shore under heavy enemy fire. Captain Grigg was not as fortunate. He went down with his ship under a barrage of enemy gunfire. The harbor resembled a blazing inferno as what had been a paradise on earth became a hell. Garibaldi, along with Anita and the other sailors, then joined the Army of Rio Grande in their retreat from Laguna.[1]

The retreat was to continue for 450 miles across a vast wilder-ness, with the Riograndense forces being pursued by Imperial troops and often harassed by local guerillas. During this retreat, an encounter with the pursuing enemy gave rise to a famous story about Anita. In a skirmish near the town of Curitibanos, an attack by Garibaldi's troops was beaten back by the Imperial forces. During the heat of battle, Anita's horse was shot from beneath her, and she was captured.[2] Her captors taunted her about the Republican cause, and even told her that Garibaldi was dead. However, when they failed to produce his corpse, Anita realized that he was still alive, and she resolved to find him. That night, when her captors were drunk with wine, she escaped into the for-est. Her incredible journey through the wilderness in search of Garibaldi stands as a monumental feat of physical endurance. For eight days and nights she pushed on, suffering the worst hardships imaginable, until she was finally reunited with him. Needless to say, their reunion was a joyous one because Garibaldi thought that Anita had been killed at Curitibanos!

By now, it was evident to Garibaldi and the others that the peo-ple of Santa Catarina Province had begun to turn against their "lib-erators." Garibaldi, himself believed that the haughty attitude and heavy-handedness of the Riograndenses had cost them the chance to bring about the fall of an empire and the triumph of Republicanism throughout South America. In the meantime, Garibaldi had adapted to his new role as a soldier, and he later referred to this period as one of the most memorable of his entire life. He stated in his *Memoirs* that he had his happiest moments "when at the head of a few men, the survivors of many battles who had honestly earned the names of heroes, I rode alongside the woman of my heart, throwing myself into a career which even more than the sea, had an immense attraction for me." [3]

On May 3, 1840, Garibaldi participated in the biggest land battle that he had fought to date—the Battle of Taquari, in which an Imperial force of 7,000 men was defeated by the Army of Rio Grande. However, Gonçalves failed to pursue the defeated enemy, thus letting a complete victory slip from his grasp. Garibaldi criticized him for not pursuing the enemy and later claimed that the one quality the general lacked was perseverance in battle.

The summer of 1840 saw the Imperial troops in Rio Grande do Sul reduced to holding a few ports on the Patos Lagoon and to waging the guerilla war of Moringue. The season, however, was not uneventful. Garibaldi was one of the three commanders selected to take part in an attack on the port of San José do Norte at the entrance to the Patos Lagoon. The attack on the town failed, but the Riograndenses captured twenty prisoners. The prisoners were to be executed, but Garibaldi's intervention saved sixteen of them. Four had already been executed before he arrived on the scene and prevented the execution of a younger soldier, believing that he might yet "render good service to the community." He then ordered that the executions be halted, thus sparing another fifteen as well. [4] Ninety years later, the son of that soldier journeyed to

Italy to pay his respects to the Garibaldi family and described how Garibaldi had saved his father's life.

After he had participated in the attack on San José do Norte, Garibaldi was sent to San Simon on the Patos Lagoon to supervise the construction of some warships for the next naval campaign. In the meantime, he and Anita, who was with child, moved into a farmhouse in the nearby village of Mustarda, where she gave birth to a son on September 16, 1840. They named him after the Italian patriot who had been martyred in 1831.

Shortly after Menotti's birth, the village of Mustarda was suddenly attacked by Moringue and his raiders. Garibaldi was away on a mission at the time. Moringue's men surrounded the farmhouse, thinking that they had trapped their catch. However, Anita, who was in her night clothes, was not about to be taken. Clutching the infant Menotti in her arms, she dashed out, leaped on a horse, and galloped off into the darkness. She eluded Moringue and hid in the forest until Garibaldi returned the next morning to fetch her.[5] Moringue fled empty handed, and the family was again reunited thanks to Anita's courage in the face of danger!

Toward the end of 1840, the tide of battle began to turn in favor of the Brazilian Imperial forces. A revolution had taken place in Rio de Janeiro, abolishing the Regency of Araujo Lima and proclaiming Dom Pedro II as Emperor of Brazil. A new constitutional government came to power and offered an amnesty to the Riograndense rebels if they ended their war of independence. The offer was refused by President Gonçalves. Thereupon, a large Brazilian army under General Barâo de Caixas advanced against Gonçalves and drove the Riograndenses inland toward the highlands. Caixas renewed the offer of amnesty as he continued his advance across the province.

The Riograndenses who were not willing to accept the amnesty offer, and the wives and families of the soldiers, all followed the retreating army. These camp-followers more than doubled the size of the retreating column, causing it to lose its maneuverability. During the perilous march, Garibaldi, Anita, and the infant Menotti would have to face even greater dangers than those experienced by the American pioneers on their trek westward.

12

The Wilderness March: November 1840—January 1841

By THE END OF 1840, support for the Republican cause in Rio Grande do Sul began to dissipate. The people of the region were weary of the civil war, which had dragged on for six years, and many of the rebels began to accept the amnesty the Brazilian Government offered them. The Rio Grande Army, already reeling from the Brazilian onslaught, was further weakened by desertions. As the Imperial forces advanced, the rebel positions near the coast became untenable.

In order to save what was left of his forces, President Gonçalves ordered his army to retreat into the interior. Following the army in its retreat was a large entourage of Republican sympathizers who

refused to accept the Brazilian Government's offer of amnesty.[1]
Also, in the entourage were the wives and children of the soldiers.
Anita and the infant Menotti were among them.

At that time in South America, it was customary for a soldier to
have his family accompany him during a campaign. Although they
slowed down the column, the women proved very helpful at camp-
sites. They unfolded the tents from the saddlebags and raised
them. They carried water from the streams, and firewood from the
forest, while the men went out in search of food. Sometimes, stray
cattle were rounded up and brought into camp. These were
butchered, bled, and skinned gaucho-style. The beef was then
quartered and roasted vertically on green branches so the juice
could roll down.[2] The barbequed meat was portioned out, and
everyone ate. When there were no cattle around, everyone went
hungry.

The retreating column was more than a mile long as it trudged
its way along the wilderness trails leading to the western highlands
of Rio Grande do Sul. Its length made it very vulnerable to attacks
by local guerilla forces or the warlike native Indian tribes. At the
head of the column was the division commanded by General
Canabarro. Garibaldi, and the other troops who had fought at
Laguna, were in this division. The center of the column was protected on each side by a cordon of mounted troops under various
commanders, while President Gonçalves' division formed the rear
guard, the point most vulnerable to attack—and that was precisely where the enemy struck.

Near a place called Villa Setembrina, the column was suddenly
attacked by Moringue, who swooped down on the edge of the column with a force of 450 horsemen. In the ensuing action, Luigi
Rossetti was killed. His horse was shot from under him, but he

went on fighting until he was struck down. Moringue was driven off, but Garibaldi had lost yet another close friend —a man he had come to consider a brother.

Food became increasingly scarce as they passed through the dense forest of Las Antas. The retreating column consumed the last of its rations, and the marchers were forced to survive on small game and wild berries. Many died of malnutrition. Others fell by the roadside, too weak to continue. Children were often abandoned by the wayside when they became ill. In many instances, the mother stayed behind with her child, and thus both were lost. There was little time to bury the dead, so many were left where they fell. This left an easy trail to follow for the pursuing Brazilian troops.

Bad weather conditions added to the marchers' misery. It was exceptionally cold for that time of year, with temperatures often dropping below the freezing point at night. Heavy rains turned the roads into mud and raised the level of the rivers and streams. All of this slowed down the march and enabled the pursuing Brazilian forces to cut off the retreat. Nevertheless, the column continued to move ahead as the Brazilians were beaten back by the forward elements led by Canabarro and Garibaldi.

Garibaldi and Anita were terrified by the thought of what might happen to baby Menotti if either of them should die. Anita was able to carry Menotti because he was only a few months old. Sometimes she carried him in a handkerchief tied around her neck like a big sling. Thus, she was able to keep him warm with her own body heat. On one occasion, when they were climbing down a steep gorge, Garibaldi himself had to carry baby Menotti in the sling tied around his neck. It was a rocky ride down, but Garibaldi managed it, keeping the baby warm by breathing on his face. At times, some of the soldiers helped out by wrapping their coats around the baby in order to keep him from getting frostbitten. Everyone thought it was a miracle that Menotti survived the ordeal.

The retreating army was fortunate that wild Indian tribes living in the region made no attempt to attack them, although the Indians probably didn't appreciate their being there. For whatever reason, the Indians chose instead to attack and slaughter the pursuing Brazilian troops, thus helping the retreating Riograndenses elude their pursuers. Along the way, the Riograndenses encountered a white woman who had been held captive by the Bugrés Indians for many years. She was allowed to tag along with the camp-followers and thus escape from her captors.

Eventually, the survivors of the Army of Rio Grande reached Cruz Alta, where they found plenty of food and warm spring water. From there, they marched south to the town of San Gabriel, ending the retreat after a horrendous trek through four hundred miles of wilderness.[3]

13

The Road to Montevideo

AFTER A MARCH IN WHICH THEY HAD SUFFERED terrible hardships, the remnants of the Rio Grande Army reached the town of San Gabriel deep in the interior. There the long retreat ended, and the marchers were assigned to construct wooden huts as temporary barracks. Once the task was completed, everyone settled back to rest and recuperate from the ordeal.

This was where Garibaldi first heard of an exiled Italian named Francesco Anzani, an officer in the Rio Grande Army whom others described as a man of great strength and courage. He had gained notoriety when he confronted and beat up an Indian chieftain who had been terrorizing the town of San Gabriel. Eager to meet another Italian expatriate, Garibaldi set out on horseback to find him. Along the road, he came upon a man stripped to the

waist, washing his shirt in a stream. Garibaldi approached the man
and said, "You must be Anzani." The man looked at the red hair
and replied, smiling, "And you must be Garibaldi." Thus, began a
great friendship.[1]

Garibaldi remained in San Gabriel for several months, and during that time, he came to believe that the Republican cause in Rio
Grande do Sul was lost. Everywhere the Imperial forces were
advancing, and many of the rebels were accepting the amnesty
offered by the Brazilian government. It appeared as though the
civil war was finally coming to a close. His chief concern now shifted to his family. He had spent more than five years in a futile struggle for Rio Grande's independence, and he had not received one
cent in pay.

In April 1841, he asked President Gonçalves for permission to
immigrate to Montevideo, in Uruguay. He told Gonçalves that he
needed a rest after five years of military service, and that he wanted his family to live in a permanent residence instead of following
an army on campaign. The president expressed warm gratitude to
Garibaldi for his years of service and granted permission. Since the
rebel government had no money to pay Garibaldi, it was decided to
do so in the one commodity that was plentiful—cattle. Gonçalves
allowed Garibaldi to collect a large herd of cattle as payment for his
services to the Republic. Within three weeks, he had rounded up
nine hundred cattle and hired several of the local *vaqueros* (cowboys) to drive the herd. His next challenge would be to get the
herd and his family to Montevideo.

The journey to Montevideo would be a hazardous one covering
a distance of more than four hundred miles. During the passage,
they encountered heavy rains and flooding, and nearly half of the
cattle drowned while crossing the swollen Rio Negro. The lack of

fodder caused more cattle to die along the way. To make matters worse, the *vaqueros* secretly sold off some of the cattle and kept the money for themselves. Suspecting that he was being defrauded by them, Garibaldi, with the help of a farmer, slaughtered the remaining three hundred cattle for their hides, which were then bundled and strapped to their horses. When they finally reached Montevideo on June 17, 1841, however, he discovered that hides were selling at a very low price.[2] Thus, the "cattle drive," which had started out with such great expectations turned out to be a fiasco that earned Garibaldi little money.

At first, Garibaldi, Anita, and baby Menotti lived in the house of an Italian immigrant named Napoleone Castellini. They later moved into an apartment house on a street called Calle del Portón. The street was later renamed Calle 25 de Mayo to commemorate the anniversary of the uprising against Spanish authority on May 25, 1810. The Garibaldi family lived in a one-room apartment, sharing the same kitchen with three other families who lived in the building. The house has survived and is open to the public as a museum.

In order to support his family, Garibaldi became a tutor, as he had done years earlier in Constantinople. He taught mathematics in a school whose headmaster was a Corsican immigrant named Pietro Semidei. Garibaldi remained on the job until war broke out between Uruguay and Argentina. He then resigned his post to join the Uruguayan Navy as an officer.[3]

On March 26, 1842, Garibaldi and Anita finally got married. The Catholic ceremony took place in the local parish church of San Francisco de Asis. Anita wore a wedding dress of various shades of green, and this time, one of her wedding slippers *didn't* fall off at the church door. The marriage certificate recorded that Father Zenón

Asperiazu had married "Don José Garibaldi, native of Italy, legitimate son of Don Domingo Garibaldi and of Doña Rosa Raimondi, with Doña Anna Maria de Jesus, native of Laguna in Brazil, legitimate daughter of Don Benito Ribeiro de Silva and of Doña Maria Antonia de Jesus." The witnesses were Don Pietro Semidei and Doña Feliciana García Villagron.[4]

The question then arises: Why did Garibaldi and Anita, after living together for nearly thirty months, suddenly decide to get married in church? Some writers have suggested that pressure from the school officials, or from the naval authorities, had forced the two to get married. After all, they did have a child born out of wedlock, and Uruguay was a Catholic country. There was also speculation that Anita had received news of Manoel Duarte's death from a sailor on a Brazilian ship that had docked in Montevideo. However, there is no evidence to support any of this, and the whole matter remains an unsolved mystery to this day.

Years later, because of the lingering controversy over the couple's marital status, a certified copy of the marriage certificate was widely publicized in Europe, to show that Garibaldi and Anita were indeed married. However, the question of Anita's status prior to her marriage to Garibaldi still remained unanswered. There were also those who questioned why Garibaldi, a known anti-cleric, would get married in a Roman Catholic church. The answer is quite simple: At that time in Uruguay, the only place where a couple could legally marry was in a Catholic church. Civil marriage was not legally recognized in that country. And then, it wasn't so surprising that Garibaldi married Anita in a Catholic church. He had been baptized into the Church, and even though he disagreed with the views of the Church hierarchy, he remained a nominal Catholic.

Church of San Francisco de Asis in Montevideo (photo by Diane Jesuele)

Garibaldi's house on Calle 25 de Mayo in Montevideo (photo by Joseph Jesuele)

Meanwhile, in Rio Grande do Sul, Republican resistance against the Brazilian government had not ended. Sporadic fighting continued for another four years, until Republican resistance was finally ceased in 1845. Benito Gonçalves eventually accepted an offer from the Brazilian Emperor to become Governor of the State of Rio Grande do Sul, once all armed resistance ended. The ten-year struggle to establish an independent Republic of Rio Grande do Sul ultimately ended in failure.

14

Uruguay and Civil War

Like most of the rest of South America, Uruguay was part of the Spanish Empire— until a movement for independence began in 1811 under the leadership of José Gervasio Artigas. A series of wars followed in which the Uruguayans fought Spain and Portugal, and later, Brazil and Argentina. The long struggle for control of Uruguay lasted until 1828, when British intervention forced both Brazil and Argentina to recognize the independence of the Republic of Uruguay. At that time, Britain was eager to end the conflict because it was engaged extensively in regional trade. The British believed that an independent Uruguay could serve as a buffer state between Brazil and Argentina.

During the long struggle for Uruguayan independence, two great figures had emerged—Fructuoso Rivera and Manuel Oribe.

Unfortunately, these two patriots held very divergent political philosophies, and an internal power struggle ensued for control of the new government. Rivera was the leader of the Unitarians, the faction that favored a strong central government; Oribe led the Federalists, who wanted a loose federation of provinces. The Unitarians, who were also known as the *Colorados,* tended to be more liberal and were concentrated in the cities. The Federalists, or *Blancos*, were more conservative and traditionally represented the ranchers and gauchos of the rural areas.[1]

In 1830, Uruguay adopted its first constitution, and Rivera was chosen as the first president of the republic. In the next election (1835), Rivera's big rival, Manuel Oribe, was elected president. Both sides polarized as the power struggle between them intensified. Upon taking office, Oribe accused the previous administration of corruption, whereupon Rivera's supporters deposed Oribe, forcing him to flee to Argentina. There, he became a protégé of Argentine dictator Juan Manuel de Rosas. In 1839, Rosas provided Oribe with an army for liberating Uruguay, thus provoking Rivera into declaring war on Argentina.[2] This marked the beginning of the so-called Great War, which lasted from 1839 to 1851. During the long bloody struggle, the conflict between the Colorados and the Blancos spilled over into Argentina and eventually led to Anglo-French intervention in the region. Garibaldi, who had previously taken no interest in the factional rivalry, now felt obligated to help defend Uruguay against an imminent Argentine invasion. He therefore enlisted to fight for Rivera against Oribe.[3]

The conflict in Uruguay was also a struggle between Britain and France for trading privileges on the La Plata River. France, fearing that Britain would monopolize trade in the region, supported Rivera and the Colorados against Oribe and the

Argentines. The British, suspecting that the French wanted to establish a sphere of influence in Uruguay, lent support to Argentina and to Oribe and the Blancos in Uruguay.

As hostilities began, there was an uprising against Rosas in the northern Argentine province of Corrientes. There, Governor Ferré declared the independence of Corrientes from Argentina and opted for union with Uruguay. The French navy supported the rebels by blockading the Argentine fleet in the port of Buenos Aires. Argentina later came to terms with France, and the blockade was lifted. In the meantime the British stood anxiously by, lending moral support to President Rosas of Argentina.

Once the French blockade ended, the Argentine fleet, under Admiral William Brown, sailed across the La Plata estuary to engage the Uruguayan fleet in battle. Brown, born in County Mayo, Ireland, in 1777, had originally emigrated to the United States with his parents in 1786. He had later joined the United States Merchant Marine but had been captured by the British and forced to serve in the British Navy under Admiral Nelson. For more than ten years he served under the British and eventually became a naval officer. After leaving the British Navy in 1809, Brown went to Argentina and helped that country gain its independence from Spain. As a naval officer, he served with such distinction in several wars that he became a national hero in Argentina, ranking second only to José de San Martin. Now, Brown was ordered by Rosas to destroy the Uruguayan fleet, which at that time was commanded by Colonel John Coe, a former U.S. naval officer who resided in Montevideo. The two fleets met in the La Plata estuary in November 1841, and Brown's fleet won a decisive battle. Most of Coe's ships were destroyed.[4]

Despite this major naval reversal, President Fructuoso Rivera ordered that the Uruguayan fleet be rebuilt and outfitted for a naval expedition up the Paraná River, one of the larger tributaries of the Rio de la Plata (La Plata River). The purpose of the expedition would be to bring relief to the Argentine break-away province of Corrientes. The rebel leadership in Corrientes had sided with Uruguay in the struggle against Argentina, but the remoteness of the province had made it virtually impossible for the rebels to receive any outside aid. Corrientes was situated in the northeast corner of Argentina, near the rebellious Brazilian state of Rio Grande do Sul. Its only access to the sea was along two rivers: the Paraná, which bounded it on the west; and the Uruguay, which formed its eastern boundary with Brazil. Both flowed southward, through Argentine territory, to the La Plata. This was why the Uruguayan government considered the undertaking such a risky naval operation.

The plan called for a naval squadron to slip through the Argentine blockade in the La Plata estuary and make its way up the Paraná to Corrientes. Besides running the blockade, the operation entailed passing beneath the guns of the Argentine island fortress of Martín García and sailing through five hundred miles of enemy-held territory. To complicate matters further, the expedition was getting underway at a time when the rivers were low because of an absence of rain. At first glance, the plan seemed suicidal—it made no provision for the fleet's return to its home base at Montevideo. Command of the entire operation was given to the one man capable of such a bold undertaking—Captain José Garibaldi![5]

Preparations for the daring expedition were carried out with the utmost secrecy. The warships that were to partake in the venture weren't even anchored together. They were interspersed among the many other ships docked in Montevideo harbor.

Garibaldi even took measures to ensure that enemy spies were misled. He hired ships' pilots who had made a career of sailing on the Uruguay River, to deceive the enemy into thinking that the expedition was going to sail up that river.[6] He thus managed to conceal the true destination of the expedition, and when his squadron sailed from Montevideo, only a few Uruguayan officials knew that his plan was to sail up the Paraná to Corrientes.

The Uruguayan squadron consisted of three ships—the *Constitución*, the *Pereyra*, and the *Prócida*. The three mounted a total of twenty cannon and carried a contingent of 510 men, some of whom had fought with Garibaldi in Rio Grande do Sul.[7] Others had fought in the wars against Spain and Brazil. Many were also convicted criminals or deserters from other armies. With this gang of cutthroats, Garibaldi undertook the extremely difficult task of eluding the Argentine fleet and sailing some five hundred miles up the La Plata and the Paraná Rivers. In doing so, he would re-enter the dangerous domain of Juan Manuel de Rosas.

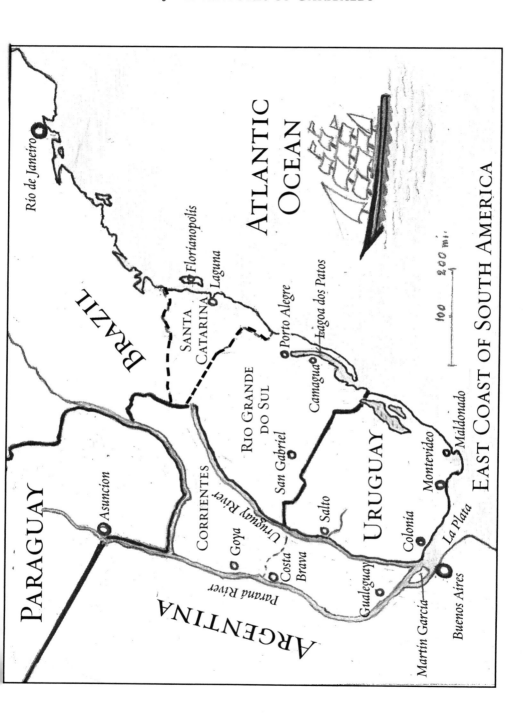

EAST COAST OF SOUTH AMERICA

15

Juan Manuel de Rosas

AFTER ARGENTINA GAINED ITS INDEPENDENCE from Spain in 1816, a dispute arose over the form of government for the new nation. Two rival factions emerged—the Unitarians, who wanted a strong central government to govern from Buenos Aires; and the Federalists, who favored a federation of provinces, each of which had a great deal of autonomy. Disagreements between the two factions led to violence and civil war.

In this struggle, the Unitarians were supported mainly by the upper- and middle-class citizens of Buenos Aires, which at that time was a city of more than 80,000 inhabitants. Their opponents, the Federalists, were favored by local leaders in the provinces and the big land owners on the Pampas, the vast grassland famous for its cowboys, or *gauchos*. These Argentine cowboys were known for their ability to ride a horse and lasso cattle. Their only diversion was drinking and gambling at the local cantina or waging war against an enemy—and in this case, the enemy was the Unitarians. An army composed entirely of gauchos was organized to fight for the Federalist cause. Their leader was Juan Manuel de Rosas. His followers were called the *Rositas*.

Juan Manuel de Rosas

Juan Manuel de Rosas was descended from a prominent Spanish colonial family. He was born on March 30, 1793, in Buenos Aires, but then lived most of his life on the Pampas. There, he learned the gaucho lifestyle, becoming a good horseman and an excellent marksman. He learned to speak like a gaucho and became their spokesman, advocating and supporting their interests.[1] Thus, he earned their loyalty and support. As a local leader, or *caudillo*, he organized a rural gaucho militia and was prepared to enter the fray when the Federalists enlisted his support in the struggle against the Unitarians.

When continued factionalism and internal strife caused the collapse in 1827 of Bernardino Rivadavia's Unitarian regime, Rosas emerged as the leader of the Federalists and was installed as governor of Buenos Aires. In 1829, he led an all-gaucho army into battle against the Indians of the northern frontier and succeeded in putting down several uprisings. Rosas then returned to Buenos Aires, where the Legislature entrusted him with "supreme and absolute" power.[2] In 1835, this move was supported by a plebiscite that gave Rosas absolute powers by a lopsided vote of more than 9,000 ayes to only 4 nays.[3] He was to dominate Argentina for the next seventeen years.

Supported through alliances with various provincial leaders, Rosas was able to exercise an iron rule over the country. He suppressed all political opposition, causing many Argentine Unitarians to flee across the La Plata River to Uruguay. Although he professed to be the champion of the lower classes, he enriched the aristocracy by selling them public lands at low prices. Officially, Rosas was only the governor of the Province of Buenos Aires, but the leaders in the other provinces had invited him to be "the protector" of the interests of the entire Argentine Confederation. In short, Rosas was the dictator of Argentina. His private army, the *Mazorca*, terrorized the city's inhabitants and even murdered Rosas' critics in their homes.[4] Wearing their red caps, the Mazorca patrolled the streets, threatening any woman who wasn't wearing a red ribbon in her hair. During the time of Rosas, the wearing of something red, such as the cap for men and the ribbon for women, showed that the person was a Rosita.

Rosas took care to observe the proper formalities of federal government and always strove to make a good impression on foreign diplomats. To further create a facade of civility and legitimacy for his regime, he used the Argentine press as a propaganda vehicle to favorably influence public opinion. Though he seldom emerged from his palace in the Palermo district of Buenos Aires, he had his beautiful daughter, Manuelita, fill in as the official hostess at gala parties, greeting all the guests and foreign dignitaries.[5] Manuelita was also the recognized leader of fashionable society in Buenos Aires and the chief sponsor of many charitable organizations. One hundred years later, Manuelita's style was imitated by Evita Perón, the wife of Argentine dictator Juan Perón.

Those Argentines who fled to Uruguay sided with the Colorados in their struggle against the Blancos. Rosas openly supported the Blancos and even provided the exiled Blanco leader, Manuel Oribe, with an army for re-entering Uruguay and challenging Rivera. The war that followed lasted thirteen years; Rosas was defeated at the Battle of Caseros in 1852, thus ending his rule in Argentina. He went into exile in England, leaving the Unitarian faction in control of the country. The victorious Unitarians were led by Bartolomé Mitre, an Argentine officer who had served under Garibaldi at Montevideo.[6] Today, Juan Manuel de Rosas is generally recognized by historians as an ardent Argentine nationalist and is often portrayed as the prototypical South American dictator.

16

The Paraná Expedition: 1842

ON JUNE 23, 1842, Garibaldi's fleet of three ships sailed out of Montevideo Harbor and slipped by the Argentine fleet which was patrolling the La Plata River. After a brief stop at the Uruguayan port of Colonia, Garibaldi sailed westward to face the most formidable obstacle on his route to Corrientes—the massive Argentine fortress of Martín García.

Admiral Brown, who had been patrolling the La Plata River, had no knowledge of Garibaldi's expedition. Rosas' spies in Montevideo had failed to inform him of the operation. However, when he did hear the news of the sailing, he immediately set out in pursuit with a fleet of seven warships. Brown assumed that the enemy ships were aiming to sail up the Uruguay River to prey on Argentine shipping, and he intended to intercept them near Martín García.

Known as "the Gibraltar of the Rio de la Plata", the island fortress of Martín García posed the greatest obstacle to any enemy incursion into the Argentine backwaters. Its strategic location at the confluence of the Uruguay and Paraná Rivers gave it command of the approaches to both rivers, and it was there that Garibaldi would face his first major test as a fleet commander.

Approaching cautiously, Garibaldi's ships hoisted the Argentine flag and entered the channel to the north of Martín García. The plan was to slip past the fortress by pretending to be an Argentine naval squadron on patrol. The trick didn't work, and when the ships came within range, the fort's batteries opened fire. The ships returned fire, precipitating a tremendous artillery duel that lasted for the duration of the passage. Miraculously, Garibaldi came through the encounter with minimal damage to his ships. He had passed his first major test as a fleet commander, but many hurdles still lay ahead.

No sooner had he sailed out of range of the fort's cannon than the *Constitución* ran aground on a sandbar in the channel. Now, he really had a problem—his ship was stuck in the sand, and the tide was going out! To make matters worse, Admiral Brown's fleet wasn't far behind. When the crew failed to pull the ship free, Garibaldi lightened the vessel by transferring its eighteen cannon to the *Prócida*. This was risky, because those guns would not be operational until the *Constitución* was refloated and her guns were remounted. In the meantime, she would be mired there like a sitting duck if Brown's fleet arrived there in the interim.

As it happened, Brown's fleet did appear in the distance while the *Constitución* was grounded with its guns dismounted. It was a scary situation as Garibaldi's men struggled to refloat the ship. Then, an incredible twist of fate occurred—Brown's flagship, the

Belgrano, ran aground as well, blocking the channel and preventing the other Argentine ships from passing. Seizing the opportunity, Garibaldi's men renewed their efforts, successfully clearing their ship from the sandbar and remounting her cannon. This having been done, Garibaldi's squadron slipped away while Brown's ships were still bottled up in the north channel. Adhering to the original plan, Garibaldi then bypassed the junction with the Uruguay River and started his run up the Paraná, unnoticed to Brown and the Argentines.[1]

Once Brown had extricated his ship, he renewed the chase, believing that Garibaldi had sailed up the Uruguay River. He knew that the Paraná flowed entirely through Argentine territory, and that, as such, there would be little chance of escaping back into Uruguay. The Uruguay River, however, formed the boundary between the two countries, and the left bank could provide Garibaldi with an emergency escape route. Logistically, Garibaldi should have chosen the Uruguay River as the route for the expedition, but as Brown later discovered, this was not the case.

The action that followed drew worldwide attention. Surprisingly, it began with Brown's fleet sailing up the wrong river. In his haste to catch up with his adversary, he was still unaware that Garibaldi's squadron had sailed up the Paraná. For four days and nights the admiral continued up the Uruguay but saw no sign of Garibaldi or his ships. On the morning of the fifth day, he finally came to the realization that Garibaldi had taken a different route and sailed up the forbidding Paraná. In his frustration, Brown reputedly commented that "Only Garibaldi could be capable of such lunacy!"[2]

Brown and his fleet now had to double back in order to resume the chase up the Paraná, and by that time, his fleet would be eight days' sailing time behind Garibaldi's. In the meantime, Garibaldi was proceeding up the Paraná, landing occasionally to seize provisions and cattle. At one village, Garibaldi forcibly took aboard a local river pilot because he needed someone to navigate the treacherous currents of the Paraná. The reluctant Argentinian had to be commandeered at sword point.[3] (The reader will recall that, back in Montevideo, Garibaldi had deceived Rosas' spies by conspicuously hiring pilots who only knew the Uruguay River. That clever bit of deception had worked well on Brown, but now it was beginning to work against Garibaldi. His unfamiliarity with the river's currents, and his reliance on an unwilling Argentinian pilot, were causing him to proceed upstream more cautiously.)

The expedition faced other problems as well. Except for the town of Rosario, the people living along the river were hostile to Garibaldi. They refused to collaborate and often fired on his squadron. At times, he was obliged to bully them into providing food and information for the expedition.[4] Needless to say, these acts again tended to reinforce Garibaldi's image as a pirate.

In mid-July, Garibaldi reached La Bajada del Paraná, where four years earlier he had spent two months in prison. There, a forbidding fortress and an Argentine naval squadron of six ships attempted to block his passage up the river. Without wasting any time, Garibaldi took the offensive by sailing straight into the Argentine formation blocking his path. After a fierce two-hour battle, his squadron blasted its way through the Argentine flotilla and past the blazing guns of the fortress. Amazingly, his ships suffered minimal damage.

The same story was repeated at a place called El Cerrito, but there, Garibaldi was able to capture several Argentine vessels. One of those seized was the *Joven Esteban*, a private yacht belonging to a rich merchant who was vacationing there with his family. The Argentine news media later accused Garibaldi of committing an "act of inhumanity" by setting the owner and his family adrift in a rowboat without any food or other necessities.[5] Garibaldi's tactics aroused much resentment in Argentina. However, the press didn't accuse him of killing civilians or prisoners—though the Argentines themselves often killed theirs. Garibaldi may have allowed his "ruffians" to loot captured towns, but he did not permit them to kill inhabitants or attack women.

Meanwhile, Admiral Brown and the Argentine fleet had resumed the chase. Once he turned up the Paraná River, he saw the havoc caused by "the pirate Garibaldi" and became convinced that he was dealing with a foe who paid no heed to logistics but relied instead on improvisation and the element of surprise. This realization caused him to proceed upstream cautiously.

As Garibaldi's expedition continued northward, there were more clashes with the local population, and at times his men had to battle the Argentine cavalry, which continued to shadow them from the river bank. The acquisition of food and fresh water became more difficult as the expedition pushed deeper and deeper into Argentine territory. Navigation was also hindered by the shallow waters above El Cerrito. By early August, Garibaldi's squadron was moving upstream an average distance of less than five miles a day.[6] With the enemy in control of both banks of the river and Brown's fleet trailing not far behind, it seemed as though Garibaldi was sailing up a "river of no return." He began to suspect that the politicians back in Montevideo had planned the expedition for the sole purpose of getting rid of him![7]

On August 6, his squadron reached the town of Caballú Cuatiá, which has since been renamed La Paz. There, they were joined by a fleet of four smaller ships that had come down from Corrientes to meet them. There was wild cheering by the crews of both fleets as the Uruguayan and Correntino forces linked up for the first time. The jubilation, however, was short-lived. Thirty miles farther north, at a place called Costa Brava, Garibaldi discovered that the Paraná River was too shallow to navigate his flagship, the *Constitución*. Uruguayan intelligence had failed to inform him of this fact and thus endangered the success of the entire operation. Realizing that Brown's fleet was getting closer, Garibaldi knew that he had to decide whether to stand and fight at Costa Brava or to abandon his flagship and proceed upstream with the smaller ships. After some debate, it was decided to stay and fight Brown at Costa Brava.

The town of Corrientes was 250 miles farther to the north, so the supplies brought for the Correntinos were sent ahead on the smaller vessels that Garibaldi had captured. The rest of his ships were then grouped against the shore on the deeper eastern bank of the river, so that Brown's fleet could not encircle them. Garibaldi put the *Constitución* up front with all eighteen cannon facing out at the river. Next to her at right angles, he placed the *Pereyra* with its two cannon, and the captured yacht, *Joven Esteban*, which had been refitted with four cannon. Behind these, Garibaldi placed the supply ship *Prócida* and three smaller warships from the Correntino fleet, under the command of Lieutenant Alberto Villegas. The formation resembled a floating fortress.[8]

Garibaldi ordered crew members who were not needed to man the guns to go ashore and take up defensive positions against a possible land attack. Once this was done, they braced themselves for the arrival of Brown and his fleet. The stage was set for the decisive battle of the Paraná campaign—the Battle of Costa Brava.

17

Costa Brava

THE ARGENTINE FLEET, commanded by Admiral Brown, reached Costa Brava on August 14, but it did not engage Garibaldi's squadron that day. Brown anchored his ships near the west bank of the river, just out of the range of Garibaldi's guns. Then he studied the situation.

Brown's fleet consisted of ten warships carrying a total of sixty-three cannon and about seven hundred crew members. Arrayed against this formidable armada was Garibaldi's smaller fleet with a total of twenty-four cannon and a contingent of five hundred men.[1] Besides numerical superiority in men and ships, Brown had another important advantage: The cannon on his ships had a longer range than those of Garibaldi. This would prove decisive, because Brown could now devise a battle strategy in which he would remain out of range of Garibaldi's guns while Garibaldi was still within range of his.[2]

As the battle opened, Brown sent ashore a landing party of a hundred men with orders to attack Garibaldi's ships from the land side. But Garibaldi had, as we have seen, anticipated such a move, and when Brown's force landed, they were met by Garibaldi's men. A fierce battle took place on the river bank as Garibaldi watched from the deck of his ship. Both sides fought doggedly till nightfall, when the Argentinians broke off the action and retreated to their ships. Garibaldi had won the first round.

The next morning, Brown's fleet opened fire on Garibaldi's formation from a distance at which it could take advantage of the longer range of its guns. Throughout the encounter, Garibaldi's ships remained in fixed positions, with their shorter-range cannon getting the short end of the artillery duel. Garibaldi made no attempt to sail into the enemy ships and do battle with them at close quarters. The spectacle of a close-range exchange of cannonades and of hand-to-hand combat was avoided. Garibaldi would later be criticized for adopting such a defensive posture.

The battle between the wily admiral and the elusive corsair continued all day and on into the evening, with Brown and the Argentinians getting the better of it. Garibaldi's flagship, the *Constitución*, was badly damaged by cannon fire, and his crew suffered considerable casualties. During the night he transferred his wounded men to the *Prócida*, which had been converted into a hospital ship. He also made several attempts under cover of darkness to set fire to Brown's ships.

In his most determined attempt, Garibaldi dispatched fifty men under the command of Captain Arana of the *Pereyra* to attack Brown's flagship from the western bank of the river. But they were spotted by the Argentinians, and Captain Arana was killed in the exchange of gunfire. His death was a severe blow to Garibaldi. The same night, Garibaldi suffered another setback when the Correntino ships under the command of Captain Alberto Villegas deserted him and sailed upstream to the safety of Corrientes. Garibaldi later denounced Villegas as a deserter commenting: "Desertion in the hour of danger is the most heinous of all crimes."[3]

In spite of these setbacks, Garibaldi made two more attempts to blow up the Argentine ships that night. Small boats loaded with gunpowder were quietly towed to the vicinity of Brown's ships and then set afire. The hope was that they would explode in the midst of the Argentine fleet. Both times, these attempts were thwarted by Brown's subordinates, who courageously boarded the "floating bombs" and extinguished the fires before the gunpowder exploded. One of those who assisted Brown in this most dangerous undertaking was a young sailor named Bartolomé Cordero. Cordero later went on to become an admiral in the Argentine navy.

At dawn, the battle resumed with greater intensity. Garibaldi, seeing that he was running short of cannonballs, ordered his men to load the guns with pieces of chain and any other scrap metal that they could find. As the cannonading continued, Brown sent a land force of more than a hundred men to attack Garibaldi's flagship from the eastern bank of the river. The fighting became desperate as the *Constitución* came under attack from both land and sea. Three times the Argentine land forces attacked, and each time they were cut down by gunfire from the *Constitución*. Eventually, the Argentines were forced to retreat.

As his losses continued to mount, Garibaldi realized that his position on the river was untenable. He therefore decided to scuttle his ships and retreat overland. He ordered that the wounded men be transferred to shore while he distributed the remaining gunpowder to his other ships. He then ordered them to be blown up—except for the hospital ship *Prócida*. Garibaldi himself remained on the *Constitución* to supervise the scuttling. The fuses were ignited after all his men had reached shore safely. Then, he dove into the water and swam to shore. The *Constitución* blew up in a tremendous explosion, staggering the enemy and preventing any immediate pursuit. Burning debris littered the river bank as Garibaldi and his men vanished into the jungle. The wounded who were well enough to be moved were helped along by their comrades; those who were more seriously wounded, had to be left behind on the *Prócida*. Fortunately for them, their Argentine captors were commanded by an admiral opposed to executing prisoners.

Supposedly, Rosas had given Brown orders to capture Garibaldi alive and to bring him back to Buenos Aires for public execution. However, when Brown's subordinates urged him to pursue Garibaldi overland, he reputedly said: "No, let him go, and may God preserve him. Garibaldi is a brave man." Brown made no attempt to pursue Garibaldi and his men.[4] Although it may seem far-fetched, there is reason to believe that Brown deliberately let his adversary escape. It was no secret that he had great admiration for Garibaldi's courageous action at Costa Brava.

The victorious Brown received a tumultuous welcome upon his return to Buenos Aires, greeted by cheering crowds as cannon were fired continuously in salute. President Rosas himself received Brown at the palace, and then hosted a great ball in his honor. While Buenos Aires society was attending the great ball in Rosas' palace, the people were celebrating in the streets, eating barbequed beef and burning effigies of Garibaldi. When Brown saw one of these, he reportedly murmured, "What an outrage, to burn a brave fellow!"[5]

Despite all the fanfare over Brown's victory, the people of Buenos Aires continued to wonder about the actual whereabouts of the "pirate Garibaldi."

18

Costa Brava to Montevideo

GARIBALDI'S RETREAT FROM COSTA BRAVA was filled with hardship. After three days of incessant fighting, his men were exhausted and their morale was low. Of the 510 men who sailed with him from Montevideo, fewer than 170 remained. They found themselves in a wilderness some 250 miles south of the town of Corrientes and about 600 miles northwest of Montevideo. They had no horses and little food. It took them three days to march through thirty miles of jungles and swamps. They subsisted on a biscuit a day until they reached the town of Esquina in rebellious Corrientes Province.[1]

The friendly people of Esquina provided food and shelter for the weary survivors of Costa Brava. It was a welcome break from the everyday pressure of the chase, but Garibaldi and his band weren't out of the woods yet. They were a long way from

Montevideo, and they were now in Corrientes under the jurisdiction of Governor Ferré.

From Esquina, Garibaldi and his men set out for the town of Goya. The hundred-mile march to Goya was made easier because they had obtained a stock of food and some horses. Before leaving Esquina, Garibaldi had sent word to Ferré that he would camp in the vicinity of Goya and wait there for instructions from him. He wound up staying at the village of Santa Lucia only a few miles from Goya. He would wait there for two months.

According to local legend, Garibaldi had a love affair there with Lucia Esteche, the beautiful daughter of a local rancher. The story goes that he met her when he stopped at her father's *estancia* to ask for a drink of water. It was love at first sight, and while Garibaldi remained in the district, he visited her regularly at the ranch. Evidently, he was infatuated with her, and after he left, Lucia gave birth to a baby girl she proudly named Margarita Garibaldi. Garibaldi never saw Lucia again, nor did he ever meet Margarita. Years later, he did carry on a correspondence with both Lucia and Margarita, and he even invited the latter to visit him at his home on the island of Caprera. Margarita, however, could not accept the invitation because she was married and could not leave her family.[2]

Garibaldi finally received orders from Governor Ferré; he was instructed to march his men eastward to the Uruguay River and then join President Rivera at the town of San Francisco near Paysandu. Rivera and his army were preparing for a decisive battle with Oribe and the Blancos—a battle that came sooner than they thought.

Garibaldi and his men arrived on the scene too late. San Francisco was deserted and looked like a ghost town. Rivera had been defeated by Oribe's forces at the Battle of Arroyo Grande

(December 6, 1842). He had lost about 1,500 men killed and 1,000 wounded.* The remainder of his men fell back in disarray toward Montevideo. Those who were taken prisoner were executed by the *degollador*. The degollador, or "cut throat," would pass down a line of kneeling prisoners and systematically slit each prisoner's throat. This was the manner in which the Rositas and the Blancos usually dealt with prisoners of war.[3]

Meanwhile, the Argentine general, Justo de Urquiza, marched on the rebels in Corrientes Province and defeated them. The rebel Governor Ferré fled to Paraguay but was refused political asylum there. He then took refuge with the rebels under Bento Gonçalves in Rio Grande do Sul. Rebel resistance in Corrientes ended, and the province once more came under control of Argentina and the Rositas.

Garibaldi, having arrived too late to partake in the battle at Arroyo Grande, was now ordered to make his way overland to Montevideo. He then set out with his men across the tall grasslands that covered most of Uruguay. Moving cautiously, he marched his men across three hundred miles of enemy territory, gathering along the way some stragglers from Rivera's defeated army. He finally reached Montevideo in late December and was reunited with his family.[4] All told, he and his men had covered a total of about a thousand miles on this combined sea and land odyssey.

During Garibaldi's absence, the Uruguayan minister of war, Francisco Vidal, had resigned and departed for Europe, taking with him in gold pieces most of the Republic's treasury. Vidal was the official who had ordered the expedition up the Paraná River. In

---

*These casualty figures are given in Jasper Ridley's *Garibaldi*, p. 130.

addition, Montevideo's chief of police, and a Uruguayan army general named Nuñez, had defected to the Blancos, all of this having occurred as the Blancos, under Oribe, were advancing on the city.[5]

19

War Comes to Montevideo

After his victory over Rivera at Arroyo Grande, Oribe advanced relentlessly toward Montevideo. The towns of Salto, Paysandu, and Colonia fell without a fight, as Rivera's battered forces made no attempt to stop him. The new Minister of Defense, Colonel Melchior Pacheco y Obes, was determined to defend the city at all costs. Later, Pacheco was to become a close friend of Garibaldi.

The City of Montevideo is located on the southern coast of Uruguay, near the point where the estuary of the La Plata River meets the South Atlantic. The city is surrounded on three sides by water, and its sheltered harbor is protected by the fortress of El Cerro, which lies just to the west of the city. A series of walls built by the Spanish in the early eighteenth century still encircled the old part of the city and presented a formidable defense line on the land side.

As Oribe and his army advanced southward, the Montevideans made every attempt to bolster their city's defenses. The remnants of President Rivera's army were recalled to Montevideo and regrouped as new regiments. Local gauchos were recruited and trained to function as a new cavalry unit. Armaments and munitions factories were opened, and clothing houses were ordered to make military uniforms. The Uruguayan Parliament officially abolished slavery, thus gaining the support of the Black community in Montevideo. Garibaldi was appointed Commander-in-Chief of the Uruguayan Navy and ordered to assemble another fleet of ships.

On February 16, 1843, Oribe reached the gates of Montevideo and camped on El Cerrito, a hill overlooking the city. Soon afterward, the Argentine fleet of Admiral Brown arrived off Montevideo to assist Oribe in attacking the city. The Montevideans braced themselves for a siege. Oribe, however, did not attack immediately, because he believed that Montevideo would surrender without a fight.[1] After all, he reasoned, hadn't the other cities in his path succumbed without offering any resistence?

Montevideo, however, was different from the provincial towns. At that time, it was a cosmopolitan community of 30,000 inhabitants, two-third of whom were foreign immigrants.[2] Many of these immigrants did not see the conflict as a power struggle between Rivera and Oribe but rather as a war between the nation of Uruguay and the forces of Argentine dictator Manuel de Rosas. The gravity of the situation now made it essential for the Uruguayan government to recruit these foreign residents in the defense forces.

As the siege began, Oribe issued a stern warning that any foreigner who actively resisted his conquest of the city would be summarily dealt with as an enemy.[3] This was generally interpreted as a
threat to execute all foreigners who fought against him. Despite
the threat, the people of Montevideo were determined to resist

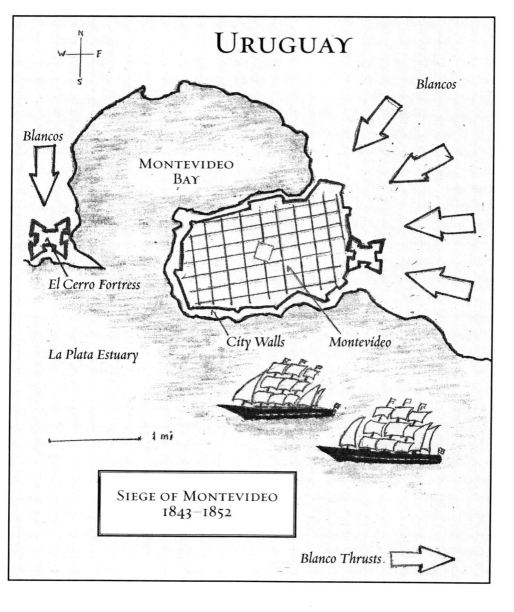

URUGUAY

Blancos

Blancos

MONTEVIDEO
BAY

El Cerro Fortress

La Plata Estuary

City Walls   *Montevideo*

1 mi

SIEGE OF MONTEVIDEO
1843–1852

Blanco Thrusts

Oribe, who had a reputation for cruelty. The very thought of execution by the *degollador* was an incentive for them to fight harder. Many foreign volunteers banded together to form foreign legions. In the meantime, most of Oribe's supporters, including the chief of police and General Nuñez, had already fled from the city—or remained behind as spies.

Oribe's army of 14,000 men outnumbered the defense forces by more than two to one, but he still made no attempt to attack the city. This was a tactical mistake, because it enabled the Montevideans to strengthen their defenses with more than 140 new cannon built in their own foundries. In addition, a large number of foreign immigrants volunteered for the army, thus swelling the ranks of the defense forces. The volunteers were given no pay, but the government promised to provide land and cattle as soon as the war was over—on the assumption that the Unitarians would win the war.

In addition to his naval commitment, Garibaldi was authorized to direct the formation of a new fighting force made up entirely of Italian expatriates. It was to be called the *Italian Legion*. The primary objective was to recruit the Italian immigrants to fight against the tyranny of Oribe and the Blancos. Garibaldi personally helped enlist the first 215 volunteers for the Legion.[4] One of the men he enlisted was Francesco Anzani, whom he had first met in Rio Grande do Sul. Anzani had since left Rio Grande to take a job in Buenos Aires. Garibaldi wrote to him there, inviting him to come to Montevideo and join the Legion. Anzani, who had great respect for Garibaldi, accepted.

The number of enlistees for the Legion soon rose to more than four hundred men, then to six hundred plus. Garibaldi himself was appointed to the three-member committee that was the ultimate authority for the Legion. Colonel Mancini was chosen as its first commander, with Lieutenant Colonel Anzani and Major Danuzio as deputy commanders. Anzani was given the task of training the men. He was a disciplinarian never known to laugh or smile. His courage and devotion to duty were to make him a role model for other legionnaires. He was to serve loyally under Garibaldi until his tragic death in Italy in 1849.

Besides the Italians, other foreign groups in Montevideo formed their own legions, the most prominent being the French, the Basques, and the Spaniards. The smaller foreign groups, such as the English and Scots, volunteered for the regular defense forces under the command of General Paz. Of all, the French Legion under Colonel Theibaud was the largest, with a contingent of 2,900 men. Because of its size, it was given a major role in the city's defense system.[5] The Basque Legion, under Colonel Brie, numbered seven hundred men and was also destined to play an important part in defending Montevideo.[6] As for the Spanish Legion, it defected to Oribe a few months after its conception.[7]

A rivalry soon developed between the Italian and French Legions. Apparently, the French legionnaires disliked the Italians, referring to them as a nation of cowards "who could only stab with a dagger in the dark or from behind." Tensions reached a breaking point when some Frenchmen made derogatory remarks about Italians at a party. Italian legionnaires took offense, intending to challenge the Frenchmen to a duel. Garibaldi, however, wishing to maintain solidarity, prevented his men from doing so. Then, in an attempt to minimize the ill-feeling, he and Theibaud tried to ease tensions by appearing together at functions.[8] There nonetheless remained an undercurrent of mistrust and suspicion.

As commander-in-chief of the navy, Garibaldi was primarily

concerned with breaking Brown's naval blockade. Montevideo depended on supplies of food and weapons from other parts of Uruguay and from other countries. Although the Blancos controlled all of Uruguay except for Montevideo, some towns along the coast of Uruguay and neighboring Brazil were willing to ship beef and other supplies to Montevideo by sea—if they could run the blockade.

In order to facilitate their efforts, Garibaldi built up a fleet of seventeen warships to protect blockade runners once they entered Uruguayan waters off Montevideo. He was even able to supply the El Cerro fortress across the bay. However, his warships were too small to engage the Argentine fleet on the open sea.

At this juncture, the British stepped in to help, dispatching a naval squadron to Montevideo under the pretext of protecting the lives and property of British subjects living in the city. The British still considered Admiral William Brown a British subject, and they pressured him into ending the blockade.[9] In order to avoid war with Britain, Brown withdrew his fleet, anchoring it some twenty miles away in the La Plata Estuary. President Rosas of Argentina protested the British interference in the struggle, but to no avail.

Meanwhile, the Italian Legion had performed poorly in battle, having been routed by the Blancos in its first two engagements. This caused the Montevideans to question the fighting ability of the Italians. The French legionnaires also resumed their criticism. Garibaldi, one of its founders, was so disappointed by the Legion's performance that he decided to take personal command. He determined that the only way to regain the confidence of the government and the people of Montevideo was for the legionnaires to distinguish themselves on the battlefield. On June 10, he himself led a force of 190 Italian legionnaires in an assault against an enemy strongpoint near the fortress of El Cerro. Charging with fixed bayonets, the legionnaires routed the Blancos and captured forty-three prisoners. In this manner, the Italian Legion wiped out the disgrace of the previous losses. (Incidentally, in this action the Legion first used the method of attack that was to make it famous—the bayonet charge.)[10]

The Montevidean press praised the legionnaires for their victory at El Cerro. On July 2, the Italian Legion proudly marched in parade in Montevideo's Plaza de la Constitución. The soldiers were commended for their valor by the minister of war, Melchior Pacheco, and given their colors—a black banner with the golden image of Mount Vesuvius emblazoned in the center.[11] The flag symbolized Italy's anguish and the fire that raged in her soul. Garibaldi always looked back with pride at the action at El Cerro when the Italian Legion restored its self-esteem.

Far to the north, President Rivera had put together an army of six thousand men and was operating in the pampas behind enemy lines, attacking the Blancos whenever he could. Oribe, who was besieging Montevideo, then sent a Blanco army under the command of General Urquiza to pursue Rivera. Rivera needed a major victory over the Blancos to consolidate his position as leader of the Unitarians in Uruguay. He also wanted to avenge his defeat two years earlier at Arroyo Grande.

Rivera, however, would suffer another disastrous setback. In March 1845, he was defeated by the Blancos under Urquiza at the Battle of India Muerta, and his army was routed. All prisoners taken by the Blancos were executed by the degollador. Rivera retreated with the battered remnants of his army into Rio Grande do Sul, but Riograndense resistance against the Imperial government of Brazil had already ended. Consequently, his troops were interned by the Brazilians, and he was asked to resign his command. He refused, despite pressure from the Brazilians. He had hoped to re-enter Uruguay and reclaim his leadership of the Unitarian forces (the Colorados) as soon as the time was right. However, the government in Montevideo, then under the control of Melchior Pacheco, ordered Rivera not to re-enter Uruguayan territory without its permission. He therefore remained exiled in Brazil, and a bitter rivalry developed between him and Pacheco.[12] This would later lead to a serious rift in the Unitarian Army between the supporters of Rivera and those of Pacheco.

20

The Red Shirts

Although the Italian Legion had gained the respect of the government and the people of Montevideo, it still wasn't the fighting machine that Garibaldi wanted it to be. The Legion was rife with internal discord, and a change of cadre was called for by the founding committee. Some of the officers, led by Colonel Mancini and Major Danuzio, formed a conspiracy to remove Garibaldi from the committee, and when they failed, Mancini and Danuzio defected to Oribe along with several other legionnaires. Garibaldi thought that the defections would only serve to strengthen the Legion, because it would be worse if the enemy remained in their midst.[1]

The committee then appointed Colonel Francesco Anzani to undertake the reorganization of the Legion. Anzani replaced incompetent officers, drilled the legionnaires incessantly, and instilled a strict discipline. To make them battle hardened veterans, he put them at the most critical point in the front line. Anzani's commanding personality was to have a tremendous impact on shaping the Legion's image as an elite fighting force. Garibaldi, as Legion commander, was so impressed with Anzani that he always addressed him as "Signor Anzani" and deferred to his opinion in most matters.

Though the Italian Legion was thus becoming a well-drilled and well-disciplined fighting force, it still lacked one very noticeable element—uniforms—or the means to purchase them, and the Legionnaires themselves received no pay from the government. They had to improvise!

Although the origin of the Legion's uniform is obscure, according to an old South American legend, some Legionnaires came across a cache of red smocks in an abandoned warehouse. The smocks had been manufactured by a Montevidean firm for export to the butchers in the slaughterhouses of Argentina. The garments were red so as not to show bloodstains. War, and the blockade, had prevented the manufacturer from shipping them to Argentina, so they remained stockpiled in the warehouse. Garibaldi, who liked to wear bright-colored clothes, decided that these red smocks could serve as uniforms for the Italian Legion. The legionnaires were ordered to wear them as slip-on outer garments belted at the waist. On July 2, 1843, the Italian Legion paraded in Montevideo's main square wearing red shirts for the first time. Thus, came into being the legendary Red Shirts.[2]

Under the leadership of Garibaldi and Anzani, the red-shirted Italian Legion became a nucleus of Italian patriotism. In fact, the outward manifestation of *italianita* in the Legion was resented by the Sardinian consul in Montevideo, who tried to use diplomatic pressure to have the Legion dissolved, but to no avail.[3] By then, Garibaldi had conceived the idea of turning the Italian Legion into an elite fighting force that could eventually be used in the struggle to unify Italy. His dream of leading the Legion in the struggle for Italian unification received a boost from his old friend Giovanni Cuneo. Cuneo, who was living in Montevideo, sent exaggerated accounts of Garibaldi's achievements to Giuseppe Mazzini in London. Mazzini published them in his newsletter *L'Apostolato Popolare*,[4] which was not only read by Italian refugees in London but illegally smuggled into Italy. Garibaldi and the Italian Legion soon became household words in Italy, thanks to the efforts of Mazzini and Cuneo.

As the siege of Montevideo continued, the Italian Legion won a series of battles against the Blancos. In the sector of the front called Tres Cruces, it was called upon to retrieve the body of a fallen colonel named Neira. He had been killed while leading an attack on the besieging forces, and it was feared that the enemy would mutilate his body. Garibaldi, with a small band of legionnaires, retrieved the body after fierce hand-to-hand combat. However, Blanco reinforcements soon arrived and surrounded them. Garibaldi ordered his men to fight to the death to prevent Neira's body from falling into enemy hands. More reinforcements were called up by both sides until about 1,500 men were involved in the battle—all for the possession of a corpse! After two hours of fierce combat, the Blancos retreated, leaving Garibaldi and his comrades in possession of the corpse of Colonel Neira.[5]

During the Spring of 1844, the Italian Legion distinguished itself in a further series of engagements against the besieging Blanco forces. Led by Garibaldi and Anzani, the legionnaires succeeded in capturing several strong points and inflicting heavy losses on the enemy. Their fierce bayonet charges seemed to strike fear into their opponents, causing them to break and run. The legionnaires were now being welcomed by cheering crowds whenever they returned to the city of Montevideo. Italian honor on foreign soil had been vindicated.

In an act of gratitude, the government of the Republic of Uruguay assigned the legionnaires gifts of land and cattle. These were, however, publicly declined by Garibaldi. He urged other legionnaires to do the same, declaring that they were not fighting for material rewards.[6] Although his comrades generally refused to accept any of these "gifts" from the government, many of the French Legionnaires did accept them, to Garibaldi's dismay.

His family lived in poverty despite his high rank as commander-in-chief of the navy. In addition, his wife, Anita, was snubbed by the upper-class women of Montevideo, who froze her out of their social activities.[7] She was mainly occupied with housework and looking after their four children—Menotti, Rosita, Teresita, and Ricciotti. The Garibaldis could not afford a servant, and Anita felt a sense of inferiority in the presence of those prim-and-proper ladies of leisure. She would soon remedy the situation.

During this period, Garibaldi had maintained a warm friendship with the British ambassador to Uruguay, Sir William Ouseley. Ouseley possessed a favorable opinion of Garibaldi, whom he had come to admire for his courage and honesty. On occasion, he would invite Garibaldi to his house for a cup of tea and a friendly discussion of local politics and international diplomacy.

Ouseley's wife, Maria, also took a liking to Garibaldi, the epitome of the handsome, swashbuckling hero. Maria, an American by birth, was a tall and attractive woman who turned men's heads wherever she went. She certainly attracted attention when she rode out to meet Garibaldi returning from the battlefront. The sight of the two of them riding together at the head of the Legion aroused Anita's anger. She may have had feelings of inferiority around high-society women, but she was always confident of her superiority on horseback. On one occasion, when the two were riding side-by-side, Anita suddenly rode out and reared her horse, frightening Mrs. Ouseley and her horse right out of the line of march. Anita then took her place at her husband's side.[8]

21

The Expedition Up
The Uruguay River: 1845

WITH THE DEFEAT OF PRESIDENT RIVERA at India Muerta, Oribe and the Blancos could now bring more pressure to bear on the City of Montevideo. A triumvirate consisting of War Minister Pacheco, General Martinez, and Garibaldi himself took command of the city's defenses. During this phase of the struggle, Garibaldi divided his time between fighting on land and sea. Whenever there was a lull in the land fighting, he was with the naval forces attacking Argentine ships on the La Plata River.

During the summer of 1844, Garibaldi captured ten Argentine merchant vessels and brought them to Montevideo. Their cargoes were placed at the disposal of the Unitarian government and any monies received from their sale used to support the war effort.

Sometimes, Argentine warships pursued him to the entrance of Montevideo harbor in an attempt to engage him in battle. On one such occasion, Garibaldi's fleet of small ships fought a running battle with two pursuing Argentine warships. The sea battle was fought right off the coast, in full view of the cheering crowds who lined the oceanfront in Montevideo.[1] The whole event had the look of a battle sequence in a pirate movie, with galleons firing cannonades and pirate ships maneuvering for the attack. The spectacle lasted four hours and ended with the Argentine ships being driven off, much to the delight of the Montevideans. The swashbuckling manner in which Garibaldi disposed of the enemy warships made him the toast of Montevideo. However, in Argentina, the press was denouncing him as a "savage" and a "pirate."

As the scope of the conflict widened, Britain and France threatened to intervene in order to ensure the independence of Uruguay and to protect their commercial interests in the region. They presented the belligerents with a plan for ending the hostilities and threatened them with military intervention if they refused to accept the peace terms. The proposal called for the withdrawal of Argentine troops from Uruguayan soil, the disbanding of the foreign legions in Montevideo, and the holding of democratic elections in Uruguay for a new national assembly, which would in turn elect a new president of the republic. The proposal was readily accepted by the Unitarian government in Montevideo but rejected by the Argentines and the Blancos. Rosas was opposed to evacuating Argentinian troops from the territory of Uruguay, and Oribe refused to end the hostilities against Montevideo. Frustrated by the Argentine and Blanco refusal, Britain and France decided to intervene on the side of the Unitarian government in Montevideo. The American press denounced Britain and France for violating the Monroe Doctrine but refused to take any action against them.[2]

In short order, an Anglo-French naval squadron sailed up the La Plata River and blockaded Buenos Aires, forcing Admiral Brown to lift the blockade of Montevideo. He was also required by the British to sign a statement promising that all British subjects, including himself, were not to continue serving in the Argentine navy. Brown resigned his command and retired from active service, ending a distinguished naval career. All this worked in favor of the Unitarians in Uruguay and to the satisfaction of Garibaldi and the Italian Legion. However, it also served to strengthen Rosas' determination to continue the struggle for control of Uruguay.

The Unitarian government in Montevideo, seeking to take advantage of the situation, decided to carry the war into enemy territory. A fleet of seventeen Uruguayan ships, under the command of Garibaldi, was to blast its way up the Uruguay River, which forms the border between Uruguay and the Argentine province of Entre-Rios. In addition to their crews, the ships were to carry a contingent of 750 legionnaires, who had orders to liberate the river towns held by the Blancos on the Uruguayan side of the river, and to raid those held by the Rositas on the Argentine side of the river. An Anglo-French squadron of ten warships was to accompany the expedition.

It set out on August 30, 1845, and for the first few days followed the same route that Garibaldi had taken some four years earlier, during the Paraná Expedition. The first objective was to liberate the town of Colonia, which had been occupied by the Blancos since the summer of 1843. When the Blanco garrison refused to surrender, Colonia was subjected to a tremendous naval bombardment that forced the garrison to evacuate the town, thus enabling the legionnaires to move in and retake it without a fight. A great deal of looting then took place, though Garibaldi had issued strict orders forbidding it. Reports of the looting appeared in the Argentine press and caused much indignation in Argentina and Europe. Garibaldi was yet again portrayed as a pirate committing atrocities—only this time, with the British and French looking on as spectators.[3]

Sailing westward from Colonia, Garibaldi's squadron soon approached the fortress of Martín García, where three years earlier his ships had run the gauntlet of enemy fire. This time, they found that the fortress had already been abandoned by the Argentines. Garibaldi left a small detachment of men to garrison the strategic bastion and then started his run up the Uruguay River, while the Anglo-French squadron headed for the Paraná River to disrupt trade with neighboring Paraguay.

On September 6, Garibaldi's squadron reached the town of Yaquari on the Uruguayan side of the river. There, he linked up with a friendly guerrilla band that had been operating behind Oribe's lines since Rivera's defeat at the Battle of India Muerta. From them, Garibaldi learned that British and French settlers in the area were being interned in Argentine prison camps. The legionnaires rescued two groups of these prisoners from their captors—one by overpowering the guards at a detention center outside of Yaquari, the other by overtaking the launch ferrying them across the river to Argentina. They expeditiously disposed of the Rosita guards by throwing them overboard.[4]

As he proceeded up the Uruguay, Garibaldi had to employ alternate plans of action depending on which side of the river the action was to take place. Uruguay was on the east bank and had to be treated as friendly territory to be liberated from Oribe's control. The Argentine province of Entre-Rios occupied the west bank, and the people there were to be dealt with as enemies. But this distinction between *friendly* and *enemy* river banks meant little to Garibaldi's men, who had to live off the land. They indiscriminately seized cattle for food wherever they found it, on either bank of the river. But they did the greatest damage on the Argentine side—looting estancias and breaking down fences so that the cattle could get out and roam around the pampas.[5] This caused the estancia owners to lose most of their livestock.

On September 19, Garibaldi landed a force of 250 legionnaires on the west bank in preparation for an attack on the Argentine town of Gualeguaychú, situated five miles inland. He enlisted the help of a friendly guide to lead them on the overland march. The legionnaires reached the town at midnight and quickly overpowered the small Rosita garrison. The commander, Colonel Eduardo Villagra, was captured in his bed and brought to Garibaldi in his underwear.[6]

Garibaldi remained in Gualeguaychú for two days, assessing each family for a contribution of food and blankets for his men. Meanwhile, his legionnaires proceeded to loot the homes of the wealthier townspeople. Stories about the excesses they committed there have become part of the local folklore. One of these stories mentions how the legionnaires stole valuables from a house that a wealthy family had allowed them to use as a hospital for their wounded. The looting supposedly had occurred while a comrade lay dying on the dining room table! Surprisingly, no complaints of rape or murder were recorded, nor did Garibaldi execute any of the captured Rosita soldiers, although that is probably what the Rositas would have done to their own captives. In fact, before he left Gualeguaychú, he released all prisoners unharmed, including Colonel Villagra.

The attack on Gualeguaychú, and the looting that followed, caused a great outcry against Garibaldi in Argentina. He was denounced in the press as an instrument of the British and French and blamed for the "horrors" that had taken place there. The Argentine government showed no gratitude either for Garibaldi's humane decision to set free the prisoners. In fact, Rosas displayed every intention of continuing the Rosita policy of executing enemy prisoners.

In Montevideo, some of Garibaldi's supporters were also dismayed by the decision to release prisoners; they wanted revenge against the Blancos and Rositas for their practice of executing prisoners. The release of Colonel Villagra caused the greatest resentment. He had a reputation for executing Unitarian prisoners, and some Montevideans believed that his release would only serve to encourage volunteers to join the Blancos or Rositas. They would feel safer knowing that, if they were captured by Garibaldi, they would be allowed to live. Garibaldi therefore received praise neither from his supporters nor from his enemies for a humane treatment of captive combatants that has long since become a civilized norm. The British and French, however, applauded his action and tried to follow his example in dealing with enemy prisoners.

There are conflicting accounts of what happened next. According to Alexandre Dumas' edition of Garibaldi's *Memoirs*, the expedition marched on to capture the town of Gualeguay, where Garibaldi had been brutally tortured some eight years before. He took the entire garrison prisoner, including the officer who had tortured him—Major Leonardo Millan. Dumas writes that Garibaldi refused even to see Millan for fear that he would recall that torture and decide unreasonably to take his revenge.[7]

Robert Cunningham-Graham, who visited Argentina in 1870,

offers a somewhat different account of Garibaldi's raid on Gualeguay.[8] According to him, Major Millan was apprehended and locked up in a room. He sat there alone for hours, awaiting the feared executioner. Suddenly, the door opened, and a man entered the room bringing him a cup of hot coffee. It was Garibaldi. Millan was so frightened that he passed out!

Very little else is known about Garibaldi's raid on Gualeguay or, for that matter, what happened to Millan. Garibaldi and his men returned to their ships on the Uruguay River and continued their course upstream. After sailing past Paysandu, where they were fired upon by Rosita shore batteries, Garibaldi's squadron finally approached its destination—the town of Salto.

It was known that the Unitarian guerrilla leader, Joseph Mundell, was already operating in the area with a force of a hundred *matreros*, or "gauchos of the mountains." Mundell, a Scotsman, had organized these matreros into a local militia he used for purposes of marauding. However, his acts of thievery had caused him to be labeled a "brigand."[9] Now, this brigand and his matreros wished to join Garibaldi's expeditionary force. Garibaldi, for his part, was eager to accept Mundell's offer of help, and the two joined forces near Salto.

At that time, Salto was a thriving river town strategically located in northern Uruguay. Control of the town was essential for the success of any military operation in the region. Salto had been occupied by the Rositas, but a Unitarian army under General Medina was also known to be operating in the area. Garibaldi planned to capture Salto and then link up with Medina's army.

As his squadron approached Salto, the Rosita commander, Colonel Manuel La Valleja, evacuated his garrison and the civilian population to an encampment a few miles to the south. Garibaldi sent Anzani, with a hundred legionnaires and a newly arrived detachment of cavalry under Colonel Baez, to attack the camp. Anzani told his men, "Don't fire until they're so close our shots burn their coats!"[10] They then proceeded to mow the enemy down. The Rositas were defeated and abandoned the field, leaving behind the civilians. Thirty British and French settlers were freed, and the townspeople were allowed to return to their homes.

In the meantime, Garibaldi had entered Salto only to find the town virtually deserted. He quickly went about making preparations for defending it against any enemy counterattack. The streets were barricaded except for the main thoroughfare, which was left open. Sharpshooters were placed on rooftops and at strategic points while civilian volunteers manned the barricades. The main body of legionnaires was deployed in a defensive perimeter around the town away from the river. Two heavy cannon were set behind the center of the defense line, and Garibaldi's fleet stood by on the river to lend support. They all awaited the onslaught.

They didn't wait long. On December 6, a Blanco army under General Justo Urquiza attacked the town with a force of more than 3,500. Urquiza was the Blanco commander who had defeated Rivera at India Muerta three years earlier. Now, he boasted that he would cross the Uruguay River in Garibaldi's ships. He also adhered to the practice of executing all prisoners. The legionnaires had no doubts about what would happen to them if they were captured.[11]

After an opening artillery barrage, the Blancos attacked with an intensity yet unseen during the war. Spearheaded by gaucho cavalry and followed by waves of infantry, they surged toward the defense perimeter. What followed resembled something out of a Wild West movie—the roar of gunfire, charging horsemen leaping over street barricades, snipers shooting from rooftops, riders falling from their horses, stampeding cattle, and the unheeded cries of the wounded. The attackers were met with a withering fire and a barrage from Garibaldi's cannon. They fell like flies. Those who did break through were cut down by Baez's cavalry. As soon as the Blanco attack faltered, Garibaldi ordered his legionnaires to launch a bayonet charge. Fierce fighting ensued, with the legionnaires forcing the Blancos to fall back.

Urquiza then laid siege to Salto, completely cutting the town off from the land side. Repeated Blanco attacks achieved little success. In eighteen days of desperate fighting, the Blancos could only force their way into the stockade and stampede the cattle—a loss that did not affect the outcome of the battle, because Garibaldi controlled the river and was able to bring in food by ship. Realizing that he had failed to defeat his opponent, Urquiza and the remnants of his army retreated northward and crossed the river into Argentina—in his own boats! Later, he would play a decisive role in the final outcome of the war.

22

Battle of San Antonio: 1846

FOLLOWING THE BATTLE OF SALTO, Garibaldi made preparations to receive the main body of the Unitarian army under the command of General Anacleto Medina.   Medina was Rivera's replacement during the latter's internment in Brazil.

Now, Garibaldi received a message from Rivera that Medina was marching his army to Salto with the intention of joining forces with him.

On February 8, Garibaldi marched out to meet Medina and escort him and his troops into Salto. He rode at the head of two hundred legionnaires and was accompanied by a hundred Uruguayan cavalrymen under the command of Colonel Baez. Around midday, Garibaldi's column was approaching a low ridge near a stream called the Rio San Antonio when, suddenly, a large Argentinian force appeared on the crest of the ridge. Garibaldi immediately realized that he was confronting an enemy force much larger than his own, and that retreat was impossible. He determined—as would George Armstrong Custer under similar circumstances—to make a last stand.

They were in open terrain, but fortunately there was an old abandoned farmhouse nearby. Garibaldi ordered his men to take cover there. All that remained on the property were the ruined house itself and a partially destroyed wall that ran along the side of the house facing the enemy. The legionnaires had just enough time to take cover as the battle got underway. It was at this desolate farmhouse that the Italian Legion made its famous stand in what came to be known as the Battle of San Antonio.

The battle opened with Colonel Baez's cavalry briefly engaging the advancing enemy and then retreating from the field in an attempt to draw off the Rosita cavalry in pursuit. The ruse didn't work. The Rositas pursued Baez to Salto and then quickly returned to the field of battle. Baez remained in Salto, and the Legion was left to fight on alone against both the Argentine infantry and cavalry. Estimates put that force, commanded by Colonel Servando Gomez, at 1,200 men, of which 900 were cavalry.* This meant that the Legion was outnumbered by more than six to one.

There are numerous accounts of the Battle of San Antonio, but they all tell basically the same story. At each sound of the bugle, the Argentines attacked in waves, each wave being beaten back by a determined fire from the Legion. The fighting continued under a blazing sun as the returning Argentine cavalry joined in the assault

---

* These figures are given in Andrea Viotti's *Garibaldi, The Revolutionary and His Men*, p. 34.

on the encircled legionnaires. In repeated attacks, Argentine horsemen leaped over the legionnaire positions at the ruined wall, only to be cut down by a withering fire from inside the farmhouse. Despite its desperate situation, the morale of the Legion remained high. Between the enemy attacks, the men joined in singing the Uruguayan national anthem, with Garibaldi using his tenor voice to lead the singing. As the battle progressed, the place was littered with the dead bodies of Rositas and their horses. In the more exposed areas, the bodies and carcasses were stacked up by the legionnaires and used as ramparts against the oncoming Rositas.

Aside from the actual fighting, the intense heat and lack of water caused the legionnaires the greatest hardship. The wounded suffered most. The Legion suffered another blow when its courageous bugle boy was killed. The fifteen-year-old had continued to sound his bugle throughout the action, until he was struck down by the lance of an enemy cavalryman. The cavalryman was in turn cut down by a legionnaire's bayonet, but too late to save the boy. Garibaldi would never forget the courageous young bugler who died at San Antonio.

Finally, after nine hours of desperate combat, Garibaldi retreated under cover of darkness. Carrying its wounded, the Legion slowly fell back, stopping to fire at enemy cavalrymen whenever they got too close. By daybreak, the legionnaires had reached the banks of the Uruguay River, where they were able to quench their thirst. They took turns drinking while their comrades guarded against encroachment by the enemy. However, the worst was over. The enemy had withdrawn, leaving more than six hundred dead on the battlefield.[1]

The victorious legionnaires returned to Salto early the next morning. Anzani, who had remained in town with a small detachment of men, was so overjoyed to see Garibaldi that he ran out to embrace him. Virtually the entire town turned out to greet the returning hero and his men. Two hours later, while the town was still celebrating Garibaldi's victory, General Medina arrived with his army, and they too were greeted by the townspeople.

The following day, after the town had quieted down, Garibaldi returned to the site of the battle accompanied by some of his men. After a thorough search, they found more wounded soldiers from both sides. These were given medical treatment and taken by wagon to Salto. Fortunately for Garibaldi, he was able to enlist the support of the "gentlewomen of Salto" to nurse the wounded. Their help proved invaluable in saving lives and boosting morale. The dead were also carted back to Salto in wagons and buried in a common grave, friend and foe alike, on a hill overlooking the town. Garibaldi ordered that a large cross be erected over the grave site, and that it bear the inscription: *Legione Italiana, Marinai Cavalleria Orientale, 8 Febraio 1846.*[2]

Around this time Garibaldi received the news that his daughter, Rosita, had died in Montevideo.[3] Rosita was four years old, and it is believed that she died during an epidemic of scarlet fever. Living conditions in Montevideo, with the family all living in one room, caused the children to be more prone to infection. Rosita's death came as a shock to Garibaldi, and he was deeply grieved.

In his report to the government in Montevideo, Garibaldi gave an account of the "terrible combat" that had taken place on February 8, 1846, at San Antonio. Legion casualties were given as thirty dead and fifty-three wounded. He noted that every Legion officer, with the exception of himself, had been killed or wounded in the engagement. Garibaldi stated that the enemy was "completely defeated."[4]

When the news of the Battle of San Antonio reached Montevideo, the press hailed it as a great victory for Garibaldi and the Italian Legion, which became the toast of the town. It had covered itself with glory and won immortal fame. Garibaldi was promoted to the rank of general, and the Montevidean government

Garibaldi after the Battle of Salto (by Gaetano Gallino)

awarded to those who had taken part in the combat at San Antonio a shield to be worn on the left shoulder with the inscription: *Invincible, they fought on February 8, 1846.*[5]

Garibaldi's friend, Giovanni Cuneo, sent news of the victory at San Antonio back to Mazzini in London. Mazzini promptly printed it in his newsletter, the *Apostolato Popolare*. When the news of Garibaldi's victory finally reached Italy, it set off a series of joyous celebrations. In Florence, donations were made for the purchase of a *Sword of Honor* for General Garibaldi in recognition of his great victory.[6] The French admiral, Laine, who had commanded the French squadron in the expedition up the Uruguay River, viewed San Antonio as a type of victory which would even fill Napoleon's Grand Armée with pride.[7] General Tomas de Iriarte of the Uruguayan Army described the victory at San Antonio as a "brilliant feat of arms" by which Garibaldi and his legionnaires had gained "immortal fame." Garibaldi himself wrote that he had "never experienced a greater honor than to have been a soldier of the Italian Legion on February 8 on the battlefield at San Antonio."[8]

News of the victory spread all over Europe and the Americas, and to this day, the two events that are most closely associated with Garibaldi's legacy in South America are his meeting with Anita and his victory at San Antonio.

23

Politics and Intrigues: 1846—1847

Soon after the Battle of San Antonio, the political situation in Uruguay began to deteriorate. A power struggle developed between Pacheco and Rivera, with each side vying for control of the government in Montevideo. Rivera was released by the Brazilians and returned to Montevideo by ship on March 18, 1846. When the Montevidean government refused to permit Rivera to land, the Uruguayan army under General Venancio Flores rose in his support and overthrew the government. The military coup was supported by the French Legion and some units of newly freed Blacks. Pacheco, whose position was weakened by the absence of Garibaldi and most of the Italian Legion, resigned his position and went into exile in Brazil.

Rivera triumphantly entered Montevideo and took command of the government. Privately, he praised Garibaldi and the Italian

Legion for their valor at the Battle of San Antonio. However, behind the scenes, he secretly contacted General Medina in Salto and instructed him to hold the town for the Riveristas. Rivera wanted to prevent the Legion from using it as a base for supporting his rival. Medina was told to proceed cautiously.

Now that he was back in control, Rivera proceeded to appoint his supporters to key positions in the government and in the military. Garibaldi and the legionnaires were excluded from any position of importance. Leaders of the new government thought of them as foreigners in their country. General Medina, a native Uruguayan, was appointed commander-in-chief of the forces of Northern Uruguay, thus placing Garibaldi and the Italian Legion under his orders. Political expediency, rather than logic and merit, now seemed to determine policy and protocol, and the efforts of devoted men were ignored.

Friction soon developed between Garibaldi and Medina. There were disagreements over military strategy and the conduct of the legionnaires. Medina was especially critical of the Legion's lax discipline. In addition, Rivera's new government refused to allow the Italian legionnaires in Montevideo to rejoin Garibaldi in Salto. Garibaldi now realized that Medina was only there for the purpose of securing the town of Salto for the Riveristas. He decided to end the farce by exercising his independent command of the Italian Legion.

It was mid-May, and Salto was once again facing the threat of an enemy attack. A Blanco force had marched north from Paysandu and camped on the Rio Daimán, some ten miles south of Salto. From there, they were attacking Garibaldi's cavalrymen whenever they tried to round up cattle.

Garibaldi now decided to seize the initiative. Without con-

sulting Medina, he and the Legion set out for the Blanco camp on
the night of May 19. The next morning, they caught the Blancos
sleeping and completely routed them, driving many of them into
the Rio Daimán. The Legion had won an easy victory—or so it
seemed. As it turned out, it was only the preliminary to the main
event. On the march back to Salto, Garibaldi encountered a much
larger enemy force. This time they were waiting to catch the
legionnaires in open terrain, where there was little cover. Upon
spotting the enemy hovering in the distance, Garibaldi ordered the
main body of legionnaires to take cover while his cavalry covered
them. The Blancos moved quickly to the attack, and a fierce battle
developed. For the better part of an hour the issue was in doubt as
both sides fought desperately. Finally, Garibaldi led his men in a
bayonet charge that sent the Blancos into headlong retreat.
Garibaldi and the Italian Legion had won yet another victory.[1]

He later commented on the bravery exhibited by soldiers on
both sides. He described how an enemy soldier fought on alone
against six legionnaires, even after he was wounded and had fallen
to one knee. Garibaldi happened to see this, and he ordered his
men to spare the soldier's life because of his courage in the face of
almost certain death.[2] It was a magnanimous thing to do and not
the first time that Garibaldi had spared a man's life.

After the Battle of Rio Daimán, Garibaldi returned to Salto to
deal with Medina. He sent a letter to the chief of police in Salto,
ordering him to take General Medina into custody. Medina was
awakened from his sleep and promptly escorted, in his slippers, to
a ship anchored in the Uruguay River,[3] and from there transported
to Montevideo. In one bold move, Garibaldi had deposed his superior officer and sent him packing back to his mentor—Fructuoso
Rivera. By then, Garibaldi was thoroughly disillusioned with

Rivera, whose seizure of power had caused a schism in the Unitarian army.

The Riverista regime in Montevideo strongly disapproved of Garibaldi's conduct, but it declined to take any action against him. His popularity had grown tremendously throughout the country, both with the civilian population and among the military. In addition, he had developed a close friendship with Admirals Inglefield and Laine, the joint commanders of the Anglo-French naval squadron. After considering the situation, Rivera decided to recall Garibaldi and the Italian Legion to Montevideo. He thought it would be advantageous for his government to have them both stationed in the capital, where they would be outnumbered by other Uruguayan forces. Garibaldi adhered to Rivera's wishes; on August 20, 1846, he departed from Salto with the remnants of the Italian Legion. Their departure was a memorable one for both the legionnaires and the townspeople because of the shared hardships and the joyous moments of glory.

Upon reaching Montevideo on September 5, 1846, the Italian Legion and its commander were honored with a tremendous victory parade. The entire city garrison marched before them in the Plaza de la Constitución. As they passed in review, the commanding officer of each corps saluted the Legion and called out: "*Vive la Patria, General Garibaldi, y sus compadres valorosos!*" (Long live the Fatherland, General Garibaldi, and his brave comrades!)[4] It was one of the most memorable events in the history of the City of Montevideo.

Although the Legion accepted these public outpourings of gratitude, it refused to accept any material or monetary rewards. Following Garibaldi's example, the legionnaires continued to serve the Republic without pay. Some of them were so poor that they couldn't even afford candles for lighting their homes. According to an old Montevidean legend, Garibaldi once encountered a legionnaire who was so poor that he didn't own a shirt. Garibaldi supposedly took off his own shirt and handed it to the man. He literally gave him the shirt off his back. When he went home and asked Anita for another, she reportedly said: "You know perfectly well that you had only one, and if you've given it away, so much the worse for you."[5] Garibaldi remained shirtless until Anita hand-sewed another for him.

The Italian legionnaires again took their place among the ranks of the defense forces in Montevideo—only now they were placed under the command of General Correa, a Riverista. Garibaldi himself was given command of a captured Argentine warship called the *Maipu* and ordered to raid Argentine shipping on the La Plata River. The *Maipu* had been captured by the British the year before, and with Garibaldi at the helm, it was to capture or destroy eighteen Argentine merchant ships.[6] All of this caused a furor in Buenos Aires—a pirate in a captured Argentine ship warring on the Argentine merchant fleet! Garibaldi had little opposition, because the British and French navies had blockaded Brown's fleet in Buenos Aires. During this time, Garibaldi was able to achieve his greatest success as a naval commander.

Despite these naval successes, the tide of war began by early 1847 to turn against the Unitarians. Argentine forces recaptured Salto and Paysandu in northern Uruguay. In Argentina's breakaway province of Corrientes, the Rositas, under Urquiza, decisively defeated the Unitarians, thus ending the rebellion there. To make matters worse, Rivera was once again defeated by Oribe and forced into exile. By the Spring of 1847, the Blancos had gained control over most of Uruguay.

With Rivera in exile again, a new provisional government came to power in Montevideo, promising to continue the war effort against Argentina and the Blancos. It appointed Garibaldi commander-in-chief of the Uruguayan armed forces. The promotion was criticized by native Uruguayans, who complained that their country was now controlled by a "foreign adventurer." Some high-ranking Uruguayan officers even threatened to mutiny. An article in a Blanco publication, *El Defensor*, detailed the tragic consequences which had befallen a people being ruled over by a "gringo pirate."[7] All of this tended to increase resentment against the Italian Legion. In an attempt to avoid any further friction in the military, Garibaldi submitted his resignation as commander-in-chief only twelve days after he was appointed to the position. He was replaced by Colonel José Villagran, a native-born Uruguayan.

The war began to wind down as the British and French once again attempted to negotiate a peace with Argentina, a peace that would guarantee the independence of Uruguay. The negotiators believed that rival military factions in Montevideo were obstructing the negotiations, and that Garibaldi and the Italian Legion were impeding the peace process. It appeared that foreign interests were now dominating the nation's affairs as the hostilities nearly came to a halt. Garibaldi again began to feel disillusionment as factional rivalries turned Montevideo into a den of political intrigue.

During this period, Garibaldi was visited by an old adversary. On July 25, 1847, Admiral William Brown arrived in Montevideo aboard a British ship. He had been compelled to resign his command in the Argentine Navy because of pressure from the British Admiralty and was on his way home to Foxford, Ireland. He was granted permission to land in Montevideo because a truce was in effect. After receiving a warm welcome at the British embassy, he paid a surprise visit to Garibaldi at the latter's home. There, the two adversaries met face to face for the first time. Garibaldi graciously invited Brown into his house, and the two had a friendly discussion over a cup of coffee. Who would have believed it? The former combatants discussed their campaigns and the lack of gratitude displayed by their respective governments. While Anita was serving the coffee, Brown told her of the high regard he had for her husband. After wishing each other well, Brown and Garibaldi parted as friends.[8] They were never to meet again.

Despite Uruguayan ingratitude and factional bickering, Garibaldi remained loyal to the Unitarian regime in Montevideo. He still believed that the cause of Uruguay was just. It was around this time that he was offered $30,000 by Dictator Rosas if he would come over and join the Argentine forces. He refused the offer. The Blanco leader, Manuel Oribe, also tried to bribe Garibaldi, and also without success. Oribe then wrote a letter to Rosas, saying, "I've used all possible means, but he can't be won. He's a stubborn savage."[9] In this atmosphere of factional discord, corrupt government, and political back-stabbing, Garibaldi began to feel that there was no honor in serving the cause of power-seeking politicians.

Then, in late 1847, reports from Italy began to revive his thoughts of returning home. He had been in South America for eleven years, and during that time, a rising tide of nationalism had begun to sweep across the Italian Peninsula. It seemed the time was ripe for revolution. A new pope, Pius IX, elected in June 1846, had immediately proclaimed an amnesty for all political prisoners in the Papal States. He had also introduced a series of new reforms, including the establishment of an elected legislative council for the

City of Rome. These new measures were greeted with great enthusiasm throughout Italy, and they served to jumpstart the Italian
nationalistic movement known as the Risorgimento.

24

The Return to Italy: 1848

THE NEWS FROM ITALY aroused a sense of pride in the Italian community in Montevideo. Count von Metternich had been overthrown in Austria, and the rulers of the various Italian states—Naples, Piedmont, Tuscany, and the Papal States—were granting constitutional reforms. They celebrated in the streets of Montevideo, singing patriotic Italian songs, while bands played. During the excitement, Garibaldi wrote a letter to Monsignor Bedini, the Papal Nunzio in Montevideo, congratulating Pius IX on his actions and offering His Holiness the services of the Italian Legion.[1] Without waiting for a reply, Garibaldi and some of his men began to make preparations for their return to Italy.

The Italians in Montevideo took up a collection to purchase a ship for the return voyage to Italy, but the money was slow coming in. In the meantime, Garibaldi decided to send his wife and children on ahead to stay with his mother in Nice. So, on December 27, 1847, Anita left Montevideo by ship for Italy with Menotti, Teresita, and Ricciotti. On board were a number of other wives and children of Italian legionnaires. Garibaldi was still under a sentence of death in the Kingdom of Sardinia for his participation in a mutiny in 1834, and he wasn't certain if the old sentence would be carried out once he returned to Sardinian territory. Therefore, he considered going to the Papal States or to Tuscany and again offering his services to Pope Pius IX or to the Grand Duke of Tuscany. If neither of them accepted his services, he intended to land somewhere on the Italian coast and engage in revolutionary activity.

In February 1848, Giacomo Medici was sent ahead to Italy with instructions to make arrangements with Mazzini for Garibaldi and his men to land somewhere in Italy. Medici had originally been sent to Montevideo in 1845 to serve as a contact between Garibaldi and Young Italy in Europe. He now returned to Italy with an important message from Garibaldi to Mazzini.

Medici was a tough soldier who would distinguish himself in future battles and become a leader of the *Garibaldini* in the struggle for Italian unification. Later, he would serve in the Italian army with the rank of general.

Colonel Anzani of the Italian Legion wrote to his brother in Italy, authorizing him to sell his property there in the hope of raising money for Garibaldi's expedition. But Anzani's career was coming to an end. An old chest injury was now causing a problem, and Garibaldi was afraid that a long sea voyage might cause his death. He told him to remain in Montevideo; but Anzani was determined to return to Italy. He wrote to a friend: "Even if I die the moment I set foot in Italy, I shall die happy, for I shall have accomplished that which I swore to do when I was young and strong and healthy."[2]

In the meantime, the Montevideo government appointed Garibaldi to the prestigious Assembly of Notables. The Assembly was a body of the most distinguished citizens of the country. Garibaldi was nominated because of his great victory in the battle of San Antonio. However, his appointment led to criticism from various factions in Montevideo, who considered him nothing more than a corsair. This criticism may have given Garibaldi another motive for leaving Uruguay.

On April 15, 1848, he and sixty-three of the Red Shirts sailed out of Montevideo on board a ship called the *Bifronte*. The Red Shirts rechristened it the *Speranza*, and the ship sailed under the Sardinian flag. On board with Garibaldi were men like Anzani, Gaetano Sacchi, Giovanni Culiolo, Tommaso Risso, and a freed African slave named Andrés Aguyar. Anzani would die shortly after the end of the voyage. Sacchi, who was wounded and had to be carried on board the ship by Garibaldi, would survive and become a general in the Italian Army. Culiolo would be present at Anita's deathbed and follow Garibaldi into exile. Risso, a fearless soldier, would be killed in a senseless duel, and Aguyar, who saved Garibaldi's life on several occasions, would die in defense of the Roman Republic. The ship also carried the coffin of Garibaldi's deceased daughter, Rosita, which he had secretly disinterred so that she might rest in Italy. The local press made only a brief mention of the departure of these men, who had done so much for the cause of Uruguayan independence. In neighboring Argentina, the press reported that Garibaldi's men had collected money for the journey "by going around begging for alms at pistol point."[3]

By then, Garibaldi was no longer the brash, idealistic revolutionary that he had once been. He was returning to Italy as an experienced military leader who believed that he could apply the lessons of South American warfare to conditions in his homeland. He believed that small, fast-moving units could carry the war to the enemy and then dissolve quickly into the countryside, only to attack the enemy again unexpectedly. In this guerrilla-type warfare, Garibaldi recognized the importance of improvisation and the ability of the troops to live off the land. Soon, he was to implement these tactics in the struggle for Italian unification.

The voyage back to Italy was to take sixty-three days, and as the coast of South America faded in the distance, the voyagers began to think only of their Italian homeland. Garibaldi and his men spent their time performing their duties on board ship and doing physical exercise to keep themselves in shape. In the evening they gathered on deck and sang the patriotic revolutionary songs composed by Luigi Cucelli, the Legion's musician.[4] The one notable mishap occurred when a fire broke out in the storage area; but the flames were quickly extinguished before any structural damage could occur.

During the long voyage, Garibaldi had plenty of time to devise an overall strategy for achieving Italian unification. Like Mazzini, he had favored unification under a republican form of government. However, he now realized that Mazzini and the Republicans were simply not capable of sustaining a prolonged revolution. All Mazzinian attempts at revolt had ended in dismal failure and considerable loss of life. The Mazzinians did not have the funds or resources to establish and maintain a formidable military force. They also lacked the diplomatic recognition needed to prevent other European nations from intervening in Italian affairs. In diplomatic circles, the Mazzinians were generally considered nothing more than terrorists.

On the other hand, the Kingdom of Sardinia, ruled by the House of Savoy, possessed a standing army and the necessary resources for spearheading such an undertaking. The Kingdom had a recognized government with diplomatic ties throughout Europe. Garibaldi concluded that unification could best be achieved by turning to the forces of a powerful monarchy, such as the House of Savoy. Once the country was unified, the people themselves would decide on the future form of government for the nation.

The *Speranza* passed through the Strait of Gibraltar in the middle of June and docked at Alicante, in Spain, to take on provisions. There they heard news of the revolts that had occurred in Naples, Venice, Milan, Vienna, and Paris. They learned that King Louis Philippe of France had been deposed, and that Metternich had been forced out in Austria. The people of Milan had revolted and defeated the crack regiments of the Austrian army after five days of street fighting. Charles Albert, King of Sardinia, had declared war on Austria and marched into Lombardy to support the revolutionary governments in Milan and Venice. The revolutionaries had accepted him as their leader and invited him to incorporate the two provinces into his kingdom.

As the upsurge of Italian nationalism spread throughout Italy, Pope Pius IX refused to support the Italians in the struggle against Austria. Though he sincerely wanted some reforms in the Papal States, he was not in favor of Italian unification, and he became alarmed at the extent of the movement he had helped unleash. He even issued a statement disassociating himself from any volunteers from the Papal States who joined in the war against Austria. The pope's statement caused Italian revolutionaries to change their opinion of him. Whereas before, they were saying, "Long live Pius IX," now they were calling the pope a "traitor" and an "imbecile."[5]

When Garibaldi heard of these events, he sailed to his home-town of Nice instead of trying to land on the coast of Tuscany. He wished to join Charles Albert's army in the fight against Austria. His arrival in Nice (Nizza) on June 21, 1848, was memorable. Cheering crowds lined the harbor front in wild anticipation. The news of his exploits in South America had preceded him. The Nizzardi welcomed their hero home after a fourteen-year absence. Coming ashore, he was reunited with Anita and his three children. Garibaldi's father had died in 1843, but his mother was still living in the same house on the Quai Lunel where the family had moved when Peppino was eight years old. Anita and the children had been living there since their arrival two months earlier. It was a happy family reunion but one of short duration.

Garibaldi was honored at a banquet in Nice attended by four hundred guests. There he announced that he planned to join King Charles Albert in his struggle against the Austrians. He recruited more than a hundred volunteers in Nice, in addition to those who had come from Montevideo. On June 28, he sailed with them to Genoa, with the intention of enlisting in the Royal Sardinian Army. He wanted to leave Anzani in Nice because of his illness, but Anzani insisted on following Garibaldi to Genoa, where he died a few days later. In his last words, he urged Garibaldi never to betray the people's cause. Anzani's death was a severe blow to Garibaldi, who had come to consider him irreplaceable. In his memoirs, he wrote: "Had we been fortunate enough to have him [Anzani] at the head of our army, the peninsula would certainly have been cleared of all foreign rulers long ago."[6]

ITALY
1848

25

The Lake District Campaign: 1848

Upon arriving in Genoa, Garibaldi and his Red Shirts received a tumultuous reception from the crowds, which included many of Mazzini's followers. Encouraged by it, they set out for Royal Army headquarters near Mantua to enlist under King Charles Albert. There, they received a chilly reception from Sardinian bureaucrats. Their ragged appearance contrasted sharply with the spit-and-polish look of the Royal Army troops, and to many of the Royalist officers, these men were nothing more than brigands.

Garibaldi was given the runaround by Sardinian officials before finally being granted an audience with Charles Albert on July 5, 1847. It was that very royal who, in 1834, had confirmed the death sentence on Garibaldi for desertion and high treason. Now, for the first time, the two met face to face, and though the king was outwardly courteous toward Garibaldi, he later wrote that "to employ this ex-pirate would dishonor the army."[1] Subsequently, Garibaldi's offer to fight for the Kingdom of Sardinia was refused.

Somewhat disappointed, Garibaldi and his men marched off to Milan, in Lombardy. The Lombards had revolted against Austria and, after bitter street fighting, had driven the Austrian troops from the city. Now, the Milanese greeted Garibaldi and his men with a parade and a popular demonstration of support. The provisional government of Lombardy appointed him to the rank of general and placed him in command of a force of five thousand volunteers. His orders were to carry on a guerrilla war against Austrian forces in the Lake District of northern Italy. With the assistance of Medici and Sacchi, he marched with this force on Lake Como.

However, just as Garibaldi was getting his campaign underway, Charles Albert was defeated by the Austrians at the Battle of Custozza, and his army fell back in disorder. At Lake Como, Garibaldi heard that the king had agreed to an armistice with the Austrians and had withdrawn from the war to liberate Lombardy, ordering his troops to demobilize. This enabled the Austrians to reoccupy the City of Milan, thus negating the efforts of so many brave Lombard patriots.

Charles Albert's order was dismissed by Garibaldi, who decided to continue the war on his own, though most of his men had deserted or simply returned to their homes. Garibaldi was left with 1,300 men to continue the struggle, and was then joined by the revolutionary leader Giuseppe Mazzini. Evidently, Mazzini had crossed over from exile in France to be "a soldier of Garibaldi's Legion."[2] Mazzini, however, was not in good physical shape and simply could not cope with the hardships of a military campaign. Exhaustion soon forced him to leave Garibaldi and cross into

Switzerland. The two were destined to meet in Rome the following year.

Undaunted, Garibaldi marched his troops to the village of Castelleto Ticino near Lake Maggiore. Here, he issued his famous appeal to the Italian people, calling on them to continue the struggle against Austria. He denounced King Charles Albert as a coward and stated: "If the King of Sardinia has a crown which he preserves by force of arms and by villainy, I and my comrades do not wish to preserve our lives by equal infamy!"[3] The Castelletto Manifesto had the immediate effect of reviving Italian nationalistic fervor and casting Garibaldi in the role of a brave patriot. Charles Albert, on the other hand, lost stature in the eyes of the Italian people.

The Sardinian government ordered Garibaldi's arrest and sent troops to the Lake District to prevent any further undertakings by him and his men. The Austrian high command also dispatched several thousand troops to find and destroy Garibaldi's force. Despite this, Garibaldi was able to keep the war going—all by himself. He knew that he couldn't do so for long, but he hoped to set an example for others so that they could continue the struggle for national unity. Desertions further reduced Garibaldi's force to five hundred men. He pressed on to Lake Maggiore regardless and won three brisk victories over the Austrians and Croatians. He was hoping that the local people would join his ranks, but few of them did. In fact, the locals were generally hostile toward him, and some even passed information of his whereabouts to the Austrians. He could do little to prevent this, but he did have two of them shot for spying.

Eventually, enemy pressure forced Garibaldi to retreat toward the Swiss border. The Austrian army, moving quickly, completely encircled his force at the town of Morazzone. Garibaldi's men bravely held out all day, despite a heavy bombardment. That night, he led a charge that broke through the Austrian lines and allowed his men to escape into the darkness. But most of his men became lost during the night, and in the morning, he found that he had only seventy men still with him. He set out for Switzerland, guided along mountain footpaths by a local priest. Even then, his men could not keep together. When Garibaldi reached the Swiss border, he had only thirty men left. He disbanded them with instructions to make their own way through Switzerland, and to prepare to continue the struggle at a later time. After a brief stay in Lugano, he himself began the long trek back to Nice, traveling through Switzerland and France. In the meantime, Austrian Field Marshal Radetsky reported to the War Office in Vienna that he had driven Garibaldi over the frontier and cleared Austrian territory of the enemy.[4]

In September 1848, Garibaldi was allowed to return to Nice despite his angry criticism of King Charles Albert. By then, he was fixed in public opinion as a sort of folk hero whose patriotism and courage were a rarity at a time of commonplace deceit and betrayal. His proclamations therefore had a popular appeal that aroused sympathy for the national cause. In October, Garibaldi was elected as one of the Ligurian delegates to the Sardinian parliament in Torino. In a letter of thanks to the electorate, he described himself as "a man of the people" and declared that he had nothing but his sword and his conscience to dedicate to their cause.[5]

However, he did not take his seat in parliament. Instead, he regrouped his men in Genoa and chartered a ship to take them to Tuscany. There, they would offer their services to the provisional government in Florence. Garibaldi suggested that he be given command of the Tuscan army and allowed to attack the Papal States. However, the new Tuscan leadership took a dim view of these suggestions. The Tuscans refused the services of Garibaldi and his men, and told them to leave the territory. One of their so-called "republican" leaders made his views plain in a letter in which he wrote: "They [the *Garibaldini*] are like a plague of locusts . . . let us do all we can to get them away quickly . . . so that they infect as few places as possible."[6] Despite this slap in the face from the Tuscans, Garibaldi was determined to continue the fight for the liberation of Italy. He now decided to march his 350 volunteers to the aid of Venice, where a republic had been established under the leadership of the Italian patriot Daniele Manin.

26

The Roman Republic: 1848—1849

THE POPE'S REFUSAL TO SUPPORT THE CAUSE of Italian unity in the war against Austria had sparked some violent reaction against the papal authority in Rome. The agitation reached a crescendo on November 15, 1848, when Papal Prime Minister Count Pellegrino Rossi was assassinated. Rossi was attacked by a hostile mob and stabbed to death outside the parliament building in Rome. It was an act reminiscent of the assassination of Julius Caesar almost two thousand years earlier.

The news was not received with sorrow and regret throughout Italy. In fact, there was rejoicing among radical groups, because Rossi had been an ardent foe of Italian unity. Margaret Fuller, an American woman living in Rome, wrote home to her mother: "For me, I never thought to have heard of a violent death with satisfaction, but this act affected me as one of terrible justice."[1]

Count Rossi's murder led to more violence as a mob stormed the papal palace, killing another papal official. The pope was now convinced that this sort of political upheaval would occur whenever people were granted a constitution and political liberties, and he became an ardent foe of liberal reform and the movement for Italian national unity. On the night of November 24, Pope Pius IX escaped from Rome disguised as a servant in the hire of the Bavarian ambassador. He fled to Gaeta in the Kingdom of Naples, where he sought the protection of King Ferdinand II. From Gaeta, the pope denounced "the violence of the gang of lunatics who are tyrannizing Rome with barbaric despotism."[2]

In the meantime, a provisional government had been formed in Rome, and it appealed to all volunteer revolutionary forces in Italy to come to its defense. Garibaldi, who had planned to go to the aid of the Venetian Republic with 350 volunteers, now decided to heed the call from Rome. He marched his legionnaires to the town of Rieti, where they were allowed to camp on the outskirts. Evidently, the new Roman government believed that they would be "less frightening" if they remained in the countryside.

Garibaldi himself went on to Rome, where he was welcomed by members of the new government. It was only the second time in his life that he had been to the Eternal City (he had visited with his father in 1825). He was given the rank of colonel and informed that he would serve under General Avezzana, the newly appointed commander-in-chief of the Roman army. Avezzana was a veteran revolutionary who had recently returned to Rome from exile in New York. It was also agreed that Garibaldi's legionnaires were to be enrolled in the Roman army and receive pay and rations from the government.

Elections for a constituent assembly for the new Roman state were set for January 21, 1849. The Eternal City would be the first in modern Italy to achieve representative self-government through free elections. The elections were denounced by Pope Pius IX as a "monstrous act of unconcealed treason and naked rebellion . . . so criminal and wicked as to arouse holy indignation."[3] Furthermore, anyone who voted in the election would be doing so under the pain of excommunication.

Papal supporters attempted to boycott the election, using the pulpit to denounce the elections as being illegal. Nevertheless, the voters elected 150 deputies to the Assembly, most of whom were Radical Republican followers of Mazzini. Garibaldi himself was one of the deputies elected from the eastern district of the Roman territories.[4]

Having failed to prevent the elections, the Pope now issued a formal appeal to France, Austria, Spain, and the Kingdom of Naples to restore him to power in Rome.

The newly elected Assembly convened in February 1849 for the expressed purpose of deciding the future government of the Papal States. One of the speakers who addressed the Assembly was Garibaldi. He spoke in favor of establishing a republic much like that which governed Ancient Rome from 509 to 48 B.C. He asked, "Are the descendants of the Ancient Romans, the Romans of today, incapable of being Republicans?"[5] In response, the Assembly passed a resolution by a vote 120 to 23 proclaiming the Roman Republic and declaring that its citizens should have a common nationality with the people of the rest of Italy. Although the resolution proclaimed the end of papal authority in the Roman state, it also guaranteed the pope all the necessary facilities for carrying on his religious functions.[6] After a lapse of nineteen hundred years, Rome was once again a Republic.

In March, the exiled revolutionary, Giuseppe Mazzini, reached Rome from Marseilles. In a speech to the Roman Assembly, Mazzini set forth a visionary program of government for what he called a "pure democracy." His proposals received much acclaim, and he was chosen by the Assembly to serve as a triumvir, along with Aurelio Saffi and Carlo Armellini. This triumvirate was to act as the executive branch of government until circumstances allowed for a formal restructuring. Since both Saffi and Armellini were disciples of Mazzini, it could be said that the executive power was in the hands of one man—Giuseppe Mazzini.

Power, however, did not alter Mazzini's lifestyle. He still lived frugally, eating in cheap restaurants and living in modest accommodations. He even continued to smoke the same cheap cigars. And when he went about town, he did so inconspicuously. However, his power was virtually absolute. The Constituent Assembly never went against his wishes. He issued decrees redefining church–state relations, but he failed to suppress popular disorders, attacks on priests, and the publication of anti-clerical newsletters. This did not sit well with many of the citizens of Rome.

While Mazzini was attempting to transform the Roman state into a pure democracy, the forces of reaction were moving to crush radical uprisings throughout Europe. Karl Marx had published his *Communist Manifesto*, sparking insurrections in some major cities, including Paris, where the French army crushed a rebellion in which 10,000 people were killed. King Louis Philippe had to flee the country, and in the election that followed, Louis Bonaparte was elected president of France. In Italy, there had been successful Republican uprisings in Venice, Rome, and Sicily. The Kingdom of Sardinia had also resumed its war with Austria. Sardinian nation-

alists had urged King Charles Albert to regain his leadership position in Italy by intervening on the side of the Venetian Republic
against Austria. However, after a few days of fighting the Sardinian
army was defeated at the Battle of Novara, and Charles Albert was
forced to abdicate. He was succeeded by his twenty-nine-year-old
son, Victor Emmanuel II. The victorious Austrians were now
ready to march south to the pope's assistance. In the south, King
Ferdinand II of Naples had ordered his army to crush an uprising
on the island of Sicily. His ferocious bombardment of the civilian
population of Messina had earned him the nickname "King
Bomba."[7] The Sicilian rebels were rounded up and executed. A
ruthless suppression of the Sicilian people followed.

At this moment, the world focused its attention on Rome. The
pope's call for help did not go unanswered. Austria, Spain, and the
Kingdom of Naples all agreed to take action against the newly proclaimed Roman Republic. In France, where Louis Bonaparte had
been elected president, there was a rising tide of anti-revolutionary
sentiment. After the bloody Revolution of 1848, many Frenchmen
were turning to the Catholic Church as the only bulwark against
Radicalism and revolutionary Socialism.

French Catholics now convinced Louis Bonaparte that it was
France's duty to restore the Pope to his rightful place as Vicar of
Rome. Thus, France would live up to its legacy as being "the eldest
daughter of the Church,"[8] a title the country had claimed since the
fifth century, when King Clovis of the Franks was converted to
Christianity. Bonaparte agreed, and the funds for the expedition to
the Papal States were approved by the French National Assembly.
On April 22, 1849, a French expeditionary force of 9,000 troops
set sail from Marseilles, bound for the port of Civitavecchia in the
Papal States. They landed there, without any opposition, two days

later. Further south, the King of Naples was preparing to invade the Papal States along with a Spanish expeditionary force. In the north, Austria had just won another war over Sardinia and was preparing to invade the Papal States from the northeast.

In the face of these ominous developments, Garibaldi had returned to his base at Rieti, where volunteers from all classes of society were coming to join his Legion: workers and peasants as well as artisans and aristocrats. There were professional soldiers, adventurous students, and even some wanted criminals. They had one thing in common—they were ardent patriots joining the struggle to expel foreigners from the Italian homeland.

Discipline in the camp at Rieti was being maintained by a tough Genoese officer named Nino Bixio. Bixio in time rose through the ranks to become second in command to Garibaldi. Another who joined the Legion was Father Ugo Bassi, a Catholic priest from Bologna who was known as a political activist. His revolutionary zeal had gotten him into trouble with the Catholic hierarchy. Now he wished to serve as the Legion's chaplain and administer the Holy Sacraments to the troops. Garibaldi's wife Anita also arrived in Rieti to be with him before the upcoming conflict. She had left their children in the care of trusted friends in Nice and was to remain in Rieti for nearly two months. It was the longest period she and Garibaldi spent together since leaving South America. During this time, new recruits swelled the size of Garibaldi's Legion to almost 1,300 men.

On April 23, General Avezzana promoted Garibaldi to the rank of general and ordered him to come to Rome with his troops. Garibaldi, having anticipated this, ordered Anita back to Nice to be with the children. Wasting no time, he hurried to Rome with his troops.

His arrival there on April 27 created a sensation. The Eternal City hadn't seen anything like it since Julius Caesar returned from the Gallic Wars in 48 B.C. The crowds who lined the Corso were heard to shout: "He has come! Garibaldi has come!" And there he was in the flesh—riding a magnificent white horse and wearing a red tunic under a scarlet-lined white cloak. Young women in the crowd were so thrilled by the sight of him that they cried out: "Oh! Isn't he beautiful! Beautiful!" Garibaldi did cut a nice picture, riding at the head of his Legion, his reddish hair falling over his shoulders and his freckled face red from the sun.[9] His very appearance seemed to bolster the morale of the Roman citizenry.

Garibaldi was followed by his black aide-de-camp, Andrés Aguyar, who was wearing a blue cloak and riding a black horse. The legionnaires who had come over from Montevideo wore their famous red shirts and also attracted much attention. The others wore the newly issued blue uniforms of the Roman army. As headgear, they all wore broad-brimmed black hats with plumes, giving them the appearance of the cavaliers who had supported King Charles Stuart I of Britain in his struggle against Parliament in the 1600s.

By then the armed forces of the Roman Republic consisted of about 21,000 men, including several volunteer corps. Of these, almost 8,000 were concentrated in Rome under the command of General Avezzana. The remainder were stationed in various cities throughout the Papal States. Apart from Garibaldi's 1,300 Legionnaires, Avezzana had 2,500 Carabinieri of the old Papal Guard, a Roman Legion of 1,400 men, 1,000 national guardsmen, and a University Legion consisting of 700 students and civil servants. These forces were bolstered by the arrival of 800 Bersaglieri

from Lombardy led by Major Luciano Manara,* men from aristocratic families who had fought under Charles Albert in the wars of
1848 and 1849 and now wanted to fight for Rome and Italy. They
were neither Republicans nor Mazzinians. Instead, they proudly
wore the Cross of Savoy on their sword belts and thought of themselves as Italian nationalists.[10] They now offered their services to
General Avezzana who gratefully accepted. The Bersaglieri were
to play a major role in the defense of Rome, and later were to
become an elite branch of the modern Italian army.

Advancing against this aggregation of defense forces were
armies from four countries—France, Austria, Spain, and the
Kingdom of Naples. On April 28, the French expeditionary force,
which had landed at Civitavecchia, began slowly advancing toward
Rome. The next day, the Neapolitan army crossed the frontier and
began advancing on Rome from the south, reinforced by nine hundred Spanish troops who had landed at Gaeta. Shortly afterwards,
the Austrians invaded the Papal States from the north, capturing
Bologna and advancing southward along the Adriatic coast. All of
these armies were heading for a showdown with "that South
American adventurer"—Garibaldi.

General Oudinot, the French commander, sincerely believed
that the Romans would not engage in battle. Papal supporters fleeing from Rome assured him that the populace was waiting to be
liberated by the French, and that all the preparations for resistance
were a bluff. Other foreign diplomats tended to confirm this view.
And then of course, there was the accepted myth that Italians
couldn't fight.

---

*These figures are given in Jasper Ridley's *Garibaldi*, p. 277.

27

The Battle of Rome: 1849

As the French expeditionary force under General Oudinot approached Rome from the northwest, barricades were set up throughout the city. In the event the French broke through the city walls, the defenders were prepared to fight in the streets and alleys. The doors of houses were to be left open so that street fighters could enter and carry on the resistance. Price ceilings were set on consumer goods and shops were ordered not to close. Telegraph stations were installed at the highest points in the city, including the dome of St. Peter's, the Capitol, and the bell tower of St. Mary Major. Military hospitals, flying black flags, were set up in churches and palaces such as St. John Lateran and the Quirinale Palace.[1]

The ancient walls that ringed Rome were nearly intact and constituted the city's main line of defense. Their strong points consisted of a series of twenty-three bastions, spaced at fairly regular intervals. The stretches of walls between the bastions were the most vulnerable part of the defenses, having no exterior embankments or trenches. The Tiber River flows through Rome, dividing the city into two parts. The center of the city is on the left bank, while the Vatican is situated on the right, along with the working-class district called Trastevere. On the right bank, the city walls run along the crest of a hill called the Janiculum, which towers over Trastevere. In Trastevere, the main road from Civitavecchia enters the city through a gate called Porta San Pancrazio. This was the sector of Rome occupied by troops commanded by General Garibaldi.

Located outside the walls in the shadow of the Janiculum Hill stood an area of residential villas and beautiful gardens, the largest and most impressive being the Villa Corsini, situated on a ridge some five hundred yards outside the city walls. It possessed a commanding view of the surrounding country, and because of its exposed position on the ridge, it was known as the "Casino of the Four Winds." The villa's gardens extended westward as far as the neighboring Villa Pamfili and northward to the Villa Valentini. A smaller villa called the Vascello stood at the eastern end of the gardens near the city walls. This peaceful setting of villas and gardens would soon be turned into a battleground.

As the French army approached the city, General Oudinot sent a message to Mazzini, asking that he and his troops be allowed to enter Rome in order to restore peace between the pope and his subjects. Mazzini presented the French proposal to the Roman Assembly, where it was rejected. Instead, the Assembly voted in favor of resisting the French with shouts of "*Viva l'Italia!*" The French command remained persuaded that the Romans were bluffing, and General Oudinot was prepared to test the validity of the accepted myth that Italians couldn't fight.[2]

Early on April 30, the French army was sighted advancing toward Rome along the Via Aurelia. The bells of the Capitol sounded the alarm first, followed by all the bells in the city. The Roman army immediately took up positions on the walls and was soon joined by civilians armed with makeshift weapons. Those who didn't have weapons climbed up on the Pincio, a hill on the left bank, in order to watch the fighting from there. Many of the spectators were women anxious for their loved ones in the coming battle. At noon, the French artillery began to bombard the city, and French troops advanced to attack the defenses in the vicinity of the Vatican and the Janiculum. General Avezzana had anticipated a French attack in this vicinity and had authorized Garibaldi to occupy Villa Corsini. Garibaldi was well aware of the villa's strategic importance in the defense of Rome. It held a commanding position over the terrain leading to the city walls and the gate of San Pancrazio. When the French attack came, he was waiting for them with 2,500 men, including 450 student volunteers. In addition to these, General Avezzana had placed another 3,800 men in reserve behind Garibaldi.*

As the French approached the city walls close to the Vatican, Garibaldi's artillery opened fire, convincing General Oudinot that the Romans would indeed fight! Even more convincing was the reception they got at the walls. The French came under such heavy fire from the Roman troops that they were forced to fall back. Many were killed. Garibaldi had shattered the myth.

However, the French did succeed in capturing the strategic

---

*These figures are given in Jasper Ridley's *Garibaldi*, p. 279.

Villa Corsini from the 450 student volunteers who were assigned to defend it. The inexperienced students proved no match for the veteran French troops. Garibaldi, who was watching the battle, rode forward on his white horse. Rising in the stirrups, he drew his sword and ordered his two thousand troops to charge with fixed bayonets. It was a scene later depicted in many paintings and sketches. Fierce fighting ensued until the French broke and retreated in disorder. During one charge, Nino Bixio captured the French commander, Colonel Picard, by seizing him by the hair and pulling him off his horse—a novel way of capturing an enemy officer!

By evening, the French forces were in full retreat along the Via Aurelia, leaving behind more than five hundred dead and 365 prisoners. Garibaldi lost two hundred killed and wounded, and had one man taken prisoner—Father Ugo Bassi,* captured while administering Last Rites to a dying soldier. Garibaldi himself had been wounded in the thigh by a bullet, but he kept it secret from his men. After he had the wound treated, Garibaldi intended to pursue the retreating French in the hope of winning a decisive victory. Mazzini, however, forbade him to do so because he wished to avoid all-out war with France. He did not want to further alienate French public opinion by inflicting greater humiliation on the "eldest daughter of the Church." For his part, Garibaldi believed that Mazzini had made a serious error of judgment, and later, he was proven right.[3]

The French, using Ugo Bassi as a go-between, then negotiated a temporary ceasefire with Mazzini, allowing each side to attend to

---

*These casualty figures in the battle for Rome are given in Andrea Viotti's *Garibaldi: The Revolutionary and His Men*, p. 54.

its wounded. Many wives and friends of the fighting men offered to serve as nurses, and many citizens donated medical supplies and linens to the hospitals. Surplus linen was sent to the French camp, along with camp beds and medical supplies. A committee of women ran the hospitals and nursed the wounded. Among its notable members were Marietta Pisacane, Giulia Bovio Paolucci, and Cristina de Belgiojoso, a Milanese noblewoman. They were joined by Anita Garibaldi, who had once again come down from Nice.

Sarah Margaret Fuller

Margaret Fuller, an American woman from Massachusetts, also helped to care for the wounded Roman soldiers. She was a brilliant writer and publisher who had argued the cause of women's rights in America. In 1846, Fuller had come to Europe, visiting England and France and then settling in Rome, where she met and fell in love with an Italian named Giovanni Ossoli, whom she secretly married. She espoused the cause of Italian freedom and, during the battle for Rome, unselfishly volunteered her services to care for the sick and wounded. When Rome finally fell to the French forces, the Ossolis and their infant son, Nino, fled to Florence and then, by steamship, to America. The story has a tragic ending: The ship on which they were traveling was wrecked by a storm off the coast of Long Island, and Margaret, her husband, and their child all perished. A manuscript she had prepared about the history of the Roman Republic was also lost at sea. Today, Margaret Fuller is recognized by the Italian people as one of the heroines of the Risorgimento, and a commemorative bronze plaque on a building facing Rome's Piazza Barberini recalls that she once lived there.[4]

The ceasefire now gave the Roman government the opportunity to concentrate its attention on another enemy army. On May 1, a Neapolitan force of 10,000 men had crossed the frontier and was advancing on Rome from the south. Led by "King Bomba," they announced that they were coming to restore peace in the Papal States. Like the French before them, their friendly gesture was rejected by the Roman Assembly, and Garibaldi was dispatched to stop the Neapolitan advance. Moving quickly with a force of 2,500 men, he engaged the Neapolitans near the town of Palestrina. In the ensuing battle, Garibaldi's legionnaires routed the enemy with a fierce bayonet charge. The Neapolitans retreated so quickly that Garibaldi suspected some sort of trick and chose not to pursue them.

The Roman victories over the French and the Neapolitans reverberated throughout Europe. In France, the government was accused of deceiving the nation when it stated that French troops were going to Rome to protect the Romans from the Austrians. Prime Minister Odilon Barrot decided to send a French official to Rome to negotiate a peaceful solution with Mazzini. The man chosen for the mission was Ferdinand de Lesseps, the French engineer who later directed the construction of the Suez Canal.

De Lesseps diligently carried out his mission. He journeyed to Rome and proceeded to negotiate a fifteen-day ceasefire agreement with Mazzini. In the meantime, French President Louis Bonaparte secretly contacted General Oudinot, promising him reinforcements and assuring him that the military honor of France would not be compromised.[5] This was done without de Lesseps' knowledge. He believed that both sides would negotiate in good faith to end the conflict.

The ceasefire went into effect on May 15, but both sides hastened to strengthen their position. Oudinot received reinforcements from France, bringing his total troop strength to 30,000 men and eighty-eight artillery pieces. Meanwhile, nearly 7,000 volunteers had appeared in Rome to join the defense forces. Included among them were five hundred foreigners who had come to fight for the Republican cause. Some of these newcomers were military officers who had served in foreign armies, men such as the Englishman Hugh Forbes, the Polish revolutionary Alexander Milbutz, the Swiss artilleryman Gustav von Hoffstetter, and the French republican Gabriel Laviron. In addition, Garibaldi's forces were bolstered by the arrival from Genoa of Medici's Legion with three hundred men,[*] all of which seemed to indicate that both sides were stalling for time to build up their forces.

On May 14, the Triumvers appointed General Pietro Roselli as the new Commander-in-Chief of the Roman Army, with General

---

* The figures on Republican volunteers may be found in Jasper Ridley's *Garibaldi*, p. 285, and in Andrea Viotti's *Garibaldi, The Revolutionary and His Men*, p. 58.

Avezzana being sent to Ancona to direct the defenses there against the Austrians. Roselli was appointed even though he lacked experience and didn't have the dynamic personality that was necessary for leading a volunteer army. He was appointed over Garibaldi because he was a Roman by birth. Thus, Garibaldi was passed over again for the position of commander-in-chief. Understandably, he resented Roselli's appointment to the position which he believed should have been his. Relations between the two became strained.

Taking advantage of the ceasefire, Roselli now prepared to engage the Neapolitan army, which had intruded into Roman territory and was camped at Velletri, just south of Rome. Roselli believed that the Neapolitans should pull back across the frontier, because a temporary ceasefire was already in effect. He sent Garibaldi on ahead with 2,000 troops to monitor the enemy's movements, but he gave him no orders to attack. However, when the enemy was sighted, Garibaldi's Lancers, under Colonel Masina, did prematurely attack the enemy's rearguard. Masina's force was repulsed and driven back. Masina himself was surrounded but fought his way clear with a display of expert swordsmanship. Garibaldi rushed forward in an attempt to halt his retreating Lancers, but he was knocked to the ground along with his horse and trampled. A Neapolitan cavalryman saw Garibaldi go down and charged at him in an attempt to finish him off. Garibaldi was saved from almost certain death by his faithful aide, Aguyar, who quickly cut down the enemy rider with his lance. The other legionnaires, led by Nino Bixio, then drove off the Neapolitans. Miraculously, Garibaldi had escaped serious injury. However, the Neapolitans who had seen him go down under the horses' hooves now believed that he was dead.[6]

The story of Garibaldi's death was readily accepted by his enemies and quickly spread to places as far away as France. When Garibaldi appeared in action a few days later, his enemies claimed that an imposter had taken his place in order to maintain the morale of his men. They said that the real Garibaldi had lost an ear in a brawl in South America, and that the fake Garibaldi really had two ears hidden under his long hair.[7] Still, rather than do battle with the real or the fake Garibaldi, the Neapolitans chose to withdraw to their own territory. Their unexplained flight gave further credence to the superstitious notion that Garibaldi was invincible.

Meanwhile, in Rome, de Lesseps was learning the cruel truth. General Oudinot, who had refused to confirm the ceasefire agreement, now informed de Lesseps that he had received orders from Paris to resume hostilities. During the cease fire, Oudinot had received 10,000 reinforcements and additional artillery pieces. De Lesseps, who had negotiated with Mazzini in good faith, was stunned. Upon his return to Paris, he was dismissed in disgrace from the Foreign Office and denounced in the press as a weakling who would betray French interests to Mazzini.[8]

On June 1, Oudinot wrote to Roselli, giving him twenty-four hours' notice that the ceasefire had ended. His communique also stated that, in order to give French civilians time to leave Rome, he would not attack the place until June 4. As it turned out, "the place" meant the City of Rome itself, and *not* the defense outposts in the villas outside the walls.[9] On the evening of June 2, just after the twenty-four-hour notice had expired, French troops began attacking the villas. General Roselli had not heeded Garibaldi's advice to fortify the villas and had told the defenders that they would be safe from attack until June 4.

The sudden French attack on the Villa Pamfili caught the defenders off guard, enabling them to take it without any resistance. Nearby, the strategic Villa Corsini (Casino of the Four Winds) also fell to the French, but only after a last-ditch defense by the Romans. By morning, the French held that vital high ground, which Garibaldi considered to be absolutely essential to the defense of Rome. Recapturing it would prove to be a very difficult task, even for him.

Having suffered from arthritis for three days, he now rose from his sick bed and went to his headquarters on the Janiculum. He believed that he could not hold Rome if the villas were lost to the enemy and decided that they must be recaptured at all costs. General Roselli put Garibaldi in command of the operation, placing 6,000 troops at his disposal. This was roughly one-third of the total force of the Roman army. Facing Garibaldi were 16,000 French troops deployed in and around the various villas on that sector of the battlefront, poised for a decisive battle.

Without question, the focal point of Garibaldi's attention was the Casino of the Four Winds. In order to retake it by a frontal assault, Garibaldi's legionnaires would have to make an open dash from the San Pancrazio Gate to the villa's garden gate, upon which all the French firepower could be concentrated. Once inside the gate, there was a 750-foot stretch of garden road, with high hedges on both sides, leading up to the Casino. In front of the Casino rose yet another wall, from behind which the defenders could fire on the attackers. The Casino itself was four stories high, with no windows on the ground floor but with a wide outside staircase leading up to the second-floor entrance. The three upper floors had windows facing the garden road, and from there, as well as from the wall in front of the Casino, the French could concentrate fire on the attacking troops.[10] Any flanking attack attempting to enter the Casino grounds from the side would entail climbing high walls under enemy fire.

The battle that was to decide the fate of the Roman Republic came on June 3, when Garibaldi ordered a series of frontal attacks to recapture the Casino of the Four Winds. On that day, Italian nationalistic fervor reached its zenith. Garibaldi and his legionnaires displayed a reckless courage seldom seen in the annals of modern warfare. He ordered one attack after another, each more determined than the last. Each time his men charged toward the hilltop Casino, and each time they were cut down by the French. The road leading to the Casino became littered with their bodies. Still, they kept coming.

Dominating over the entire battle scene was Garibaldi on his white horse, his drawn saber glistening in the sun. He was constantly in the line of fire, and though several enemy bullets pierced his poncho, he remained unscathed. His very presence seemed to instill in his men a sense of invincibility. This was particularly exemplified in the valor exhibited by his officers."

Nino Bixio had his horse shot from under him while leading a charge up the garden road but immediately got up, mounted another horse, and continued the charge. He led his men up the staircase to the Casino's front door, only to be shot down by a barrage of French bullets. Badly wounded, he continued to fight until his men managed to carry him to safety.

After repeated attacks, Major Luciano Manara and the Bersaglieri broke through, capturing the Casino and driving out the French defenders. But within an hour, the French recaptured it by attacking through the orchards located behind the Casino. Captain Enrico Dondolo was killed in the action, his body left lying where it fell. Later that day his brother, Emilio Dondolo, led another charge to recover Enrico's body—a reckless bravado that caused several more deaths and ended in failure.

Another Legion attack, led this time by Colonel Francesco Daverio, finally retook the Casino, but before Daverio could consolidate his position, he faced the brunt of yet another French counterattack. Despite overwhelming odds, Daverio refused to abandon the Casino and fall back with his men. He was subsequently killed in the action.

Masina's Lancers then made an attempt to recapture the Casino—this time against Garibaldi's orders. Masina had already led four attacks that day and had previously been wounded. This time, his charging Lancers reached the Casino and were about to retake it when Masina was shot down by a burst of fire. His frightened horse ran off, dragging him for more than two hundred feet. His body was later found, riddled with bullets, lying in a hedge alongside the road.

The news of the deaths of Daverio and Masina served to arouse the Roman troops to greater feats of daring. Shouting the names of their dead officers, the legionnaires, led by Major Gabriel Laviron, once more captured the Casino, only to be driven back one more time by a French counterattack. As the day ended, the Casino of the Four Winds still remained in the possession of the French. Garibaldi realized that Rome was lost, and that all he could do was to hold out as long as possible.[12]

The battle of June 3 lasted for seventeen hours and resulted in heavy losses for Garibaldi—over 1,000 men killed and wounded out of a total force of 6,000. Among the dead were some hundred officers.* French casualties were somewhat lighter. Nevertheless,

---

*These casualty figures are given in Andrea Viotti's *Garibaldi: The Revolutionary and His Men*, p. 62.

the Romans were determined to continue the fight. They were angered by the treachery of the French, who had attacked without warning while the cease-fire was supposedly still in effect.

It should be noted that Garibaldi's tactics during the battle of June 3 did not go without criticism. It has been argued that he lost the battle because he ordered repeated attacks by small units on the same enemy position. His critics contended that he would have overwhelmed the French if his troops had attacked the enemy positions *en masse*. As it is, we will never know for sure.

Confident of victory, the French now began making plans for the capture and occupation of Rome. They had come to respect the Roman army, whereas before they had regarded the Roman soldiers as "revolutionary rabble" who would collapse at the first major attack. General Oudinot never encircled Rome, because he believed that his force of 30,000 men was insufficient to ring the city with its eighteen miles of walls. Oudinot therefore massed his forces on the west side of the city and sent cavalry units to harass supply columns coming into Rome from the east. He placed his artillery on the ridge at the Casino of the Four Winds and bombarded Garibaldi's position on the Janiculum Hill. Garibaldi impressed people with his coolness during the French bombardment of his headquarters on the Janiculum. He would stand on top of the defenses in full view of the enemy and calmly light a cigar as their shells exploded around him.[13]

The French recklessly bombarded civilian areas of the city along with some of the historic landmarks. Their shells even damaged the facade of St. Peter's Basilica. A number of foreign diplomats protested to General Oudinot about the bombardment, but to no avail. In Britain, the press condemned the French incursion into Italy, but it also admonished the revolutionary Republicanism of Mazzini.

In France, the opposition leader, Ledru-Rollin, called for the impeachment of Louis Bonaparte and his government. Ledru-Rollin believed that it was unconstitutional for the French government to suppress the liberty of the Italian people. However, the motion for impeachment was decisively defeated in the French Assembly and Ledru-Rollin was forced to flee from France. Nevertheless, Garibaldi was beginning to acquire a large following abroad as a gallant champion of the oppressed. His early image as a bloodthirsty corsair was now being eclipsed by his heroic exploits in the defense of the Roman Republic. These events helped gain much sympathy throughout Europe and America for the cause of Italian unification.

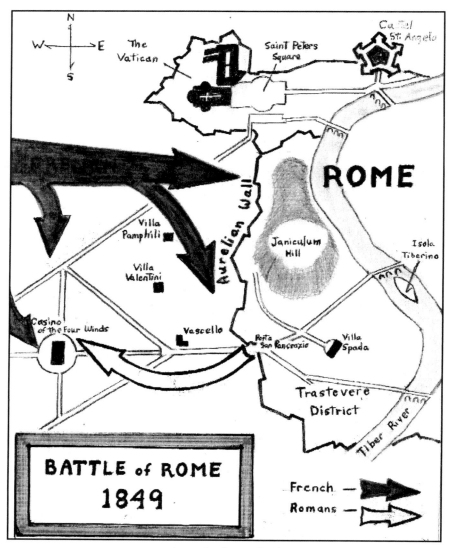

The Battle of Rome (1849)

28

The Fall of the Roman Republic

IN JUNE 1849, THE FRENCH FORCES edged closer to the Janiculum Hill and the San Pancrazio Gate by digging trenches and erecting fortified advance posts close to the Roman defense positions. Each night small detachments of legionnaires attacked the French at their work, but they were unable to stop the enemy's progress.

On June 21, the French forces launched a general assault on Garibaldi's position. Fierce hand-to-hand combat ensued around the San Pancrazio Gate, the legionnaires refusing to retreat and dying at their posts without any thought of surrender. The French managed to capture several strong points, forcing Garibaldi's men to fall back to the old Aurelian Wall near the Trastevere section of the city. However, his men still held the Janiculum Hill and the fortified Villa Vascello, which was located just outside the walls near the San Pancrazio Gate. Garibaldi's headquarters on the Janiculum had been so badly damaged in the bombardment that he had been forced to move it to the Villa Spada, a modest structure located some 150 feet behind the Aurelian Wall.

In the meantime, French forces also managed to cross the Tiber River to the north of the Vatican, and despite fierce resistance from the University Legion, they had advanced to the edge of the Villa Borghese on the north side of the city. As the fighting became more desperate, many ordinary citizens joined in to help the defenders at the barricades. They formed into groups known as "Seven Hills Squads"[1] and were assigned to take messages, carry ammunition, and retrieve unexploded shells. Many of the squad members were youngsters in their early teens.

During this period in late June, the most intense fighting continued in the area of the San Pancrazio Gate, where Garibaldi's legionnaires continued to hold the Janiculum and exchange cannon shots with the French. Nearby, the Villa Vascello was still held by a Genoese officer named Giacomo Medici, and nothing short of a direct order from Garibaldi would make him abandon it. Although the villa had been reduced to rubble, Medici and his men continued to beat back one French assault after another. One of the men defending the Vascello described the action:

> It is horrendous to be inside a house where a bullet might ricochet off any surface at any moment; where if a cannonball didn't get you, you might be crushed by falling masonry; where the air was full of smoke and dust and the moans of the wounded; where the floor was slippery with blood; and where the entire building shook under the impact of a cannonade.[2]

Medici continued his heroic defense of the villa and abandoned it only upon receiving Garibaldi's direct order to do so. He was later to be promoted to the rank of general, and the King of Italy was to bestow on him the title of Marchese del Vascello.

While Medici was gaining immortality for his heroics, the Roman leadership was locked in debate over strategy. Mazzini proposed that the entire adult population attack the French positions *en masse*. This would include soldiers and civilians, both armed and unarmed. The idea was to overwhelm the enemy through sheer weight of numbers, regardless of the casualties suffered in the assault.[3] At that time, revolutionary theoreticians considered this an ideal tactic. Garibaldi, however, opposed the plan, claiming that such an attack would fail with heavy loss of life, and that a disorganized mass of people would make an easy target for enemy gunners.

Garibaldi then proposed an alternate plan under which he would sortie from Rome with his Legion and attack the French near the port of Civitavecchia. He would aim to destroy their supply base and line of communication, and thus foil the French battle plan against the city. The idea was rejected by both Mazzini and General Roselli. In doing so, Garibaldi believed that the two of them had made a great strategic blunder. He was later proven correct, when General Oudinot admitted that Garibaldi's plan would have completely disrupted the French campaign. According to Oudinot, the French did not have a sufficient number of troops to secure their supply line.[4]

At 2:00 a.m. on the morning of June 30, the French began an all-out attack on the city. A violent artillery barrage was followed by a massive infantry assault. General Oudinot had ordered his troops to give the Roman defenders no quarter because of the inconvenience of handling prisoners.[5] This attitude was to set the tone for the entire battle. Fierce fighting ensued, with the French attack repulsed and then renewed. Garibaldi threw in his last reserves in a desperate attempt to hold the Aurelian Wall, the last line of defense before the barricades in the streets. Medici was ordered to abandon the Villa Vascello, where he had been barricaded for twenty-five days and nights. Garibaldi wished to consolidate the defenses around the Villa Spada inside the walls, a position defended by the Bersaglieri under Major Manara.

The Roman defenses reeled under the shock of the French assault. The Aurelian Wall was breached as the French advanced to the doors of the Villa Spada only to be beaten back by the Bersaglieri under Manara. The French then encircled the Villa, forcing the Bersaglieri to barricade themselves inside the building. Major Manara was killed during the action, but his men continued to hold out, firing from the windows. The French were in turn dispersed by a charging force of Red Shirts led by Garibaldi. Bitter hand-to-hand combat followed, with Garibaldi himself leading the defenders. Shouting *"Viva l'Italia!"* his men battled the French with their guns and bayonets, and then with their fists. In reality, these brave men were now fighting for their country—Italia!

An officer of the Lombard Brigade described the battle scene as "a swaying mass of men killing each other." Garibaldi remained in the midst of the melee, cutting down enemy soldiers with his saber and inspiring his men with superhuman feats of bravery. Agosto Vecchi, one of Garibaldi's men, later wrote: "Garibaldi was greater than I have ever seen him, greater than anyone has ever seen him! His sword was like lightning. . .the blood of a fresh adversary washed away the blood of one who had first fallen."[6]

George M. Trevelyan, in his book *Garibaldi's Defense of the Roman Republic*, and Andrea Viotti, in his *Garibaldi, The Revolutionary and His*

Men, cite numerous examples of incredible courage on the part of the defenders. On the Janiculum, Garibaldi's artillerymen battled the enemy down to the last man. Lieutenant Casini kept firing his gun until he was cut down, his skull split by ten saber strokes. Another gunner, who had run out of ammunition, defended his post with a cannon brush until the brush was hacked to shreds and he was bayoneted to death. Lieutenant Tiburzi withstood seventeen bayonet wounds before he finally fell. Corporal Parucco fought on with his rifle stock until he was nailed to a wall by twenty-three French bayonets. Other gunners were found dead by the French, still clinging to their cannon. Even the drummer boys picked up weapons and joined in the fight, only to be cut down like the rest.[7]

The French were impressed by the courage of these men and, in some cases, did offer them quarter. In one instance, three officers of the Lombard Brigade and a Roman girl found themselves surrounded by the French. The French offered them their lives if they would lay down their weapons. All four refused and went down fighting. Other trapped defenders weren't given any option—they were either shot or bayoneted to death. By late afternoon, the French were in possession of the Janiculum Hill, where virtually all of Garibaldi's artillerymen had died defending their posts. The French had also broken through the Aurelian Wall, and the fighting now spilled over into the Trastevere district, where the surviving Roman troops prepared for a last stand.

That night, Garibaldi was summoned by the Roman Assembly to give his opinion on the feasibility of further resistance. Coming straight from the battle zone, he arrived covered with dust and oozing blood, his uniform in shreds and his saber bent out of shape. He stated that no further defense was possible and asked for permission to withdraw his troops from Rome in order to continue a guerrilla war against the French. The Assembly decided to end all resistance in the city, and now appointed Garibaldi as commander-in-chief of the Roman army. He was given permission to withdraw with as many volunteers as were willing to accompany him. The Triumvirate then resigned, and a new government, led by Enrico Cermischi, was assigned to carry out the degrading task of surrendering the city to the French.

Many of the revolutionary leaders, including Mazzini, made plans to escape. A number of the revolutionaries were given passports by the British consulate, enabling them to escape to Britain or Gibraltar. Others were offered asylum by the Swiss government. Lewis Cass, the United States ambassador to Rome, offered Garibaldi safe passage to the United States on an American warship.[8] Garibaldi refused; he had decided to fight on in Italy and was planning to march his army out of Rome.

On July 2, 1849, the Roman Republic capitulated to the French while Garibaldi assembled his volunteer army in St. Peter's Square. He addressed his men:

> *Fortune, which today has betrayed us, will smile on us tomorrow. I am leaving Rome. Whoever wishes to continue the war against the foreigner, let him come with me. I offer neither pay nor quarters nor provisions. I offer hunger, thirst, forced marches, battle and death.*[9]

More than 4,700 men followed him out of the city at 7:00 p.m., by the Porta San Giovanni on the Tivoli Road. That army included the remnants of the Italian Legion with their red shirts, the Bersaglieri, the University Legion, Masina's Lancers, and various other units that had defended Rome. Anita, who had cut her hair short, rode alongside Garibaldi dressed as a legionnaire —red shirt, dark trousers tucked into her boots, and a slouch hat with black feathers. Across her breast she wore a red, white, and green sash.[10] Father Ugo Bassi joined the march in a red shirt and a traditional priest's hat. He wore a crucifix around his neck and carried a sack with the sacred vessels for the Catholic Mass.

They left behind more than 3,500 dead and wounded comrades, the casualties of the ten-week battle. Among the dead were Daverio, Masina, Manara, Enrico Dandolo, and Andrés Aguyar, the Black former slave who had accompanied Garibaldi from South America. Left behind were Nino Bixio, who was badly wounded, and Giacomo Medici, who was suffering from exhaustion. Dr. Pietro Ripari also remained in Rome to care for the wounded.

On July 3, the French army triumphantly entered Rome. They received a cold reception as the population stood by in absolute silence. The French troops tore down the Republican tricolor flags from the balconies and arrested a number of prominent Republicans, including Dr. Ripari. Romans who insulted or attacked the occupying forces were beaten up or even executed. Mazzini, who had remained in Rome, now decided to escape with the aid of a British passport. Disguised as a ship's cook, he made his way by sea to Marseilles, and then eventually to London.[11] Aside from this, the only thing that spoiled the French victory was the fact that Garibaldi and his men had made their escape.

29

The Retreat to San Marino

After leaving Rome on the night of July 2, 1849, Garibaldi's plan was to march his troops to Venice on the Adriatic side of the Italian Peninsula. Venice had earlier declared itself a republic under Daniele Manin and was holding out against an Austrian siege. Garibaldi knew that getting there would not be easy. His troops would have to cover five hundred miles of difficult, mountainous terrain with four enemy armies converging on them. General Oudinot, upon learning of their escape from Rome, sent 7,000 French troops to pursue them. A Spanish expeditionary force of 7,000 men joined in the pursuit from the south, while 7,000 Neapolitan troops guarded the Neopolitan frontier against any incursion into their territory by Garibaldi. Coming down from the north were 15,000 Austrian troops under the command of General D'Aspre. Other Austrian armies were poised in Lombardy and Venetia. The commanders of these pursuing armies considered Garibaldi nothing more than a brigand making war on his own account.

Garibaldi's retreat from Rome has been described as a masterpiece of military elusiveness. Some even believe that his skillful maneuvering rivaled that of Napoleon Bonaparte during his retreat from Moscow in the winter 1812–13. Garibaldi realized it would be extremely difficult for a retreating army with limited mobility to dodge several pursuing enemy armies. Yet he attempted to do just that. Exhibiting great tact, he zigzagged his way across the mountains of central Italy, repeatedly eluding his pursuers. The events of this spectacular retreat constitute one of the most exciting, and one of the most tragic, chapters in the resurgence of the Italian national identity.

Knowing that he would have to run the gauntlet of French, Spanish, Austrian, and Neapolitan armies, Garibaldi hoped to deceive the enemy as to his whereabouts. He first marched his army eastward, toward Tivoli, and then turned south, leading the French to believe that he was heading for the Abruzzi and Molise. But after marching southward for a short distance, he turned sharply to the northeast and disappeared into the mountains. He soon reached the town of Monte Rotondo, where he halted his march and requisitioned food and wine for his troops. When he offered to pay in paper currency printed under the Roman Republic, he found the townspeople reluctant to accept banknotes issued by a defunct government.[1] They became less friendly, and refused to further supply his army. Garibaldi now got his first glimpse of what lay in store for him and his men. He even had to post guards at the town gate to prevent the locals from reporting his position to the French. Evidently, mistrust existed on both sides.

Upon leaving Monte Rotondo, Garibaldi received some welcome reinforcements. Near the town of Terni they were joined by Colonel Hugh Forbes and his well-trained detachment of 650 men.[2] Forbes, an Englishman, had served in the British army and later settled in Florence with his Italian wife. There, he had recruited a battalion of volunteers to fight for the Roman Republic. He had hoped to take part in the defense of Rome against the French, but General Avezzana had ordered him to stay to the north of the city and harass the invading Austrians. Forbes now gladly joined forces with Garibaldi.

After a quick feint toward the Tyrrhenian coast, Garibaldi led his troops due north. His troop column stretched for about three miles along the road. He rode in front with Anita and thirty cavalrymen. Behind them marched the infantry; then came the wagons carrying the supplies, the ambulance, and the only cannon Garibaldi had. The remainder of the cavalry brought up the rear. While marching, they only spoke in whispers and were not allowed to smoke. They usually marched during the night, from 2:00 to 10:00 a.m., and rested during the heat of the day, while food was requisitioned and eaten. They set out again from 5:00 to 8:00 p.m., stopping to rest at dusk.[3]

Using the powers bestowed on him by the Roman Republic, Garibaldi claimed authority to requisition food and supplies from the local communities. However, the people in these towns again objected to being paid in the paper currency of a Republic that no longer existed. They looked upon Garibaldi's men as marauders and sometimes shot at them. Nevertheless, Garibaldi would not allow his men to loot or pillage. He issued strict orders forbidding theft, and warned that any man caught stealing would be summarily shot.

However, obtaining food continued to be a major priority. Wagons were sometimes exchanged for cattle, thus providing the marchers with a mobile milk and meat supply. On one occasion, the retreating column acquired an unexpected quantity of food when a detachment of its cavalry captured a convoy of provisions bound for the French army. The captured cargo included 5,000 live chickens and 50,000 eggs. All of this made for a welcome change of diet from the usual bread, cheese, and salami.[4]

Desertion remained a major problem as many of the men ran off during the night. Some of the deserters turned highwaymen, robbing people and terrorizing the countryside. During the first week, there were more than 2,000 desertions as the men began to sense they were fighting for a lost cause.[5] Garibaldi was saddened by these desertions but unable to prevent them. He was also disappointed by the lack of support he received from the local people: None volunteered to join him. A most annoying factor was the ease with which the pursuing armies were able to obtain information about his whereabouts. There seemed to be no shortage of spies and informers.

Through all of this, Anita remained a shining example of female courage and determination in the face of impending disaster. She endured all the hardships and disappointments of the retreat and still managed to remain cheerful. She chatted with the troops during the march and helped serve the food at mealtimes. They were inspired by her example and went out of their way to render small services to her. Anita's exemplary behavior during this final chapter of her life made her the legendary heroine of the Risorgimento.

With the pursuing armies converging on him, Garibaldi abandoned the territory of the Papal States and crossed the border into Tuscany. Aware that the Tuscans would certainly not accept his paper currency, he required local bankers in the towns through which he passed to exchange Roman banknotes for gold or silver coins, which would be more readily acceptable as legal tender. Of course, the bankers thought they were being swindled. The French high command in Rome had already issued a proclamation declaring that all Republican paper money was valueless and should not be accepted as legal tender. All of this served to turn the local people against Garibaldi.

With the Austrian army blocking the road north to Tuscany, Garibaldi turned westward toward Orvieto, though this meant moving into the path of an oncoming French column. Orvieto was close to the Tuscan frontier; Garibaldi felt certain the French would not pursue him there, since, at the time, Tuscany was considered part of the "Austrian zone."

On the road to Orvieto, one of his men stole a chicken from the house of a peasant woman. Garibaldi, who was passing by as the woman was protesting the theft, had the thief shot on the spot.[6] In doing so, he demonstrated to his troops that he meant what he said—no stealing!

Continuing on to Orvieto, Garibaldi found the town preparing to celebrate the arrival of the French army. A group of prominent citizens came to ask him not to enter. They would rather have welcomed the French! Garibaldi refused to listen to them and rode into Orvieto to the cheers of the townspeople. That night the town was illuminated in his honor, and he and his troops dined on the food that had been prepared for the French.[7] Next morning, the French arrived— only in time for the coffee! By then, Garibaldi was marching his well-fed troops over the mountains toward the border between the Papal States and Tuscany.

In Tuscany, the revolution of 1848 had caused Grand Duke Leopold II to grant the Tuscans a constitution. A moderate government came to power under the leadership of Giuseppe Montanelli and Francesco Guerrazzi. However, when they proclaimed a Tuscan Republic, Emperor Franz Joseph of Austria sent in troops to restore Leopold to his throne. Now, Leopold was alarmed by the approach of Garibaldi's force at the Tuscan frontier. He feared that their arrival would touch off another Republican uprising. The Austrian forces in Tuscany were put on alert and given orders to destroy Garibaldi's "band of brigands."

Despite the impending danger, Garibaldi's force of 2,500 men crossed the frontier into Tuscany on the night of July 17. Garibaldi was hoping to find more support in Tuscany than he had gotten in the territory of the Roman Republic. At the Tuscan town of Cetona, he and his men received their friendliest reception since the retreat began. They were even allowed to sleep in people's houses! Anita purchased a new dress in Cetona and wore it instead of the men's clothing in which she had ridden from Rome. She was now pregnant, and it better befitted her condition to be dressed like a lady.[8]

The reception Garibaldi met in other Tuscan towns was not nearly as friendly. At Chiusi, the Garibaldini were fired upon by Tuscan national guardsmen. At Montepulciano, they were greeted by cheers from the local girls—but that was the extent of it. The townspeople didn't even offer them a glass of the fine wine for which their town was famous. At Arezzo, Garibaldi found the gates slammed shut and the local militia prepared to stop them from entering. It was a reawakening for the man who would liberate Italy.

Tired and hungry, Garibaldi and his troops waited outside Arezzo for twenty-four hours, hoping to be admitted. However, the council refused them entry into the town. Angered by the refusal, his men urged him to attack the place, but, using better judgment, Garibaldi decided to march his weary men away, unwilling to provide his enemies with a further excuse to portray him as a brigand terrorizing the people. As it was, his troops were dejected, and a mood of defeatism began to spread among them. It had become evident that the people of Tuscany were not going to rise up and fight for freedom under Garibaldi's banner.

He now decided to march eastward to the Adriatic coast and then set out for Venice by boat. Executing a series of zigzag maneuvers that baffled the pursuing Austrians, his column headed toward the Apennine Mountains. Among his demoralized troops, the number of desertions increased. He suffered a bitter blow when two of his cavalry officers, Bueno and Müller, deserted the column. Captain Bueno had served with Garibaldi in Montevideo. Major Müller, a Polish revolutionary, had distinguished himself in the defense of Rome. Despite these personal disappointments, Garibaldi remained steadfast in his determination to reach Venice. He was at this point joined by Captain Giovanni Culiolo, who had been wounded and left behind in Rome and who, sufficiently recovered, had hurried to join the retreating column.[9] Captain Culiolo, was also known as "Leggero, the nimble." He would certainly live up to his nickname during the march.

Continuing eastward, Garibaldi reentered the Papal States and reached the town of Citerna on July 24. There, he quartered his men in the local monastery, forcing the monks to supply food for his hungry and exhausted men. By then, three Austrian armies had virtually encircled him. In spite of the encirclement, he slipped through the cordon of Austrian troops along a seldom-used mule trail that was not marked on Austrian military maps.[10] Once again, he had eluded his pursuers.

Over the next few days, the Garibaldini continued their march across the rugged Apennines toward the Adriatic. The Austrians followed close behind, capturing and shooting a number of stragglers. Some of these were boys, aged twelve to fourteen, who had come from Rome with Garibaldi. When asked who they were, they proudly replied that they were "soldiers of Garibaldi" and were summarily shot by the Austrians.[11]

By that juncture, many of Garibaldi's best officers had been knocked out of action by wounds or sickness. Even Anita was in a state of exhaustion from the long, hard march. His force had been reduced to less than 1,800 men, and his chances of reaching the coast and escaping to Venice seemed remote. With the Austrians closing in fast, he realized that his only chance lay in crossing the border into the Republic of San Marino, which had been an independent state for 900 years and could provide asylum. The San Marinese, unwilling to give Austria any cause to invade their state, were reluctant to admit Garibaldi's force when it reached the gates on July 30.

After waiting all day for permission to enter, Garibaldi himself rode up the mountain into the main square of the town of San Marino. Entering the chamber of the Grand Council, he formally entreated that body to allow his men to enter as political refugees, surrendering themselves and their weapons to the state authorities. The request was granted, but not before the Austrians attacked Garibaldi's troops at the frontier. During this action, Garibaldi's rearguard was wiped out, though the remainder of his shattered force managed to enter the territory of San Marino. The pursuing

Austrians halted at the frontier in compliance with the requirements of international law.

Garibaldi and his men were received hospitably by the people of San Marino, who offered food and other necessities. The Capuchin monks even provided quarters in the monastery. The next afternoon, Garibaldi wrote an order officially disbanding his army. It read: "Soldiers, I release you from your duty to follow me. Return to your homes, but remember that Italy remains in slavery and shame. The Roman War for the independence of Italy has ended."[12] Throughout Italy, it seemed as though the purple curtain of doom had descended on the Risorgimento. Garibaldi, although disillusioned, remained determined to continue the struggle for Italian unity.

Meanwhile, the government of San Marino sent envoys to negotiate the future of Garibaldi and his men. The Austrian commander, General Hahn, demanded unconditional surrender. Garibaldi and Anita were to be shipped to exile in the United States, and those who had fought under him were to be granted amnesty and allowed to return home. However, General Hahn also demanded the arrest and punishment of those Garibaldini who had committed crimes during the battle for Rome and the subsequent retreat to San Marino. He awaited a reply while his envoys discussed these terms with Garibaldi himself. Garibaldi rejected unconditional surrender and the detention of suspects, fearing that the Austrians might use this as justification for prosecuting some of his men for murder or theft. It was in any case against his principles to enter into any negotiations with a foreign invader. The final outcome at San Marino would serve to justify his defiance.

He decided instead to escape from San Marino with a band of volunteers. He secretly recruited about two hundred Garibaldini who were willing to follow him in an attempt to reach Venice. His wife, Anita, insisted on going along, though she was ill with a fever,[13] having contracted malaria or some other disease prevalent in those parts of Italy.

Garibaldi enlisted the services of a local guide named Zani, who made a living conducting tours through the mountains around San Marino but, on this occasion, he offered his services for free. The stage was set for another daring escape.

30

Death of Anita

ON THE NIGHT OF JULY 31, Garibaldi, accompanied by Anita and two hundred of his men, made his escape from San Marino. Having persuaded the gatekeeper to secretly let them out at midnight, his departure went unnoticed. Half of his men were mounted, the other half on foot. Led by the guide Zani, they slipped unobserved through the Austrian lines and headed west away from the Adriatic Sea. Marching silently in single file, they made their way along mountain paths used by shepherds. The footing was difficult, and some of the men fell to their deaths. Others, including Gustav von Hoffstetter, lost their way in the darkness and were unable to rejoin Garibaldi. Hoffstetter made his way to Switzerland and later published a book about the retreat from Rome. All told, about fifty men were lost during the perilous night march.

Early the next morning, the small band descended from the mountains and turned northeast toward the Adriatic. They continued marching all day, except for a small break near Mussano. Around midnight, they reached the Adriatic coast at the small fishing port of Cesenatico, about twenty miles south of Ravenna. Desperate to escape by sea, Garibaldi requisitioned thirteen fishing boats in the harbor and ordered the mayor to supply him with pilots to transport his men to Venice. Needless to say, rounding up the reluctant pilots was no easy task, and it caused much resentment among the townspeople. It appeared as though Garibaldi was resorting to his old pirate tricks.

Once the local pilots took the helm, the Garibaldini boarded the ships, leaving their horses behind. But a storm developed, making it difficult for them to put to sea. Garibaldi, undeterred by the adverse weather, ordered the boats to set out for Venice anyway. They left Cesenatico at dawn, sailing into the teeth of the storm in boats piloted by unwilling fishermen.[1] An hour later, the Austrians arrived in town to find only the horses that had been left behind.

Meanwhile, the Austrians were still demanding the unconditional surrender of the remaining Garibaldini in San Marino. This presented a problem for the San Marinese, who were now burdened with a thousand refugees, some of whom tried to escape by slipping through the Austrian lines. Others remained in the tiny Republic until the Austrians withdrew many months later. Those captured by the Austrians were summarily shot; some were tortured and imprisoned, others severely whipped before being released.[2] Eleven years later, some of the survivors rejoined Garibaldi during the campaign in Sicily.

Although Garibaldi and his men had been able to get away

from Cesenatico in boats, they were still in Austrian-controlled waters. After sailing north for almost two days, they passed Ravenna and reached the marshes of Comacchio. They were still about fifty miles south of Venice when they were spotted by Austrian patrol boats and ordered to halt. When they refused, the Austrians gave pursuit. Realizing that they could not elude their pursuers, Garibaldi signaled his boats to put to shore. Only three, including the one carrying Garibaldi and Anita, managed to land safely. The other ten were captured, and more than a hundred of the Garibaldini were taken prisoner.

Anita was so weak that Garibaldi had to lift her out of the boat and carry her ashore near Magnavacca. With him were Ugo Bassi, Angelo Brunetti and his two sons, and Captain Giovanni Culiolo, known as "Leggero." Garibaldi divided his men into small groups of two or three and told them to make their way overland to Venice. He didn't know that they had landed on an island near the mouth of the Po River, and that it was impossible to get to the mainland without a boat. They all said their goodbyes and disappeared into the brush, leaving Garibaldi, Anita, and Leggero alone on the beach. For most of them it would be a final goodbye. Garibaldi stayed with Anita while Leggero went off in search of help. Anita, whose fever had worsened, repeatedly asked for water, but Garibaldi had none to give her.

Then a miracle occurred. Leggero returned with a man Garibaldi recognized—Giacomo Bonnet, who had fought in Rome under Garibaldi's command. He had been captured when Rome fell to the French but, like many of the Roman soldiers, had been allowed to return home. Bonnet explained that he heard gunfire coming from the direction of the sea and had rushed to the shore to investigate, arriving in time to see Garibaldi and the others reach the beach and disperse into the brush. He had shouted to them from the distance but had been too far away to be heard. So he had gone searching for them and met Leggero.[3]

Garibaldi Disembarks with Anita at Magnavacca (by Emilio Paggioaro)

Although the Austrians hadn't come ashore, Bonnet realized that they would soon begin a systematic search of the area. He quickly led the three to a nearby hut, where Garibaldi and Culiolo changed out of their red shirts and put on peasants' clothing. Anita was too ill to walk and had to be carried across the fields to a farm managed by a friend of Bonnet, where they laid her on a bed to rest and brought her warm broth. She was unable to take it, because she could not swallow. Her condition was deteriorating rapidly.

Bonnet took Garibaldi aside and warned him that there was little chance of reaching Venice. He suggested to him that he head south toward Ravenna, where he could hide with friends until he could escape abroad. Because Anita appeared too weak to continue, Bonnet urged Garibaldi to leave her behind at a nearby farmhouse called Casa Zanetto. At least there, she could be cared for by a local doctor.

Garibaldi reluctantly agreed, and she was moved the short distance to the Casa Zanetto. Once there, however, Garibaldi had misgivings about leaving her. He couldn't contemplate the idea of abandoning her to the Austrians while he made his escape. If he did, he would never forgive himself. He decided to take her with him and asked Bonnet to get someone to transport them to the mainland. Before leaving the Zanetto farm, Garibaldi shaved off his beard and changed into one of Bonnet's suits, to further reduce the chances of being recognized by the authorities.

The two boatmen who were summoned to transport them did not realize who their passengers were until they had rowed them almost half way to the mainland. Then, fearing that they would be shot by the Austrians for aiding fugitives, they refused to take them any further. Instead, they hurriedly dropped them off on a small island in the middle of Lake Comacchio and rowed away, leaving the three fugitives marooned. At that point, Garibaldi and Leggero could do nothing but watch over Anita and wait for the Austrians to come.

But the cowardly boatmen, afraid of being implicated in a plot to rescue Garibaldi, never told the authorities! Instead, they went bragging around town about how they had gotten rid of Garibaldi. One of those who heard them boasting was Bonnet's sister-in-law, who at once informed Bonnet of what had happened. He quickly alerted a patriot named Michele Guidi and convinced him to intercede. It was Guidi, not the Austrians, who found the three on the island and escorted them to safety.[4]

Anita was delirious when they reached the mainland. Guidi secured a cart from a nearby farm and transported her, Garibaldi, and Leggero for eleven miles to an isolated dairy farm belonging to the Marquis Guiccioli. In the marquis' absence, the farm was being managed by two brothers, Giuseppe and Stefano Ravaglia; both brothers were there to meet Garibaldi and the others upon their arrival. Also present was a doctor named Nannini, who had already been summoned by Guidi. Garibaldi appealed to him to save Anita. They all helped carry her to a bedroom on the first floor. As they put her down on the bed, she spoke her last words to Garibaldi: "Peppino, the children!" Then, she expired.[5]

Devastated, Garibaldi fell to his knees at the bedside and cried out: "No! No! She is not dead! It is only another fit. She has suffered so much, my poor Anita. She will revive, she is strong. . . . She is not dead, say she is not dead. It is impossible! Look at me, Anita, speak to me, speak to me."[6] Those present tried futilely to console him.

Circumstances dictated that Garibaldi leave there at once—the Austrians were closing in. It was with a heavy heart that he consented to leave. He only asked that Anita be given a decent burial; and then he and Leggero left the Guicciolo farm. The Ravaglia brothers had only enough time to bury Anita in a shallow grave behind the farmhouse.[7] Garibaldi and Leggero then set out on an escape odyssey that would take them 250 miles across Italy.

31

Escape Odyssey

THE AUSTRIAN VICTORY over the Garibaldini was dampened by the fact that Garibaldi had escaped. On August 5, the Austrian high command branded him a wanted criminal and warned that anyone who aided or sheltered him would face summary military justice. People feared they would be shot if they tried to help him.

Within days, the press reported that the Austrian authorities had recovered the body of Anita Garibaldi. A peasant girl, tending cattle on the Guiccioli estate, had spotted a human hand protruding from what appeared to be a shallow grave and reported the gruesome find to the police. A postmortem examination of the corpse had revealed some neck abrasions, causing the examiner to conclude that the woman had been strangled to death. The body was reinterred "for reasons of public health." The official police report identified it as that of "the wife or woman who accompanied Garibaldi, and who was reported to have landed in this district."[1]

Further police investigation established the presence of the two Ravaglia brothers and Dr. Nannini at the Guiccioli farmhouse when the woman died. All three were arrested and charged with murder. The police arrested Giacomo Bonnet and charged him with aiding the fugitives. Then, in a strange twist of events, the medical examiner who had originally concluded that Anita had died by strangulation, retracted his opinion and adopted the view that she had died of natural causes. The courts eventually released the Ravaglia brothers and Dr. Nannini for lack of evidence.[2] Bonnet was later released as well, after serving some time in prison.

The press also announced the capture of the other Garibaldini who had landed on the coast, including Ugo Bassi and Captain Livraghi. Father Bassi, who had acted as chaplain for the Garibaldini, had never borne arms. Nevertheless, an Austrian military court condemned him to death along with Captain Livraghi, an Austrian subject fighting for the Italian cause. They both faced a firing squad. Before his execution, Bassi was degraded from the priesthood by the ecclesiastical authorities and brutally tortured. Nine other Garibaldini were also executed by the Austrians. These included Angelo Brunetti and his two sons, and Captain Parodi, who had come with Garibaldi from Montevideo. They had managed to reach the mainland and were making their way northward when they were betrayed to the Austrians by an informer.[3] They also faced a firing squad.

Those Garibaldini who were captured during the retreat to San Marino faced an equally ignominious fate. They were marched off under heavy guard to the prison at Pietole outside of Mantua. During this "death march," prisoners who stopped or faltered along the way were brutally clubbed. Those too weak to walk were strapped to gun carriages and literally dragged along the road. Those who survived these horrors were interned at the infamous prison at Pietole, where most of them died from torture, malnutrition, and disease.[4]

But the man whom the Austrians wanted most had not been captured. Garibaldi, most wanted of criminals, had eluded them again. He would prove more elusive than ever, because few people actually knew what he looked like. He had shaved his beard and discarded his red shirt. Donning peasant garb, he and his companion Leggero set out on one of the most incredible escape odysseys of all time.

Following Anita's death at the Guiccioli farm, Bonnet's friend Michele Guidi had taken them to the village of SaintAlberto, where they hid in the house of another friend. They made contact there with a clandestine Republican organization that ran a sort of underground railroad for fugitive revolutionaries. This organization would provide them with shelter and guidance during their journey across the peninsula.

One dark night, Garibaldi and Leggero were taken to a hiding place in the pine forest where a group of men was sitting around a campfire. The guide first signaled their approach with a code whistle; and upon entering the campsite, he introduced the two fugitives to those present. The men around the campfire were not the lumberjacks they pretended to be, but members of the revolutionary underground. One of the group then led Garibaldi and Leggero to another hiding place, where they remained the next day. At nightfall, he led them through the forest to another guide at yet another campsite.

Upon reaching Ravenna, they hid in another house for several days and then headed southwest toward Tuscany—the direction in which the authorities would least expect them to go. They traveled by night, led by one guide after another, passed from house to house—and no one revealed their whereabouts to the Austrians. One of their guides was a Catholic priest, Father Giovanni Veritá, who sheltered them in the church rectory in the town of Modigliana.[5] Then, one night, something went wrong—the guide they were to meet failed to show up, and the two fugitives lost contact with the underground. They suddenly found themselves on their own in a region where they did not know the footpaths and byways. The deadly game of hide-and-seek now began in earnest.

Continuing on their own through the night, Garibaldi and Leggero soon found themselves on the main road to Florence. They hitched a ride on a farmer's cart, along a thoroughfare heavily patrolled by the Austrians. At one point, they passed a corps of Austrian soldiers marching in the opposite direction, but the soldiers didn't even give them a second glance.

At dusk, they were dropped off at an inn in the small town of Santa Lucia. There, they ordered a cup of strong Italian coffee and sat down at a long table in the dimly-lit dining room. Garibaldi was so tired that he put his head down and fell asleep at the table. An incredible event ensued—a group of Austrian soldiers entered the inn and sat down at the same long table! Garibaldi, awakened by a sudden nudge from Leggero, raised his head, saw the Austrians sitting there, and lowered his head, pretending to fall asleep again. The soldiers ordered drinks and bragged about how they would soon capture "the infamous Garibaldi." But they only had eyes for the innkeeper's daughter who was waiting on them; they didn't notice the two men sitting in the shadows just a few feet away. When they finally left, Garibaldi and Leggero emerged from the shadows and were shown to a farmer's hut where they found shelter for the evening.[6]

This is the story that Garibaldi wrote in his memoirs. A somewhat different version was recorded years later by the innkeeper's daughter, Teresa Baldini. Twenty years old in 1849, she said that she had recognized Garibaldi as soon as he entered the inn, remembering him from the year before when he stopped by on his way to Ravenna. In an attempt to warn him of the impending danger, she'd said to him, "The Austrians and Tuscans are looking for you." But before he could hide, the Austrian soldiers had entered the inn and sat down at the same long table with him and Leggero. The inn was rather dark, having only one lamp to light the place, and it was shining on Garibaldi. Teresa recounts how Garibaldi went to the lamp under the pretense of lighting his cigar and deftly adjusted it so that he and Leggero would not be in the light. Then he sat down and silently smoked his cigar in the shadows while the Austrians boasted of his impending demise. Teresa had deliberately distracted them while she was serving their drinks, making sure they had eyes only for her. After they left, she had escorted Garibaldi and Leggero to the safety of a friend's house.[7]

Although Baldini's version of the story makes for interesting reading, some doubt its authenticity. Garibaldi never failed to acknowledge anyone who helped him—especially a beautiful girl; it has therefore been suggested that Teresa identified her father's inn from Garibaldi's description of it in his memoirs and gave the story a more romantic twist.

It seemed that the whole world was awaiting news of Garibaldi's whereabouts. Some newspapers published sensational, wholly invented reports. One such described Garibaldi's arrival in Venice with Anita, and had him standing on the Doges' balcony, acknowledging the cheers of the crowd in St. Mark's Square. Another had Garibaldi and Anita still hiding in San Marino, waiting for a chance to escape to the coast and sail to the Ionian isles. Probably the most absurd claimed that Anita had been murdered by the Republican revolution-aries because she was impeding Garibaldi's escape![8]

Traveling along lonely country roads, Garibaldi and Leggero moved across Tuscany, sometimes fed and sheltered by humble peasants. These brave patriots were moved by admiration for the man who would ultimately unify their country. But now that the two fugitives had lost contact with the revolutionary underground, they were at greater risk of apprehension by the Austrian authori-ties. It was absolutely essential that they reestablish contact.

They entered a taverna and overheard a young man named Sequi drinking wine with friends and bragging that he would do anything to help Garibaldi escape from the Austrians. They won-dered whether the man was a patriot or an informer, but decided to trust him at his word and, at the right moment, Garibaldi drew him aside and identified himself. Sequi fainted! After he was revived, he made good on his offer to help Garibaldi by promptly putting him in contact with the Republican underground.[9]

Garibaldi and Leggero were once again aided by reliable local guides who led them from one hiding place to another across Tuscany. Their new contacts warned them that the Tuscan frontier with the Kingdom of Sardinia was too well guarded, and that it would be safer to head for the coast further south. There, they could find a fisherman who would take them to Liguria by sea. Following their contacts' instructions, they turned south, passing by Volterra and stopping at the village of San Dalmazio, near the sea. They remained there for several days while arrangements were made for their departure by boat.

The details were soon completed for them to move out on the

night of September 1. Accompanied by a few companions, they carried sporting guns and pretended to be hunters on a night foray. After hiking through a dense forest, they reached the Tyrrhenian coast at an isolated spot called Cala Martina. There Garibaldi and Leggero boarded a waiting fishing boat and sailed away, waving to their friends on the shore and shouting "Viva l'Italia!"

Three days later, they landed at Porto Venere in the Kingdom of Sardinia. From there, they traveled by cart northward along the coast to the town of Chiavari. Garibaldi's relatives, the Gustavini family, lived in Chiavari, and that morning, they were startled by a commotion in the streets; they looked out and saw a cheering crowd escorting two men toward the house. The two were Garibaldi and Leggero, and their safe arrival in Sardinian territory was cause for great jubilation. Within two days, the whole world knew of Garibaldi's incredible escape.

The government in Torino, however, was not so happy to hear of it, having previously announced that anyone who fought in the defense of the Roman Republic had forfeited his citizenship and would not be allowed to enter Sardinian territory. Garibaldi was no exception. He was promptly arrested, charged with entering the country illegally, and taken to a prison in Genoa. But his role in the defense of Rome had made him a popular hero, and the news of his arrest aroused popular indignation. It also sparked a heated debate in the Sardinian parliament, where the overwhelming majority voted for a resolution declaring that his expulsion was unconstitutional. The resolution read as follows:

> The arrest of General Garibaldi and his threatened expulsion
> from Piedmont is contrary to the right assured by the statute, to the
> sentiments of patriotism, and to the glory of Italy.[10]

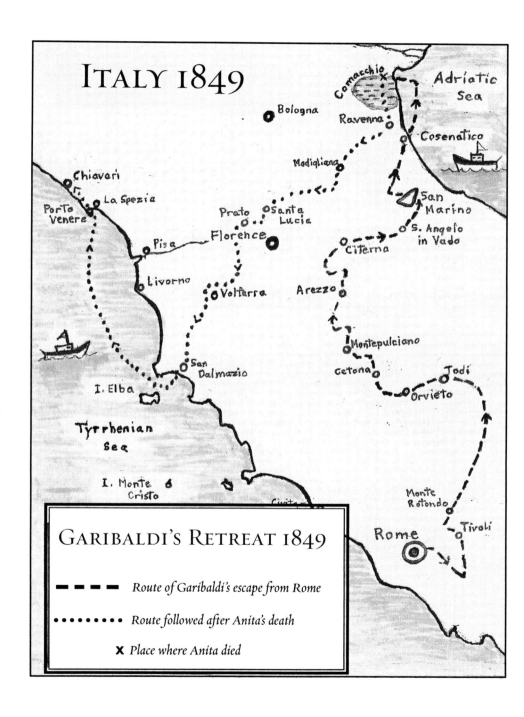

ITALY 1849

Adriatic
Sea

Comacchio ✕

Bologna

Ravenna

Cosenatico

Modigliana

San Marino

Chiavari

La Spezia

Porto
Venere

Prato

Santa
Lucia

Florence

S. Angelo
in Vado

Citerna

Pisa

Livorno

Volterra

Arezzo

San
Dalmazio

Montepulciano

I. Elba

Cetona

Todi

Orvieto

Tyrrhenian
Sea

I. Monte
Cristo

Monte
Rotondo

Civita

Rome

Tivoli

GARIBALDI'S RETREAT 1849

‐ ‐ ‐ ‐ ‐ *Route of Garibaldi's escape from Rome*

•••••••••• *Route followed after Anita's death*

✕ *Place where Anita died*

Only eleven members of parliament opposed the resolution—
one of them was Count Camilo di Cavour, a deputy from
Piedmont. King Victor Emmanuel remained conspicuously silent
throughout the whole affair. Apparently, the king did not wish to
antagonize the Austrians by befriending Garibaldi, nor did he want
to outrage public opinion in his country by repudiating him.

The government dared not treat Garibaldi badly. Even as a
prisoner, he was granted almost every privilege by the military governor of Genoa, General La Marmora. Garibaldi could receive as
many visitors as he wished. He was even allowed to talk to the
press. He said nothing that would embarrass the government.
After five days of imprisonment, the government decided to allow
him to emigrate to America. As a sweetener, it promised a pension
to maintain his family and agreed to allow him twenty-four hours
to visit his relatives in nearby Nice. He also received the sum of
2,000 francs to cover the cost of his visit. But he had to give
General La Marmora his word of honor that he would seek no publicity and return promptly." So, five days after his arrest and detention, Garibaldi embarked by ship to visit his family in Nice.

Upon his arrival, he found the harbor filled with boats and the
shorefront crowded with people awaiting his return. Even the fishermen had remained in port that day (September 13) in order to
greet him. He stepped ashore to a tumultuous welcome and was
escorted by the crowds to his mother's house on Quai Lunel. His
reunion with her was joyous. She had seen him go into exile as a
wanted criminal, and now she witnessed his return as a national
hero.

Next, he went to see his children at the home of his good friend
Giuseppe Deideri, where his beloved Anita had boarded them
before joining him during the battle for Rome. The three chil-

dren—Menotti, age nine; Teresita, age four; and Ricciotti, age two—had not yet been told of their mother's death. They all greeted their father warmly, but when they asked for her, Garibaldi broke into tears and couldn't answer them. It remained for Signora Deideri to break the news.[12]

After spending the night at his mother's house, Garibaldi returned to the ship as he had promised. He would never see his mother again; she died soon afterward. But he kept his word, returning to Genoa at the agreed time and not seeking publicity despite the large crowds that had gathered to cheer him. All this made a favorable impression on General La Marmora.

Before sailing into exile, Garibaldi accepted, on behalf of his family, a cash sum of 1,200 lire as the first quarterly installment of his government pension.[13] As an additional sweetener, two of his old comrades-in-arms, Leggero and Cucelli, were allowed to sail away with him—and all at government expense. Why all this generosity? Apparently, Prime Minister Massimo d'Azeglio believed that it was a small price to pay for the removal of such "a disturbing personality" from Sardinian territory.

32

Exile in New York: 1850—1851

GARIBALDI SAILED INTO EXILE FROM GENOA on September 16, 1849. With him were Giovanni Culiolo, also known as "Leggero," and Luigi Cucelli, the former bandleader in the Italian Legion in Montevideo. Culiolo had been with Garibaldi during his retreat from Rome and present when Anita died. Cucelli was one of the sixty-three legionnaires who had returned to Italy with Garibaldi. All three faced a future filled with uncertainty.

Their first port of call was Tunis, in North Africa—though the Turkish governor there would not allow them to land because of pressure from the French government. Since the ship had a schedule to follow, the three exiles were taken to the port of Cagliari on Sardinia. There too they were refused entry, and the ship was diverted to the small island of La Maddalena, where, on September

25, the three exiles were at last allowed to land, and temporarily lodged in the home of the military governor, Colonel Falchi. Falchi did not hold his guests in detention, but he did keep them under close surveillance.[1]

La Maddalena lies a few miles off the northeast coast of Sardinia and was already known as an island resort then. To the east of La Maddalena lay the smaller island of Caprera. A narrow channel less than half a mile wide separated the two islands. Caprera got its name from the wild goats that roamed the island and was uninhabited except for an Englishman named Collins, who had initially purchased it for its hunting and fishing rights and later built a house there. The island seemed to hold a special attraction for Garibaldi, who was now a man without a country. Five years later, he bought land there.

At that time, however, the Sardinian government had no intention of allowing Garibaldi and his companions to remain anywhere in the kingdom, and they negotiated with the British to send the exiles to either England or Gibraltar. They were refused entry to both. Besides feeling unwanted, Garibaldi was still struggling with his greatest grief: He had lost his beloved Anita and was now separated from his three children. He was a man without love, without family—and without a country.

Finally, the King of Morocco allowed the exiles to land at Tangier, on the coast of North Africa, where they were welcomed by the Sardinian consul, Giovanni Battista Carpeneto. Carpeneto, a true patriot, allowed the three exiles to stay at his house. However, he offered his hospitality without first consulting his government, and for this was later reprimanded by Prime Minister Massimo d'Azeglio.

During his stay in Tangier, Garibaldi began to write his memoirs. The original manuscript only covered the period from his birth in 1807 to his departure from Montevideo in 1848. He managed to cope with his sudden inactivity by writing. Otherwise, exile in Tangier proved a boring existence except for the occasional wild boar hunt. Along with his faithful dog, Castor, he spent days in the wilds, sleeping in the open and living on the game he shot. He still hoped to receive a call from Torino summoning him to take command of an army of national liberation. The call never came.

Seven months later, he decided to try his fortune in the United States as so many of his fellow countrymen had done before him. He had concluded that only in America would he be able to secure employment as a sea captain. So in June 1850, he left Tangier for the United States of America. Culiolo and Cucelli remained in Tangier because he could not afford to pay for their passage. After a brief stop in Liverpool, England, the ship sailed for New York, arriving there thirty-three days later after a rough ocean crossing.

Garibaldi's arrival in New York did not go unnoticed. The Italian Committee in the United States had already made preparations for a civic reception, followed by a banquet in his honor at the Astor Hotel. However, Garibaldi, who was kept in quarantine for five days on Staten Island, declined to attend any civic reception or banquet in his honor. When the period of quarantine expired, he took a ferryboat to Manhattan and went to live with a compatriot named Felice Foresti, at a house on Irving Place.[2] Foresti was an old revolutionary who had spent a total of eighteen years in Austrian prisons. Upon his release, he had emigrated to New York, where in 1837, he became the Chairman of the Department of Italian Literature at Columbia College.

The New York of 1850 was a city of approximately 700,000 inhabitants, many of whom were European immigrants—Irish,

Germans, Italians, Polish, and others. The commercial hub stretched from the Battery and Wall Street to Fourteenth Street and Union Square. Extending northward to the vicinity of Seventy-second Street lay a newer area of the city containing the townhouses of the wealthy and some imposing new buildings. Beyond that stretched woods and fields. The Bronx was mainly farmland, and of the other boroughs, only Brooklyn had a fairly large and concentrated population.

While Garibaldi was living on Irving Place, he was visited by writer Theodore Dwight, who asked for permission to translate and publish the Tangier memoirs. Garibaldi eventually gave his consent, thus enabling Dwight in 1859 to publish an English translation of the memoirs under the title *The Life of General Garibaldi*. This text became a valuable source of information on Garibaldi's life in South America.

In October 1850, Garibaldi moved to the house of Antonio Meucci, across the bay on Staten Island. Meucci, born near Florence, Italy, in 1808, had studied design and mechanical engineering at Florence's Academy of Fine Arts. He had then worked in local theatres as a stage technician. In 1835, he emigrated to Cuba, where he accepted a job as a scenic designer at the Teatro Tacon in Havana. He left Cuba for New York in 1850 and took up residency on Staten Island. There, Meucci was earning a meager living operating a candle factory he had constructed in his own backyard. He spent his spare time experimenting with a new gadget that could transmit the human voice over a copper wire charged with electricity—a gadget he called the *teletrofono*.

While living at Meucci's house, Garibaldi earned his keep by working in the candle factory. He was not skilled in the trade, so he performed the menial work of carrying barrels of tallow from the docks to the boiling vat at the factory. For recreation, he sometimes played bocci ball with other Italians at a bowling ground near the water's edge. He also frequented Ventura's Bar on Fulton Street in Manhattan, where he engaged in lively conversation with other customers. When there were get-togethers at the house, Garibaldi played popular Italian songs on Meucci's piano and sometimes joined in a sing-along. He often went fishing with Meucci or hunting by himself in the Staten Island woods. While engaged in the latter on one occasion, he broke a local ordinance and had to appear in court. When the frightened judge discovered who the defendant was, he slammed down his mallet and dismissed the case!

Eventually, Garibaldi came to feel that he was of no real use in the candle factory, and that he was living on Meucci's charity. He went down to the New York waterfront instead, in search of a job. He offered to sign up as a longshoreman but was told that his services were not needed and that he was too old to do heavy physical work. This last barb really hurt Garibaldi, because he was only forty-four. He did not tell Meucci about failing to find a job on the docks.[3]

He also filed an application for a job with the U.S. Postal Service but there too failed to secure a position. Around this time, he applied for U.S. citizenship and was given a passport. But he never actually completed the formalities, and his naturalization was never confirmed by the Department of Immigration and Naturalization.

Throughout the period, Garibaldi took a keen interest in the welfare of the Italian community in New York. He attended numerous fund-raisers and allowed his name to be used in connection with charitable appeals. Though he personally had little money, he remained willing to literally give someone the shirt off his back. A raggedly dressed visitor once told him that he had no money to buy a new shirt. Garibaldi, who possessed only two shirts, offered one of them to the poor man. Meucci, who was present, objected to Garibaldi dispossessing himself of what he thought to be a valuable souvenir, and offered the poor man one of his own shirts— if Garibaldi would let him have the red one as a memento.⁴ Garibaldi agreed, and today, that red shirt is on display at the Masonic Lodge of the Borough of Richmond (Staten Island).

In April 1851, Garibaldi received news that an old friend, Francesco Carpanetto (not to be confused with Giovanni Carpeneto), had arrived in New York from Genoa. Carpanetto and his associates had recently purchased a ship in San Francisco, and they wanted Garibaldi to be its captain.⁵ The ship would sail down the Pacific coast to Peru, where it was to be registered under the Peruvian flag, and he would take command there. Called the *Carmen*, it had originally transported prospectors to California to partake in the Gold Rush. Now, it was lying idle in the harbor because the crew had abandoned it to search for gold. Carpanetto and his associates had thus been able to purchase the ship at a reasonable price. Once again, Garibaldi had to take leave of his friends and journey into the unknown. This time, however, he was setting out to take command of a new ship.

His friend Meucci remained behind and was to dedicate his life to perfecting a device that would become a key element in our modern culture—a device that came to be known as the *telephone*.

As early as 1855, when his wife began to suffer from arthritis, Meucci had set up a telecommunication system connecting his basement laboratory with her second-floor bedroom. In 1860, he had successfully demonstrated his invention before a large gathering and had a description of his device published in a New York newspaper. His demonstration, however, had failed to attract the financial backing necessary for its commercialization. Unable to find backers in New York, Meucci attempted to produce his invention in Italy. A friend took a model of his telephone there for that express purpose. This venture also failed to attract investors, and nothing came of it.

Unable to continue his project for lack of funds, Meucci was obliged to seek other employment, and on July 30, 1871, while commuting to work, he was badly scalded in an explosion on the Staten Island ferry. He remained hospitalized for nearly three months, and during that period, his wife sold his prototype model telephone to a secondhand junk dealer for six dollars! Apparently, she needed the money to pay the bills. When Meucci tried to repurchase the valuable device, he was told that it had been resold to an "unknown young man."

Despite this terrible setback, Meucci was determined to pursue his quest for the development of a system of communication based on his invention. Using old notes and diagrams, he worked frantically to reconstruct another prototype model telephone. Several more months passed before this was achieved, and he grew fearful that someone else might steal the idea before he could patent it.

His fears deepened when he was unable to raise the sum of $250 to take out a definitive patent on his telephone. His only recourse was to apply for a patent caveat, a one-year renewable notice of intention to take out a patent. Meucci registered the caveat in December 1871, and renewed it in 1872 and in 1873, but not thereafter. Tradition has it that he didn't have the $10 to pay the renewal fee.

In 1872, Meucci sought to gain the backing of the newly formed Western Union Telegraph Company. He sent a working model of his device to a company official, offering to demonstrate its potential on the wires of the Western Union system. The official, a certain Edward B. Grant, expressed an interest in the project but made no further commitment. Months passed, and when Meucci contacted Grant about scheduling a demonstration for his device, he was given the brush-off and told that Grant had no time to schedule it. Two years later (in 1874), when Meucci demanded the return of his apparatus, he was told that it had been "lost." Betrayed and bewildered, now Meucci had to face his most formidable adversary—Alexander Graham Bell.

In March 1876, Bell filed his patent for the telephone, and when Meucci brought suit against him and the Bell Company, a series of lengthy court cases ensued. During the course of litigation, it was learned that all the documents filed in Meucci's caveat had also been mysteriously lost. An investigation into the matter uncovered evidence linking two employees of the U.S. Patent Office to high-ranking officials of the Bell Company. Even more startling was the revelation that Bell himself had conducted experiments in the same laboratory at Western Union where Meucci's materials had been stored. To top it all off, it became known that Bell had agreed to pay Western Union twenty percent of the profits from the commercialization of the telephone for a period of seventeen years. With millions of dollars involved, the case took on greater ramifications, and it appeared that the Bell forces would stop at nothing to gain the patent for the telephone.

In the court case that began in 1885, the court ignored important evidence supporting Meucci's claim and was instead enthralled by the rhetoric of Bell's Ivy League lawyers. Meucci himself was portrayed as a "delusional fool with wild dreams and a string tele-phone." In the end, the court ruled in favor of Bell, and he was thereafter credited with inventing the telephone.

Meucci, in turn, received no recognition for inventing the tele-phone despite a preponderance of evidence indicating that he was decades ahead of Bell in the development and use of telephone technology. He died penniless on October 19, 1889, a victim of fraud and injustice.

Since Meucci's death, various Italian-American organizations have joined in the quest to assign him rightful credit for his great invention. One of the groups at the forefront of this movement has been the Order Sons of Italy in America, whose tireless efforts, with the combined efforts of countless other individuals, eventual-ly led to the inventor's vindication. On June 11, 2002, 113 years after Meucci's death, the U.S. House of Representatives passed Resolution 269, sponsored by Representative Vito Fossella (R-NY), officially recognizing Antonio Meucci as the true inventor of the telephone. A similar resolution (223) sponsored by Senator Jon Corzine (D-NJ) was passed by the U.S. Senate in September 2003.

Meucci's legacy has been preserved in the Garibaldi-Meucci Museum, located in the house where the two men had lived. The museum is administered by the Order Sons of Italy in America and includes some of the original furnishings. Also on display are two models of Meucci's original telephone as well as numerous docu-ments, letters and, photographs dating back to the mid-1800s. The museum is located at 420 Tomkins Avenue, Staten Island, New York 10305, and is open to visitors during afternoon hours from Tuesday to Friday.

The house of Antonio Meucci on Staten Island, New York (now the Garibaldi-Meucci Museum)

Piano and rocking chair in Meucci's living room

The boiling vat Meucci used in candle-making.

Model telephones designed by Meucci in 1854, now on exhibit at the Garibaldi-Meucci Museum

Monument to Meucci erected in 1923 on Staten Island, New York

33

Odyssey to the Far East: 1851–1853

GARIBALDI AND HIS FRIEND FRANCESCO CARPANETTO set out for Peru on April 28, 1851. On the first leg of their journey, they sailed from New York to Chagres, on the Caribbean coast of Panama. Although there was no Panama Canal at that time, the Isthmus offered travelers the shortest overland route to the Pacific. It was the route taken earlier by the Forty Niners on their way to prospect for gold in California.

Since Carpanetto had to go north to Nicaragua on business, Garibaldi accompanied him and spent several months sightseeing in Central America. They encountered a region of spectacular natural beauty, dotted with old Spanish colonial towns. They canoed up the San Juan River to Lake Nicaragua and across the lake by ferry to the town of Granada. From there, they made their way to León, where Carpanetto negotiated a business transaction for the company that he represented.

Returning to Chagres four months later, the two hiked across the Isthmus of Panama, following the route taken by the Spanish explorer Vasco de Balboa in 1519—a fifty-mile journey through a tangled jungle infested with malaria. Garibaldi fell seriously ill with a tropical fever and for a few days was delirious. He recovered sufficiently to complete the crossing to Panama City on the Pacific coast. There, he and Carpanetto boarded a steamship for Callao, in Peru.[1]

Sailing down the west coast of South America, their ship stopped at Guayaquil in Ecuador, and then at Payta in Peru, where Garibaldi went ashore to visit Señora Manuela Saenz. Manuela Saenz had been the mistress of Simon Bolivar, the liberator of much of South America, and had fought at his side the way Anita had fought at Garibaldi's. When they met at her home, she was ill and confined to her bed. The two spent the afternoon reminiscing. Garibaldi felt a great affinity with Manuela and described her as a charming and graceful lady.[2]

In early October, they reached the port of Callao in Peru and then traveled inland to the capital city of Lima. There, they were given a rousing welcome by the Italian community, many of whom were political exiles. The Sardinian consul, however, wasn't nearly as happy about their arrival. He feared that Garibaldi would fall under the influence of the local Mazzinians and possibly engage in the recruiting of militants. As a precaution, he had someone shadow Garibaldi and report his every move. This angered Garibaldi, who snubbed the consul when they met at a social function.[3]

Shortly thereafter, the newly purchased *Carmen* arrived from California, and Garibaldi took over as her captain. The new owner of the four-hundred-ton schooner was Pietro Denegri, a businessman in New York who had put up most of the money. The vessel was to be loaded with a cargo of guano for a shipment to Canton in China. At that time, Peru held a monopoly in the flourishing trade based on the exporting of guano, a fertilizing manure. Carpanetto, who had made all of the arrangements, now left Peru for Nicaragua, and later died of cholera; Garibaldi never saw him again.

During his stay in Lima, Garibaldi attended a wedding in which a prominent member of the Italian community married the daughter of a wealthy Peruvian. At the reception that followed, Garibaldi exchanged barbs with a wealthy French businessman named Charles Ledo. There are conflicting stories about what passed between the two, but it appears that Ledo deliberately provoked Garibaldi with sarcastic comments. He went so far as to depict the Italians who had fought in the defense of the Roman Republic as "traitors" and "cowards." Garibaldi did not wish to quarrel at a wedding reception, so he ignored the comments. But while he was discussing the battle for Rome with some of the guests, he was interrupted by Ledo, who asked him to admit that "the French fought like heroes." Garibaldi replied, "I don't know. I never saw more than their backsides!"[4] His reply brought a roar of laughter from the other guests.

A few days later, an article appeared in a local newspaper condemning Garibaldi's conduct in the defense of Rome and during the retreat to San Marino. The anonymous article referred to him as "a hero of the mob" and described him as a "a pygmy" whom some journalists were trying to "make into a giant." The article also depicted Garibaldi as a caricature of a brave man possessing no intellect. The article was signed "A Gaul," but Garibaldi guessed that it was written by Charles Ledo and determined to deal with the matter personally.

He went searching for Ledo at his place of business and, finding him there, proceeded to beat him with his cane. Ledo's assistant, who happened to be there at the time, hit Garibaldi in the back of the head with a crowbar. Although he was badly hurt, Garibaldi continued to batter both Ledo and the assistant until he saw "both their backsides fleeing out the door."[5]

Garibaldi had preserved his honor, but the brawl caused much antagonism between the Italian and the French communities in Lima. Tensions mounted when Ledo brought assault charges against Garibaldi. The court fined Garibaldi two hundred pesos but reversed its decision under pressure from Italian demonstrators. A national crisis was narrowly averted when Peruvian army troops were called in to maintain order. In the end, Garibaldi emerged the victor, having defended Italian national honor. Nevertheless, he was severely reprimanded for his part in the fracas by the Sardinian consul. He himself later described the entire incident as "regrettable."[6]

At this juncture, Garibaldi was to embark on one of the longest sea voyages of his career. On January 10, 1852, he sailed for China on the *Carmen* with his cargo of guano. During the long journey across the Pacific, he had a disturbing dream. He dreamt that his beloved mother, Rosa, had died back in Nice, and saw a long procession of women following her casket.[7] A year later, he was to learn that his mother had indeed died, and on the very day he had had the dream—March 19, 1852.

The voyage across the Pacific Ocean took ninety-three days and enabled Garibaldi to broaden his knowledge of the Far East. He sailed past Hawaii and countless other islands before reaching Canton on April 12, 1852. At that time, China was in a crisis, having just lost the Opium War to Britain and its allies. The victors were in the process of forcing her to open her ports to foreign trade, including the trade in opium. China had also been forced to cede Hong Kong to the British.

Garibaldi, unaware he was entering a war zone, found himself in the midst of a naval battle between a Chinese naval vessel and a pirate ship in Canton harbor. What little is known about Garibaldi's stay in Chinese waters was later recounted by W. C. Hunter, a representative of the American shipping firm Perkis and Company. Hunter came aboard the *Carmen* during the battle to alert the ship's captain to the danger and was surprised to discover that the ship's captain was none other than Garibaldi himself. The two conversed on deck as bullets whizzed past their heads.*

Unable to make a transaction in Canton, Garibaldi sailed five hundred miles up the China coast to Amoy, where he succeeded in selling his cargo of guano. He then sailed back to Canton and began his return voyage to Peru on October 15, 1852. This time, he took a more southerly route, sailing down to the Indian Ocean and around Australia. He proceeded eastward along that continent's southern coast. Sailing through the Bass Strait between Melbourne and the island of Tasmania, he stopped at one of the Hunter Islands to pick up provisions.

The island that he put into was a paradise, covered with lush vegetation and humming with the sounds of indigenous birds. There were numerous clear-flowing streams and an overabundance of wild flowers. However, there were no people, only an abandoned farmhouse with a vegetable garden.[8] An inscription on

---

*Hunter's account of what happened in Canton is described in Jasper Ridley's *Garibaldi*, p. 372; and B. Lubbock's *The Opium Clippers*, p. 326.

a tombstone indicated that the farmer had moved because of the death of a loved one, so Garibaldi had no qualms about gathering up the vegetables in the garden.

He was so charmed by the beauty and solitude of the island that he often thought of it when he was distraught over the betrayals and double dealings of "civilized society." It probably was the memory of that beautiful and lonely island that later inspired him to make a home for himself and his family in a somewhat similar island setting.

Continuing on, Garibaldi sailed south of New Zealand and across the South Pacific to Peru. Although they encountered contrary winds during the last part of the journey, the ship finally docked at Callao on January 24, 1853, about a hundred days after leaving China. From there, he sailed southward to Valpariso, Chile, where he loaded his ship with a cargo of copper and wool, and set sail for Boston. He rounded a tempestuous Cape Horn and continued northward along the east coast of South America. We have no knowledge of any stops in those regions where Garibaldi had fought so many battles a few years earlier. On September 6, he sailed into Boston harbor after a journey of about 10,000 miles.

Garibaldi travelled by train to New York to square his financial accounts with the ship owners. When he did so, he discovered that he was short a considerable sum of money. Denegri realized that Garibaldi had not embezzled the money and believed that the discrepancy was due to an honest accounting mistake. It was common knowledge that Garibaldi had never been a good businessman. Denegri's accountant, however, made some demeaning statements, implying that Garibaldi was dishonest and incompetent. This angered him so much that he resigned the command of his ship. The dispute over the correct sum of money due Denegri from

Garibaldi's China voyage continued until 1866, when it was finally settled.[9]

34

New York to Nice: 1854

WHILE IN NEW YORK, Garibaldi heard some encouraging news from Italy. A new government had come to power in the Kingdom of Sardinia, headed by a prime minister named Count Camillo di Cavour. Under its young king, Victor Emmanuel II, Sardinia was the only state in Italy that had maintained a liberal constitution after the revolutions of 1848–1849 were put down. Sardinia thus became the exception in a Europe dominated by powerful forces of reaction and repression. Italians now looked forward to Sardinia's leadership in a war of liberation from Austrian domination. Cavour was destined to become a key figure in the upcoming conflict everyone knew to be inevitable.

In the autumn of 1853, the Sardinian consul in New York notified Garibaldi that he would be allowed to return to his home in

Nice. Since Garibaldi had not become a U.S. citizen, he chose to return to Italy.

Around this time, Captain Antonio Figari, an old friend, arrived in New York from Europe. He and Garibaldi had met in Tagonrog, Russia, in 1832, when Garibaldi was a mate on the *Clorinda* and Figari a cabin boy. The latter, now a sea captain in the Italian merchant navy, was in the United States to purchase a ship and offer Garibaldi a job.[1]

Figari successfully negotiated the purchase of a ship, named the *Commonwealth,* in November. Garibaldi was appointed as her captain, and preparations got underway for the voyage across the Atlantic. On January 16, 1854, the *Commonwealth* sailed from Baltimore, bound for London and Genoa. After an absence of almost five years, Garibaldi was again returning to the land of his origin.

The ship first docked in the port of London on February 11, 1854, where Garibaldi contacted Mazzini. The two had not seen each other since the downfall of the Roman Republic five years earlier. Through Mazzini, he met many other prominent exiled revolutionaries including Alexandre Ledru-Rollin of France, Lajos Kossuth of Hungary, and Alexander Herzen of Russia. During his stay in London, he met with Herzen on several occasions. He told the Russian about his life at sea and spoke of "a floating revolution ready to put in at any shore, independent and unassailable." Later, in his writings, Herzen described Garibaldi as "a hero of antiquity, a figure out of the *Aeneid.*"[2]

Garibaldi was also to meet several prominent British supporters of Italian freedom, including George Holyoake, William Ashurst, Jessie White, and Sir Anthony Panizzi. Panizzi had come to Britain as a political refugee in 1823 and later rose to the office of Principal Librarian of the British Museum. Both Holyoake and Ashurst were active in supporting radical causes such as women's rights and Italian unification. Holyoake was later to help recruit British volunteers to fight with the Red Shirts during the liberation of Sicily.

Jessie White, the beautiful daughter of a British shipbuilder, also championed women's rights as well as Italian freedom. She was an ardent follower of Mazzini who later married an Italian revolutionary named Alberto Mario. In 1856, she became the first woman journalist in Britain when she was appointed by the *Daily News* as its foreign correspondent in Genoa.[3] During her stay in Italy, she accompanied Garibaldi on his campaigns and often assisted in caring for the sick and wounded. She later wrote a biography of Garibaldi's life titled *Garibaldi e i suoi tempi* (*Garibaldi and His Times*), published in 1884.

While he was in London, Garibaldi and several other exiled revolutionaries attended a dinner party at the United States Embassy, where he met James Buchanan, formerly secretary of state under President James Polk. Buchanan had since held several other important government posts and at that moment was trying to secure the Democratic presidential nomination. During their conversation, Buchanan declared that Garibaldi was as famous in America as he was in Europe. Garibaldi was flattered. Two years later, Buchanan was elected president, and his administration adhered to the pro-slavery policy that drove the nation toward civil war. Subsequently, Alexander Herzen was to describe the dinner, which was attended by many revolutionaries, as "the *red* dinner, given by the defender of *black* slavery."[4]

Since Anita's tragic death in 1849, Garibaldi had shown little interest in other women. He became romantically involved again when he met and fell in love with Emma Roberts, a beautiful English socialite, at a London house party. Mrs. Roberts, wealthy and widowed, was quite active in the London social circuit. She was charming and cultured, and had a keen appreciation for the finer things in life. After their first meeting, she and Garibaldi carried on a whirlwind romance and soon announced their engagement, which received much press.[5]

On March 17, Garibaldi sailed from the Port of London for Tynemouth to take on a cargo of coal. He remained there for three weeks and struck up a friendship with Joseph Cowen and his family. Cowan was an MP for the city of Newcastle and a champion of social reform. He organized a public meeting in Newcastle to honor Garibaldi as the "glorious defender of the Roman Republic." At the ceremony, Garibaldi was presented with a sword of honor, a telescope, and a declaration of welcome. Funds for the gifts and travel expenses had been provided by the contributions of more than a thousand working men, none of whom contributed more than a penny.[6]

On April 12, Garibaldi sailed from England for Genoa, arriving on May 7 to a warm welcome from the townspeople. He proceeded on to Nice, where he saw his family after an absence of almost five years. His mother Rosa Garibaldi had died during his absence, and her nephew, Angelo Gustavini, had taken over the old family home on Quai Lunel. Garibaldi and his seven-year-old son, Ricciotti, moved into a small house close by. His older son, Menotti, was attending a boarding school in Genoa, while his daughter, Teresita, continued to live with the Deideri family in Nice.

Garibaldi had intended to pass a pleasant summer with old friends in Nice, but recurring insurrections by Mazzini's followers caused him to condemn the poorly planned uprisings. He described them as "premature insurrections" incited by "cheats and swindlers" who would discredit the cause of Italian freedom.[7] He believed that these ill-conceived uprising had resulted in the unnecessary death of many Italian patriots. For his part, Mazzini, a Republican, was critical of Garibaldi's favoring Italian unity under a powerful monarch—King Victor Emmanuel II of Sardinia. In consequence, Mazzini and Garibaldi drifted apart and were no longer considered friends. Another disagreement between the two revolutionaries arose over Sardinia's participation in the Crimean War on the side of the Allies. Mazzini disapproved of Sardinia entering the war; Garibaldi supported the move, because he believed that the Sardinian army would gain valuable military experience for a future war with Austria.

In the summer of 1854, Garibaldi obtained his master's certificate from the Sardinian naval authorities and took command of a steamship named the *Salvatore*. He engaged in a coastal trade, sailing between Genoa, Nice, and Marseilles, earning some much-needed money. Soon, he was entertaining the idea of settling down on the little island of Caprera (which still belonged to the Englishman named Collins who had earlier served under Admiral Nelson during the Napoleonic wars) and becoming a farmer.

When Garibaldi's brother, Felice, died in November 1855, he left Garibaldi an inheritance of 35,000 lire (£1,400). With this money, Garibaldi purchased half of Caprera for £360.[8] The following year, he began building a house on the island with the help of several friends and his older son, using materials brought over from Genoa. They camped in a tent until they finished building the house, a four-room stone bungalow in the South American style with white walls and green doors, high ceilings, and a flat roof.

Over the front door, they put a metal grill with the date 1856. They also built a windmill, a small observatory, and several outhouses.[9] Flower gardens and vegetable patches were planned for later. Garibaldi finally had his dream house.

35

Private Love Affairs

Writers have portrayed Garibaldi as a romantic figure with an emotional appeal that transcended national boundaries. Men idolized him, and women loved him with a passion bordering on cult worship. To them, he was the epitome of the swashbuckling hero—only he was real! A legend in his time, Garibaldi was the embodiment of the disinterested hero. His handsome bearing and personal charm seemed to captivate those in his presence. Understandably, women flocked to his banner, passionately pledging their loyalty and devotion to him.

Women always played an important role in Garibaldi's life, from his early childhood to his later years. His love for his mother was such that he always kept a picture of her on the wall above his bed. As he grew older, rumors of his love affairs with various women established an image as a womanizer. Accounts of these affairs are included in his own memoirs as well as in the many love letters later found among his personal effects.

From his own account, Garibaldi's first love was Francesca Roux, a girl from his hometown of Nice.[1] At the time, he was a young merchant seaman sailing back and forth across the Mediterranean, and he promised to marry her when he returned from a voyage to Turkey. However, he became ill during the voyage and was stranded in Istanbul. Upon his return four years later, he found that Francesca had married someone else and just given birth to a baby. Although the initial shock was unsettling, Garibaldi was now able to return to his other love—the sea.

During his exile in South America, he met the "woman of his heart," Anna Maria de Jesus Ribeiro da Silva, or "Anita," the dark-haired beauty he first saw walking on the beach in Laguna, Brazil. The events of their first meeting remain somewhat obscure, but their love affair has been romanticized in story books and paint-ings. Despite rumors that Anita was already married to another, the two eloped and were eventually married in Montevideo, Uruguay on March 26, 1842. Garibaldi's first meeting with Anita and their subsequent elopement are described earlier in this work.

Garibaldi appears to have been faithful to Anita, though he was known to make her jealous by flirting with other women. There is no indication of him having extramarital affairs—except for the story of Lucia Esteche, in Corrientes Province in Argentina.[2] Although that story is based mainly on local tradition, it is true that Esteche gave birth to a daughter shortly after Garibaldi left Santa Lucia dos Antas in the autumn of 1842. In later years, her daugh-ter, who proudly called herself Margarita Garibaldi, carried on a cordial correspondence with him on Caprera.

After Anita's tragic death in Italy in 1849, Garibaldi appeared to show no interest in women. His interest in women revived after his return from exile in 1854. He was forty-seven years old and about to enter the period of his life when most of his famous love affairs took place. By then, his reputation as a swashbuckling adventurer had made him somewhat of a celebrity; his presence was much requested at social events, and he was often pursued by designing women. This was especially true in England, where on a visit in 1854 he met and fell in love with a London socialite named Emma Roberts.[3] The two began a relationship that had all London buzzing with excitement—the wealthy socialite and the swash-buckling pirate.

After announcing their engagement, she joined Garibaldi for a visit to Sardinia. There, they enjoyed a delightful stay at the estate of a wealthy landowner who was a friend of Garibaldi. Emma and Garibaldi seemed very much in love. They went horseback riding in the wilds and even participated in boar hunts. The affair seemed like a prelude to a happy marriage—but it was not to be.

Shortly after she returned to England, it was announced that the wedding was being indefinitely postponed because of her son's opposition to the marriage—a lot of money and property was involved. Evidently, she was too rich and too sophisticated for Garibaldi, who found it difficult to adjust to high-society life. He himself later commented that a month in Emma Roberts' house would have killed him.[4] Nevertheless, the two were to remain friends, and Mrs. Roberts even offered to take Garibaldi's son, Ricciotti, to England for his schooling. Garibaldi agreed, and young Ricciotti was soon packed off to a boarding school in Liverpool.

Although Emma and Garibaldi carried on an affectionate correspondence for many years, relatively little is known about their love affair. Garibaldi did visit her again in London, but he failed to mention her in his memoirs. For her part, she remained very discreet about him. The fact that they both kept the matter private suggests that she meant a lot more to him than did the other women with whom he established friendships.

Another woman with designs on Garibaldi was the Italian Countess Maria Martini della Torre. Somewhat of an eccentric, she had also met Garibaldi at a London society party. She fell madly in love with him, but since she was already married nothing came of the affair. Some years later in Italy, however, she donned a red shirt and joined Garibaldi during the campaign of The Thousand to liberate Sicily. She followed him into battle only to collapse from exhaustion, and later be committed to an insane asylum.[5]

Cupid struck again in October 1857, when the regal-looking Baroness Marie Esperanza von Schwartz came to the island of La Maddalena, seeking an interview with Garibaldi on nearby Caprera. She was a wealthy divorcée who traveled around Europe in search of love and adventure, and wrote about her travels in a series of entertaining books published under the pen name Elpis Melena. She had come to Caprera in search of another adventure story. She would get everything that she asked for—and then some!

Her first meeting with Garibaldi was electric: It was love at first sight. She and Garibaldi spent the following two days sightseeing and enjoying each other's company. They saw La Maddalena as well as nearby Caprera. By the time the baroness left to return home, Garibaldi had not only given her permission to translate his memoirs into German and publish them, but had also promised to take her on a trip to Sardinia at some future date.[6]

The baroness returned ten months later, and this time, she and Garibaldi were together on Caprera for nearly a week. One day when they were walking along a footpath, he proposed marriage. Taken somewhat by surprise, she asked for time to consider the proposal, but she never gave him an answer. Somewhat miffed, Garibaldi didn't ask again. Their love affair degenerated into a love–hate relationship that droned on for several years.*

In the end, nothing came of the relationship, but the baroness did publish his memoirs in 1861 under the title *Garibaldi's Denkwürdigkeiten.*

Garibaldi also had an affair with a young peasant woman named Battistina Ravello, who had come from Nice to work for him as a cook and housekeeper. Visitors who came to Caprera surmised that she was Garibaldi's mistress because of her tantrums whenever he showed another woman any special attention. Rumors of the affair turned out to be true when, in May 1859, she gave birth to their love child, a girl they named Anita. But Garibaldi was not in love with her, and he didn't marry her. However, he did sign a document acknowledging the baby Anita as his legitimate child. Under Italian law, this had the effect of legitimizing the child and of making him her legal guardian. Later that year, while on a campaign in northern Italy, Garibaldi learned that Battistina was having an affair with a young man on La Maddalena. His anger over the affair caused her to leave Caprera with the infant Anita and return to her hometown of Nice, where she and the child lived on an allowance he provided.[7]

At the end of the war with Austria in October 1859, Garibaldi

---

*The love affair between the Baroness von Schwartz and Garibaldi is elaborated on in later chapters.

met and fell in love with the Marchesa Paulina Zucchini—a beautiful young widow and the granddaughter of the former king of Naples, Joachim Murat. They met at a social gathering at the Villa Letezia in Bologna, and fell in love, and while walking with the marchesa in the garden, he asked her to marry him. She politely refused, but she did pledge her undying devotion to his cause.[8] Once again, he had established a lasting friendship but failed to find a wife.

Later the same year, he became infatuated with a beautiful girl he had met the previous summer, during the war against Austria. She had been given the dangerous task of carrying messages through enemy lines, an assignment she handled very well. Giuseppina Raimondi was the daughter of the Marquis Raimondi of Fino on Lake Como. Garibaldi was so impressed by her courage and expertise that he fell madly in love with her. He wrote her passionate love letters until she consented to marry him, though she was actually in love with one of his young army officers. She admired Garibaldi as a national hero, however, and felt that it was her duty to marry him. Her father strongly approved of the marriage.[9]

After a formal announcement, Garibaldi and Giuseppina were married in a Catholic church on the shores of Lake Como. The whole event seemed like a fairytale—the beautiful spy and the invincible hero! A bizarre turn of events followed, straight out of an Alfred Hitchcock thriller; as the newly married couple stepped outside the church, a mysterious note was thrust into Garibaldi's hand. It read that Giuseppina had had sex with another solider the previous night. Stunned, he turned to his bride and asked her if this was true. When she nodded that it was, he flew into a rage, raising his hand as if to strike her—but didn't. Instead, he handed her back to her father, telling him that she was not his wife! He never spoke to Giuseppina again.[10] *

Though he was deeply hurt, Garibaldi did not brood for too long. In May 1860, he led an expedition which invaded Sicily and soon liberated almost all of southern Italy. He briefly ruled as dictator over his conquered territories and returned to Caprera after relinquishing power to King Victor Emmanuel II. By then, Garibaldi was a national hero and, as such, was visited by a steady stream of dignitaries, journalists, and well-wishers. He also received an enormous amount of correspondence, the volume so great that he had to employ three personal secretaries. A major portion of the correspondence was fan mail from women of every age and status, most of whom expressed their support for his cause. There were also letters of admiration and passion. Among these latter were the correspondances of Mrs. Charles Seely, the Duchess of Sutherland, Florence Nightingale, and his former fiancée, Emma Roberts. Evidently, distance made Garibaldi seem more enchanting to these women. This infatuation with Garibaldi by wealthy high-born women seems to have been an important feature of his private life.

Garibaldi finally married again on January 26, 1880. His marriage to Giuseppina Raimondi had officially been dissolved on the grounds of non-consummation, and he wed his housekeeper, Francesca Armosino. She had been his mistress for many years and had borne him three children, one of whom had died during infancy. It was Garibaldi's third and last marriage.

---

* Garibaldi's marriage to the Marchesina Giuseppina Raimondi is elaborated on in a later chapter.

It should be mentioned that, in later years, many young men and women wrote to Garibaldi, claiming that he was their father. Because of the volume of letters from these real or pretended love children, Garibaldi asked an old friend, Luigi Coltelletti, to handle it. The Coltelletti family continued to handle this correspondence for fifty years, but after World War I, Coltelletti's son, Giuseppe Garibaldi Coltelletti, burned all the letters, thus ending this rather amusing correspondence.[11]

36

Baroness Marie Esperance
von Schwartz

GARIBALDI WENT TO ENGLAND AGAIN in March 1856 to visit
Emma Roberts and his son, Ricciotti, who was in boarding school.
During this visit, he and Mrs. Roberts officially broke off their
engagement. They nevertheless remained friends, and as a parting
gift, she gave him a forty-two-ton yacht, which he reluctantly
accepted. He named her *Emma* and used the boat to travel back and
forth from Caprera to the mainland.

On his way back from England, he stopped at Nice to attend to
personal matters—signing his cottage over to his cousin, Angelo
Gustavini, and taking his children, Menotti and Teresita, to live
with him at his newly completed house on Caprera. His other son,

Ricciotti, had remained in boarding school in England. Garibaldi also hired a young woman named Battistina Ravello as cook and housekeeper for him on Caprera. She was later to become his mistress and bear him a daughter, whom they named Anita. But the two quarreled, and Battistina was dismissed by Garibaldi. Little Anita was sent off to an exclusive girls boarding school in Winterthur, Switzerland, and the Baroness Marie Esperance von Schwartz was appointed as her guardian.

The baroness had first come to visit Garibaldi on Caprera in the autumn of 1857. A tall, beautiful blonde, she was the daughter of a German banker but claimed to be English because she had been born in England. She had been married twice. Her first husband had committed suicide; her second, Baron von Schwartz, had divorced her. As a woman of leisure, she traveled widely and wrote about her escapades in a series of travel books published under the *nom de plume* Elpis Melena, a literal translation in Greek of her real name. She had come to Caprera to obtain Garibaldi's permission to translate his memoirs into German and arrange for their publication in Hamburg.

After arriving by steamer on La Maddalena, she arranged for an interview with Garibaldi through a Captain Dodero. Garibaldi, eager to meet this woman author, came over from Caprera in his dingy. Dodero literally played Cupid when he introduced the two. The adventure-seeker had finally met her swashbuckling hero—and on a lonely isle! The starstruck lovebirds spent two days together, sightseeing on Caprera and La Maddalena. By the time she left, Garibaldi had given her permission to translate and publish the memoirs, and had invited her to visit him again on Caprera.[1] What had transpired between the two can best be surmised from the contents of his first letter to her:

My Speranza,

How can I possibly convey to you all the gratitude and affection you deserve? If ever I have wanted to lay all that I am and have at the foot of a woman, it is certainly now. It was only natural that I should love you before ever I knew you. You were already interested in me, and in my imagination, I cherished a precious vision of you. But the reality has transported me with delight and I am really happy and proud for one moment to occupy the thoughts of so dear, so tender, so noble a woman.

The promise I made you in front of your landlady's door was rash. I can't say more in a letter but, as soon as I have the joy of seeing you again, I will tell you what holds me back. In any event, when you want to start your journey, write to me. I shall be heartbroken if I can't come with you. In future, I am proud to be yours, completely and utterly, therefore, the more use you make of me, the happier I shall be.

Teresa is delighted with the beautiful clothes. All you sent were most gratefully received and our only regret is that we could not give you the welcome here that you deserve. Accept the thanks and love of all of us. Au revoir!

I kiss your hand and am always,

Your,

G. Garibaldi[2]

He wrote the baroness fourteen more love letters during this period, all of which she later published in her book *Garibaldi: Recollections of his Public and Private Life.*

In August 1858, "Speranza," as Garibaldi called her, visited Caprera again; this time she stayed with him for nearly a week, near the end of which Garibaldi asked her to marry him. For whatever reason, she stalled for time and never gave him a final answer. Hurt by her indecision, he did not propose to her again.[3] Their love affair, which had started out so promising, now drifted into limbo. So although he was surrounded by adoring women, Garibaldi could not find one to his liking, that was willing to marry him!

Even so, he and Esperanza continued to have strong feelings for each other. This became evident when she journeyed to Torino in April 1859 to visit him just before the beginning of hostilities with Austria. She knew that he had been appointed a general in the Sardinian army and would soon be leaving for the battlefront. After much difficulty, she managed to get to see him. Their reunion was a passionate one—the beautiful baroness and the handsome officer in his gold-braided uniform. Garibaldi expressed his love for her, and she for him, but it was the last day before his departure for the front. In her *Recollections*, she describes that final night with Garibaldi and how she was "so kind" to him. The next morning, she accompanied him to the train station and saw him off to war.[4]

Although Garibaldi had not renewed his proposal of marriage, Esperanza believed that he still wished to marry her. After all, she had neither accepted nor rejected his original proposal of marriage on Caprera! She failed to realize that she had missed her chance. Garibaldi soon found himself entangled with two other women— Battistina Ravello, with whom he had a child; and Giuseppina Raimondi, whom he suddenly married in January 1860. Each of these relationships would have tragic endings.

Through all of them, Esperanza and Garibaldi still remained friends, though their relationship was severely strained. She was deeply disappointed over Garibaldi's affair with Battistina and his marriage to Giuseppina. She subsequently vilified both of these women in her *Recollections*.

However, as time passed and the scandal gossip subsided, the relationship between Esperanza and Garibaldi began to warm up again. During 1863, their correspondence became more affectionate, and Garibaldi began his letters with *Speranza carissima* (Dearest Speranza).[5] In 1864, she visited him on Caprera with the express purpose of providing for the welfare of his young daughter Anita, his love child by Battistina Ravello. She urged him to entrust the five-year-old to her care, so that Anita could be reared as "an educated lady of quality." After much hesitation, Garibaldi agreed, using his parental authority to appoint Esperanza as Anita's legal guardian.[6]

In 1875, Anita, then sixteen, returned to Caprera to live with her father. She had faced problems of adjustment at her girls' boarding school at Winterthur, as a result of which Esperanza had brought her to live at her house in Crete. There, the girl was to work as an unpaid servant for the baroness—a demeaning experience for the youngster who longed to be with her father. Anita secretly wrote to him lamenting how unhappy she was living with Esperanza. She simply addressed the envelope to "General Garibaldi" and threw it out the window of her room. Somehow, it was picked up in the street and then delivered to Garibaldi on Caprera!

Upon reading it, Garibaldi immediately dispatched his son, Menotti, to Crete with strict orders to bring the girl back to Caprera. When Menotti reached the island, he discovered the cruel truth: The baroness indeed *had* Anita working as her servant. He also found that the girl's hair was crawling with lice. When he and Anita returned to Caprera and reported what had happened, Garibaldi was greatly disturbed by the callous manner in which the baroness had treated his daughter.[7] He wrote her several more letters concerning his daughter Anita's condition, but the letters went unanswered.

Anita spent six happy weeks with Garibaldi and his family, and then tragedy struck—one day while she was playing by the seashore, she contracted a malarial fever and died. It was a double tragedy for Garibaldi. Not only had he lost his daughter, Anita; he had also lost faith in Esperanza von Schwartz, on whom he had depended for a lasting friendship.

Despite her strained relations with Garibaldi, the baroness wrote another book, entitled *Garibaldi: Recollections of his Public and Private Life*, in which she published some of his love letters and in which extended praise of Garibaldi is interspersed with demeaning revelations about his private life—as though the baroness intended to tarnish the image of the man who had not repeated his proposal of marriage. She ended the volume with this comment:

> *In accordance with her father's wish, Anita left Crete. I prefer to throw a veil over the treatment with which father and daughter requited me for all I had done for them, as well as over Anita's mysterious death. I owe it to the memory of the dead . . . In history, Garibaldi will always shine resplendent as the sun; but even the sun has its spots.*[8]

There was no further correspondence between the two. The baroness continued her travels, living comfortably off her book royalties. While vacationing in Switzerland in August 1899, she died in a room of the Adler Hotel at Ermatingen. She remains one of the most enterprising of Garibaldi's many mistresses.

37

War With Austria: 1859

IN AUGUST 1856, Garibaldi traveled to Torino for a meeting with Camillo Benso di Cavour, the Prime Minister of the Kingdom of Sardinia. The meeting was arranged by the National Society, an organization pledged to bringing about the unification of Italy. Garibaldi was a member, and Cavour had close ties with it.

At that time, the Kingdom of Sardinia ruled over five states in Italy—Piedmont, Savoy, Nice, Liguria, and island of Sardinia, whence it got its name. Sometimes, however, the name "Piedmont-Sardinia" is used to denote what officially was called the Kingdom of Sardinia. In an attempt to acquire new territories, the Kingdom had fought in the Crimean War (1855) against Czarist Russia. Sardinian troops fought with valor and won the admiration of the major powers. The Kingdom of Sardinia had also gained a seat at the peace conference held in Paris—and nothing more. Sardinian ambitions for gaining overseas territories were brushed aside.

Cavour then focused his attention on extending Sardinian control across northern Italy. However, there was one major obstacle—Austria. The Austrian Empire ruled over most of northern Italy, either directly or indirectly through puppet rulers. Cavour knew that Sardinia was not strong enough to defeat so great a power; it would need the help of a strong neighbor. He also recognized the necessity for arousing public sentiment at home for any future conflict with Austria. In order to achieve this, Cavour decided to enlist the support of that radical revolutionary, most wanted criminal, and fugitive from justice—Giuseppe Garibaldi! Who could better arouse nationalistic fervor than he? Garibaldi was, consequently, to meet Cavour for the first time.

Count Cavour was a Piedmontese diplomat whom many consider to be the architect of Italian unification. In actuality, he was a skeptic who hadn't converted to the nationalist cause until the eleventh hour.[1] Scion of an aristocratic family, he had a natural distrust for radical movements and was determined to foil any radical attempt to do away with the power of the king or the pope. However, he was also a shrewd diplomat who had come to realize that nationalism made for practical politics. It was only a matter of creating the right situation in which to *use* Garibaldi's services.

The "Piedmontese Machiavelli" was now to come face to face with the world renowned revolutionary. Recall that, in 1849, after the Battle of Rome, Cavour had been one of the members of the Sardinian parliament who called for the arrest and imprisonment of Garibaldi as a wanted criminal.[2] Now, he treated Garibaldi with courtesy and familiarity. In the discussion that followed, Cavour led Garibaldi to understand that plans were underway for the reconstruction of Italy. He didn't reveal any details, but he did urge Garibaldi not to participate in any premature Mazzinian revolt.

Actually, Cavour's grand design called for a war against Austria, in which the Kingdom of Sardinia would liberate the Austrian-held provinces of Lombardy and Venetia, and thus unite northern Italy into a strong kingdom. But in order to achieve this, the small Kingdom would need the help of a major power—France.

Cavour's immediate objective was to persuade French Emperor Louis Bonaparte (Napoleon III) to wage war on Austria. This would be a difficult task because France had nothing to gain from such a conflict. Cavour, however, was to play on the Bonaparte family's pro-Italian sympathies. After all, hadn't his uncle, Napoleon Bonaparte, liberated Italy from foreign domination some fifty years earlier? And hadn't Louis Bonaparte himself, as a young man, joined the Carbonari Society and taken part in an Italian uprising back in 1830? Yes, Louis Bonaparte might just be persuaded to go along with Cavour's plan—if France stood to gain some valuable territory.

In July 1858, Cavour, brandishing a false passport in the name of Giuseppe Benso, crossed the border into France,[3] to meet secretly with Louis Bonaparte at Plombieres; the two were to discuss a plan for France to engage in war against Austria on the side of the Kingdom of Sardinia. According to the plan, Sardinia would provoke Austria by invading the Duchy of Modena, an Austrian puppet state. Austria would come to the support of the duke, and then France would enter the fray on the side of Sardinia. Following Austria's defeat, the provinces of Lombardy and Venetia were to be ceded to the Kingdom of Sardinia. In return, Sardinia was to cede the provinces of Nice and Savoy to France. The plan seemed plausible, but there was one major stumbling block—Nice was the birthplace of Garibaldi.

It was also agreed that the Italian peninsula should be divided into four states—the Kingdom of Sardinia, the Grand Duchy of Tuscany, the Papal States, and the Kingdom of the Two Sicilies. The Duchies of Parma and Modena would be taken over by Sardinia at a later time, along with Romagna, the northernmost part of the Papal States. The remainder of the Papal States and Tuscany were to remain separate political entities—although Grand Duke Leopold of Tuscany was to be turned out because of his close ties with Austria.

Napoleon III of France

Even if there were no immediate plans for the Kingdom of the Two Sicilies, Napoleon III hoped eventually to overthrow King Ferdinand of Naples and replace him with his cousin, Prince Lucien Murat. Napoleon also expected Lucien to marry Princess Clotilde, the daughter of Victor Emmanuel II. The proposed marriage would link the Bonaparte family to the Royal House of Savoy.[4]

The Plombieres Agreement was kept secret for several months, but in December 1858, Cavour informed Garibaldi that a war of national liberation would soon be waged against Austria, and that he should hold himself in readiness. He made no mention of his agreement to cede Nice and Savoy to France. (Later, this would cause much animosity between the two men.)

Two months later, in February 1859, Garibaldi was again summoned to Torino by Cavour and, this time, introduced to King Victor Emmanuel II. Through the House of Savoy, one of the oldest in western Europe, the royal family traced its origins back to the 11th century and Count Humbert I of Savoy, also known as "Humbert of the White Hands." Over the centuries, Savoy gradually extended its power into Italy and France. It evolved into a duchy, and eventually into a kingdom. In the early 18th century, it became known as the Kingdom of Sardinia after it acquired the large island of the same name.

Victor Emmanuel was a dashing young monarch known to his people as *Re Galantuomo*, or the "Gentleman King."[5] He enjoyed hunting and partaking in sporting events. He also loved to eat wholesome peasant food and was attracted to beautiful women. When he visited England, he charmed Queen Victoria and the royal court by his gentlemanly behavior. In Paris, he delighted the emperor's courtiers with his down-to-earth manner and great sense of humor. Victor Emmanuel was a master at the art of handling people, and now he sought to win Garibaldi's loyalty.

At their first meeting, Victor Emmanuel convinced Garibaldi that he (the King) was a true patriot who intended to lead the struggle for Italian national unity. Garibaldi was much impressed. The two seemed to have a great deal in common, and Garibaldi was now prepared to give the king his allegiance. This would prove very important in the formation of a united Italy, for after this moment Garibaldi adhered to the idea of unification under a powerful monarch. He believed that such an outcome would put an end to the seemingly endless squabbles of the politicians and parliament. "The national will had already chosen the King as our supreme duce,"[6] he later said. Naturally, the politicians, including Cavour, were opposed to this extension of royal power, because it would diminish the parliamentary role.

In spite of his misgivings about nationalism and republicanism, Cavour became a participant in the movement for national unity, fearing that Mazzini and the radicals might otherwise monopolize it and use it for political advantage. Cavour also realized that the Kingdom of Sardinia was not strong enough to free northern Italy from Austrian domination, and that a volunteer army would be needed to help achieve that goal. It was his belief that a popular hero like Garibaldi could create the momentum for such an army by rallying people to the Sardinian cause. In March 1858, Garibaldi was therefore appointed a major general in the Royal Sardinian Army and given command of a volunteer brigade called *Cacciatore delle Alpi*. Because Sardinian military regulations banned the wearing of the red shirt, the volunteers were issued the bright blue and gray uniforms of the royal army.[7] Garibaldi himself had to trim his beard and wear a gold-braided general's uniform. He was permitted, however, to wear his off-white poncho and red neckerchief.

As preparations for war got underway, it became apparent, however, that Garibaldi was not running the show; Cavour was. According to Cavour's design, the volunteer brigade was to consist of not more than 3,000 men, nor was it to include cavalry, artillery, or service troops. Furthermore, Garibaldi was assigned to a training base some forty miles outside Torino, so as not to embarrass the Sardinian government in its dealings with Napoleon III. Garibaldi realized that Cavour was exploiting him mainly for the purpose of attracting volunteers to the cause. As it turned out, many volunteers who had joined the army in order to serve under Garibaldi were actually being sent to serve under other commanders.[8] And of those assigned to Garibaldi's own brigade, many had been rejected for duty in the regular Sardinian army.

Despite all this, Garibaldi did gain the services of some experienced officers, among them being Medici, Sacchi, Bixio, and Dr. Bertani—all veterans of the Battle of Rome in 1849.

One of the more promising new recruits was Enrico Cosenz, a young officer who had previously served in the Neapolitan army and then, in 1848, gone over to join Daniele Manin in the defense of the Venetian republic. Among the other volunteers who stood out were the five Cairoli brothers—Benedetto, Ernesto, Enrico, Giovanni, and Luigi. Their mother had instilled in them a deep love of their country and encouraged them to join in the struggle for national unity. Four were later killed in battle. Only Benedetto was to survive the wars and go on to become prime minister of Italy in 1880. Other volunteers who gained subsequent fame included Francesco Simonetta, Giuseppe Missori, Antonio Mosto, and Stefan Türr, the last a Hungarian who had deserted from the Austrian army. Volunteers continued to pour in, eventually swelling Garibaldi's forces to more than 11,000 men.

Because of the urgency of the situation, only a few days had been allowed for training the volunteers. Nevertheless, Garibaldi was able to create a good esprit de corps and prepare his men for a guerrilla war. The troops were trained to travel light and live off the land. Garibaldi would have the opportunity to make use of tactics he had learned in the brutal school of South American war.

In the meantime, the British government, trying to maintain the peace, persuaded Napoleon III to submit the Italian question to an international conference. An important element of the British plan was that Sardinia should agree to disarm. Cavour was concerned that the plan to provoke Austria into war would fail to materialize. But the Austrian government, intending to take advantage of France's hesitation, instead presented Sardinia with an ultimatum, threatening war unless Sardinia agreed within three days to disarm.

Cavour, of course, rejected the ultimatum, causing Austria to declare war on Sardinia. France kept its agreement and entered the war on the Sardinian side. The Austrian army, under Marshal Gylai, quickly advanced toward Torino, but the capital was saved by the arrival of 100,000 French troops. As French and Sardinian troops advanced to meet the enemy, Garibaldi was ordered to attack the Austrian right flank in the Lake District near the Alps. His brigade was to create a diversion while the main force of 60,000 Sardinian and 120,000 French troops faced the main Austrian army.

He moved out quickly with 3,600 men, soon leaving his own lines of communications far behind. Marching by night, he crossed the Sesia River after preventing an Austrian raiding party from seizing the ferry. He advanced toward Lake Maggiore, sending out

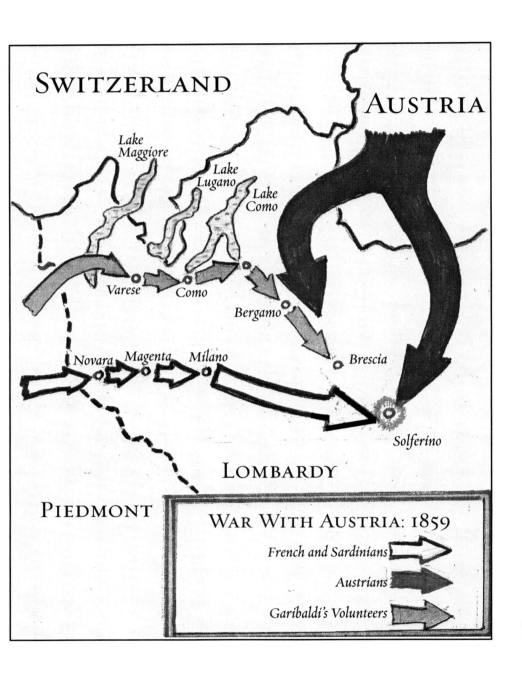

SWITZERLAND

AUSTRIA

Lake
Maggiore

Lake
Lugano

Lake
Como

Varese   Como

Bergamo

Brescia

Novara   Magenta   Milano

Solferino

LOMBARDY

PIEDMONT

WAR WITH AUSTRIA: 1859

French and Sardinians

Austrians

Garibaldi's Volunteers

volunteers in civilian clothes to spy out the land ahead of him. On May 24, Garibaldi, with no cavalry or artillery support, defeated an Austrian force at Varese and so opened the way to Lake Como. He went on to defeat the Austrians at San Fermo, Laveno, Lecco, and Bergamo, thus liberating the lake region of northern Italy from Austrian control.[9] It was precisely where he had encountered so much local apathy and hostility during the campaign of 1849. Now, he was received in the same places with great enthusiasm.

During this campaign, Garibaldi met a beautiful young girl who brought him a message from Como telling him that he should advance at once on the town to prevent it from falling into Austrian hands. The girl was Giuseppina Raimondi, the seventeen-year-old daughter of the Marquis Raimondi, who lived at the town of Fino near Como. She was an ardent patriot who secretly served as a messenger for the local Italian revolutionaries. Apparently her status enabled her to get through the Austrian checkpoints without being stopped. Impressed by her courage and beauty, he fell in love with her.

He *did* march on Como and secured the town from the Austrians. The inhabitants came out to cheer him, and the beautiful Giuseppina even visited him at his headquarters at the Albergo del Angelo. He expressed his love for her, but she remained cool and noncommittal. Feeling dejected, Garibaldi tried to dismiss her from his thoughts and resolved "to forget the beautiful daughter of the Lake."[10]

Meanwhile, having been cut off from news and supplies, he knew nothing of the movements of the Sardinian and the French armies. He read in the newspapers that the Austrians had been defeated at Palestro on May 31 and at Magenta on June 4. The stage was now set for the decisive battle of the war. Emperor Franz

Josef of Austria had reached Italy to take personal command of his forces. On June 24, a gigantic battle took place at the village of Solferino, to the south of Lake Garda. The French and Sardinians were victorious, but the losses were heavy, with the French losing nearly 12,000 men, the Sardinians 5,500, and the Austrians 22,000.* The wounded suffered greatly because of the inadequacy of medical supplies and the ambulance service. Many lay on the battlefield for three days before being taken to a hospital. The awful carnage caused a young Swiss stretcher-bearer named Henri Dunant to start a campaign to establish the International Red Cross. That organization was founded in Geneva, Switzerland five years later.

---

*These casualty figures appear in Jasper Ridley's *Garibaldi*, p. 413.

38

The Armistice of Villafranca

Emperor Napoleon III was so appalled by the carnage and suffering at the Battle of Solferino that he decided the war had gone far enough. He opened secret peace negotiations with Emperor Franz Josef of Austria, thus bringing the war to a premature end. The French were dissatisfied with the Sardinians' contribution to the war effort and distrustful of revolutionaries like Garibaldi. The French emperor had also concluded that it was not in the best interests of France to create a strong kingdom on her southern border.

On July 11, 1859, Napoleon III and Franz Josef met secretly near the small town of Villafranca and agreed on armistice terms. Under their agreement, Austria would cede Lombardy to France, which, in turn, would give it to the Kingdom of Sardinia as a gift. This was done in order to save "Austrian face." However, Austria was to retain Venetia, even though Napoleon III had promised it

to Sardinia in the secret agreement reached at Plombieres the previous year. In addition, the Hapsburg rulers who had fled to
Austria during the hostilities were to be restored to power in
Modena, Parma, and Tuscany. The Kingdom of Sardinia was to
cede Nice and Savoy to France. This last clause would cause the
most controversy.

The Armistice of Villafranca was forced on an unwilling
Cavour several weeks later. He had not been consulted or, for that
matter, even warned of the settlement. He protested vigorously to
King Victor Emmanuel, who, unlike himself, had been informed of
the negotiations. The king calmly smoked a cigar as his prime minister insisted that he renounce the agreement and continue the
fight against Austria. Cavour even went so far as to call the king a
traitor. The king ordered him out of the room for his abusiveness,
commenting that "vanity and pride" had turned Cavour's head.[1]
His resignation was gladly accepted by the king, who by then envisioned himself playing a more dominant role in the government;
until that point, he could not truly boast that he was a king who
governed "in fact as well as in name."[2]

Knowing that it would be folly to continue the war against
Austria alone, Victor Emmanuel signed the treaty as the price of
peace. However, he let it be known that, while he consented to the
first clause (the gaining of Lombardy), he would not guarantee
Sardinian adherence to the other clauses of the treaty.[3]

When news of the armistice spread, the people of Italy felt that
they had been betrayed by the French and, to a lesser degree, by
Cavour. Anti-French fervor swept through the country.

Garibaldi did not share the general outrage over the armistice.
He instead issued a statement of gratitude to Napoleon III and the
heroic French nation for their part in the war.[4] Apparently, he did

not yet know that Nice was to be ceded to France!

His campaign in the Alps had aroused great interest throughout Italy and the rest of Europe. He had won a string of victories over an Austrian force of 11,000 men and diverted it from joining the main Austrian army in the battles against the French and Sardinians. Cavour's plan to keep Garibaldi in the background had backfired as well, since the Sardinian press praised his exploits. Garibaldi even received favorable cover in some French newspapers. Popular biographies of him soon appeared in many countries, and Theodore Dwight published Garibaldi's memoirs in New York. All of this served to erase his image as a black-bearded "Calabrian brigand" and helped establish his reputation as a "responsible" military commander.[5]

For his victories during the Alpine campaign, Garibaldi was awarded the Gold Medal for Valor by King Victor Emmanuel II. He was also made a Grand Officer of the Military Order of Savoy. The king decorated the officers and men who served under Garibaldi during the campaign as well. Although Garibaldi's relations with the king were excellent, Cavour and his friends were hostile to Garibaldi and jealous of his success. For his part, the latter was also growing increasingly distrustful of Cavour.

39

Command of Intrigue

DURING THE MONTHS following the Armistice of Villafranca, the question of Italian unity was mired in international diplomacy. In the territories of Parma, Modena, Romagna, and Tuscany, popular revolutionary movements demanded union with Sardinia. Although the Sardinian government wished to annex them, it feared that France would oppose the move because of the Villafranca commitment to restore their former Hapsburg rulers to power in each of these states. In addition, the pope was refusing to cede Romagna, which was part of the Papal States, to Sardinia.

Sardinian troops had occupied these states during the war with Austria, but they had withdrawn after the Armistice of Villafranca, handing over power to provisional revolutionary governments. The new leaders were prepared to work closely with the Sardinian government in Torino, because they opposed the return of the former Austrian-backed rulers—a political arrangement that would enable the Kingdom of Sardinia to control these states indirectly. In Modena, the new leaders stated that, if Duke Francis tried to return, he would be treated as a "public enemy." He had fled from the city, but not before emptying the public treasury.[1] Meanwhile, in neighboring Romagna, the Bolognese were prepared to resist any attempt to reestablish papal control over their state. Tuscany, after deposing the grand duke, adopted the same policy as Romagna and Modena. The tide of Italian nationalism was beginning to sweep southward.

In order to strengthen Sardinian military control over these disputed states, the new leaders proposed that Garibaldi be appointed commander-in-chief of the forces of the provisional governments of Parma, Modena, Romagna, and Tuscany, with the task of organizing an army there. They intended to use his fame and prestige to bolster popular support for their provisional governments. Garibaldi gladly accepted the assignment but, upon arriving in Florence, discovered that he had been passed over for the position. The leaders of the newly formed Central League had chosen General Manfredo Fanti to lead their joint armies, relegating Garibaldi to the position of deputy commander-in-chief under him. The politicians had finessed Garibaldi out of the top command because they feared that he might use the superior position to order an attack on the Papal States. Fanti, on the other hand, was an instrument of the Sardinian government who would make no move without a nod from Victor Emmanuel. The question became whether the chief purpose of the Army of the Central League was to guard the frontiers or invade the Papal States. As for the pope, he had no intention of relinquishing control of any of the territories of the Holy See.

General Garibaldi, from a portrait by Orsini

Meanwhile, Garibaldi made no secret of his intention to liber-ate the Papal States. He was confident that he could defeat the Pope's Swiss troops and capture Rome. However, any such plan of invasion was summarily rejected by General Fanti. Garibaldi began to suspect that the military and political leaders in the Central States were secretly plotting against him. He had been infuriated when they appointed Fanti over him at the last minute. Then he discovered that some of his own subordinates had received secret instructions to disobey his orders.[2] He also noticed that other orders were being inexplicably countermanded. His command appeared to have been caught up in a web of secret intrigues, with outside forces undermining his authority. Several face-to-face meetings with General Fanti and other leaders seemed to achieve no change in these conditions.

Though irritated by the machinations engulfing him, Garibaldi was greatly encouraged by the devotion of the local people. He was cheered by the populace wherever he went in the Central States: in Florence, in Ravenna, in Rimini, and in Modena and Cremona. In each town he gave a speech from the balcony of the town hall, and in each, large crowds responded to his patriotic appeal with thun-derous applause. He tried to devise a plan for the liberation of Marche and Umbria from papal control, but each time his efforts were thwarted by General Fanti and the Sardinian government.

In September 1859, Garibaldi visited the places in Romagna where he had been with Anita before her tragic death ten years ear-lier. He met Zani, the guide who had led him and his men out of San Marino. He visited the house where he had stayed in Saint Alberto on the night of Anita's death. He saw Bonnet and some of the others who had helped him elude the Austrians. Finally, he attended a banquet at the Guiccioli farm in Mandriole where Anita had died. When an old man spoke of the great loss of Anita, Garibaldi broke down and cried. Afterwards he visited Anita's grave, where a small chapel had been erected, accompanied by his son Menotti, his daughter Teresita, and Baroness Speranza von Schwartz, whom he had invited to come.[3]

He made arrangements to move Anita's body to Nice,* for he still had no knowledge of the secret agreement that had ceded Nice to France. Her remains were carried the twenty miles from Mandriole to Ravenna by a total of forty pallbearers, escorted by the village band of Saint Angelo playing the usual funeral march music. During the procession, Garibaldi was met by crowds of people expressing their devotion to him, and displaying shirts, handkerchiefs, and a host of other objects that they claimed he had left behind in 1849.[4] Amazing, the number of collectibles left behind by someone who was known to travel light!

In October 1859, Garibaldi was elected president of the National Society, a rather prestigious organization which was dedicated to the unification of Italy under the Sardinian monarchy. As the Society's spokesman, he gave patriotic speeches denouncing the foreigners, politicians, and priests who were obstructing Italian unity. He declared that, if Italy had a million armed men, it would not need to rely on foreign powers and international diplomacy. It appeared he was trying to raise a private army with the blessing of Victor Emmanuel. The only problem was that he couldn't get the king's permission to advance into the Papal States.

Cavour and his associates were so convinced that Garibaldi *would* march into the Papal States that they pressured the king into

---

* In 1932, Anita's body was again moved, from Nice to Rome, and buried beneath her statue on the Janiculum Hill.

asking Garibaldi to resign his command. On November 14, Victor Emmanuel summoned Garibaldi to Torino and told him that he was asking him to resign his command because of international pressure. The king added that it would be better if the Army of Central Italy were commanded by someone "less frightening" to the foreign powers. He offered to reappoint Garibaldi as a general in the Sardinian army, but Garibaldi declined the offer and resigned the command. As a parting gift, the king offered him his personal hunting gun, which the latter readily accepted. Afterwards, Garibaldi issued a statement praising the king as the "soldier of national independence."[5] He also announced his intention of returning to Caprera. Since he was no longer wearing the king's uniform, he would be free to undertake the greatest enterprise of his life—the liberation of southern Italy.

40

Giuseppina Raimondi

After resigning his command in the army of the Central League in December 1859, Garibaldi did not return to Caprera as everyone had expected. Instead, he went to Lake Como to see Giuseppina Raimondi, daughter of the Marquis Raimondi. After exchanging passionate love letters for several months, Garibaldi's feeling for Giuseppina bordered on utter infatuation. He visited her and her family for two weeks in December and, while there, asked her to marry him.

Giuseppina accepted his proposal, because she felt that it was her patriotic duty to marry a national hero. Her father strongly approved of the marriage. She did not tell her betrothed that she was in love with another man, a young army officer named Luigi Caroli.

On January 6, 1860, the press announced the forthcoming marriage. She was eighteen, Garibaldi fifty-two.

On January 24, the marriage took place in a Catholic ceremony in the Marquis Raimondi's private chapel at Fino, on Lake Como. Teresita Garibaldi was one of the bridesmaids, and Garibaldi's friend Lorenzo Valerio, the newly appointed governor of the Como district, was the *testimone* (best man). Friends and relatives of the bride filled the chapel.

Then occurred a scene the kind of which you would expect to see in a Verdi opera: The bride and groom were leaving the chapel when a young army major named Rovelli stepped out of the crowd and handed Garibaldi a disturbing unsigned note that accused the bride of making love to another man on the eve of the wedding.

Garibaldi turned to Giuseppina and asked her if the accusation was true. She said it was, whereupon Garibaldi, in an outburst of rage, called her a "whore" and raised his hand as if to strike her. She faced him without flinching and said that she thought she had married a hero but now knew he was only a "brutal soldier."

Garibaldi did not strike her but led her to her father. He told the marquis that she was not his wife, and that she must never use his name. Turning back to her, he declared, "I leave you for ever!"[1] It was the last time he ever spoke to her.

Although the events of the wedding were reported in the press, public comment on the tragic breakup was somewhat muted. Most people believed that Giuseppina, not Garibaldi, was to blame. An intriguing question also arose: Garibaldi had never been concerned about past love affairs. His first wife, Anita, had been another man's wife. The Baroness von Schwartz had been twice married when he proposed to her. Even his mistress, Battistina, had had a previous lover before she came to Caprera. It seemed contrary to his nature to be jealous of former lovers.

But illicit sex with a lover on the eve of a marriage to another was a different matter. Garibaldi had been publicly humiliated and deeply hurt. He had been made to look ridiculous—an old man duped by a young flirt! Even the king joined in the chorus of laughter that followed the news of the circus-like wedding.[2]

Neither Garibaldi nor Giuseppina was willing to comment on the affair, and the press shed little light on the contents of the mysterious note. Only Lorenzo Valerio was able to give a precise account of what had actually occurred at the wedding. He identified the author of the note as Major Rovelli and implied that Rovelli himself was the lover mentioned in the note. As it turned out, he was a rejected suitor who hoped to wreck the happiness of Giuseppina's marriage to Garibaldi—apparently "overcome by jealous passion" at the sight of the beautiful Giuseppina being married to an old man."[3]

It subsequently became known that Giuseppina had been the mistress of several men, all with the knowledge of the tolerant Marquis Raimondi. One of the more recent had been Lieutenant Luigi Caroli, who had served under Garibaldi. Caroli regularly came to visit Giuseppina at the Villa Raimondi, and the two would spend the night together in a small room in the villa's tower.[4] Their passion had been in full bloom when Garibaldi first expressed his love for her at the Albergo delAngelo during the campaign against Austria. She was enamored of Caroli and, therefore, inevitably cool and indifferent toward Garibaldi. Nevertheless, she had reluctantly bowed to her father's wishes and agreed to accept Garibaldi's proposal of marriage.

As it turned out, the matter proved unfortunate for all concerned. Giuseppina gave birth to a stillborn infant seven months afterwards; it remains uncertain whether Caroli, Rovelli, or Garibaldi was the father. Caroli—genuinely devoted to his general—had broken off his association with Giuseppina when he heard that she was about to marry Garibaldi. Soon afterwards, he was one of the Garibaldini who volunteered to fight for Polish independence from the Czar of Russia. He was later taken prisoner by the Russians and sent to Siberia, where he died in 1863.

The contemptible Rovelli gained little satisfaction from his interference, though he did succeed in destroying Garibaldi's marriage to Giuseppina. Nineteen years later in 1879, he tried to make amends with Giuseppina by denying that he had written the note to Garibaldi. But he was refused when he pleaded with her to meet with him.[5] It was a rebuttal befitting the jealous scoundrel who nearly ruined the lives of several people.

The Marquis Raimondi, who had hoped to gain prestige as Garibaldi's father-in-law, now found himself an object of public ridicule. Many people thought that he was to blame for the whole fiasco, and that he had been entirely too permissive in Giuseppina's upbringing. He in any case fell out of favor with Garibaldi, who would have nothing more to do with him.

Garibaldi, deeply hurt by her deception and her preference for one of his young officers over himself, considered the whole affair a calculated plot to make a public fool of him. He never forgave her. When she wrote to him after he was wounded at Aspromonte in 1862, he did not reply. On the one occasion that she went to Caprera to visit him, he refused to see her.[6]

Garibaldi was finally granted a divorce from Giuseppina in 1880, allowing him to marry again.

She herself suffered greatly. She lost her position as Garibaldi's wife as well as her lover Caroli. She never made an attempt to tell her side of the story, and she did not contest the divorce proceedings in 1880. Apparently, she did not wish to embarrass the man whom she admired as a national hero, though she had never been in love with him.

After the divorce, Giuseppina married Ludovico Mancini, with whom she lived happily until his death in 1913. Around then, she made her only public statement about her relationship with Garibaldi:

> It has been suggested that I should have persisted in my refusal of marriage [to Garibaldi] to the very end. But although, in those days, as a girl of eighteen, I was allowed sufficient liberty. . .and was permitted to choose the men whom I would love, nevertheless the choice of a husband was jealously guarded. How can one expect so much courage from a girl who was abandoned by everyone? Even Caroli, who was sure of my love, left me on my own at the end. [7]

Giuseppina Raimondi-Mancini died in 1918, after having presented to the state archives in Mantua the love letters Garibaldi wrote to her in 1859.

41

Nice and Savoy

In early 1860, Cavour returned to power. Although Victor Emmanuel privately disliked him, political pressure from the Right had forced the king to reappoint him as prime minister. He replaced Urbano Rattazzi, who had proven himself inept in handling the consequences of the aborted plan to invade the Papal States.

As soon as Cavour returned to power, he worked to conclude the agreement he had previously made with Napoleon III at Plombieres. Sardinia was to annex the central Italian states of Parma, Modena, Romagna, and Tuscany; Umbria and Marche were to remain part of the Papal States; and Sardinia was to cede Nice and Savoy to France. In each case, the cessions had to be approved by a plebiscite in the ceded territory. This marked the first time that the principle of self-determination of peoples, as expressed by plebiscite, had ever been accepted as a means for determining national borders.

Plebiscites held in Parma, Modena, and Romagna on March 12, 1860, showed that the people favored annexation to Sardinia by a vote of 426,006 to 1,506. In Tuscany, the vote in the plebiscite favored annexation by 366,571 to 14,925.* However, there were nearly 153,000 abstentions, and the Sardinian government was accused of applying improper pressure on the Tuscan voters.[1]

At this juncture, France stepped back into the picture. Napoleon III, afraid of being outmaneuvered by Cavour, insisted that Sardinia surrender Nice and Savoy to France in keeping with the agreement reached at Plombieres. He demanded that Cavour sign another secret agreement pledging that cession before France recognized Sardinian annexation of any of the states in central Italy. Although Cavour readily agreed to cede Savoy, he was rather reluctant to relinquish Nice, because of its strong ties to the national movement. Nevertheless, he acquiesced in order to maintain his friendship with Napoleon. So while he publically allowed that Nice was "essentially Italian," he secretly instructed the local authorities there to help secure a favorable vote for cession to France in the upcoming plebiscite.[2] Later revelations of Cavour's double-dealings would serve to portray him as a Machiavellian and cause him to lose popular support.

The whole matter was kept secret until March 24, 1860, when it was announced that the plebiscites for ceding Nice and Savoy to France were to be held on April 15. It was then that the public first learned of the secret agreement made at Plombieres some twenty

---

*These figures are given in Ridley's *Garibaldi*, p. 430.

Count Cavour

months earlier. The announcement outraged many Italians, including Garibaldi, who was indignant about the loss of his hometown of Nice.

Cavour's "secret intrigues" also came under fire by some members of the Sardinian Parliament. Included among them were Urbano Rattazzi, Massimo d'Azeglio, and Baron Bettino Ricasoli. Rattazzi contended that the cession of Nice to France was a negation of the principle of Italian nationality on which the Risorgimento was based. General Fanti, the minister of war, expressed concern that Cavour was surrendering the nation's natural frontiers to France, thus making northern Italy more vulnerable to invasion. Others considered Cavour's secret agreement with Napoleon III "unconstitutional," and even "treasonous."[3] King Victor Emmanuel, who had already agreed to the cession of Nice and Savoy, remained noticeably quiet about the matter.

As a result, public opinion swung away from Cavour and in favor of Garibaldi. Vowing not to let the former's decision go unopposed, Garibaldi formed the Nice Committee, an organization of prominent opponents to the cession of Nice. He even agreed to argue against it before the parliament in Torino. Despite obstructionist tactics by Cavour, Garibaldi was finally permitted to debate the issue before parliament. The Sardinian MPs would have to decide whether to endorse Cavour's cool logic or Garibaldi's appeal to nationalistic sentiment.

Garibaldi argued that the agreement between Cavour and Napoleon III was fraudulent, illegal, and unconstitutional because it had been signed in secret without any parliamentary discussion. He accused Cavour of alienating an inherent part of Italy because the very idea of a nation-state meant nothing to the man. He insisted that Nice had always been Italian, and that it should remain so. Garibaldi's proposal to cancel the plebiscite received a lot of applause but few votes. To his dismay, the government plan was approved by a large majority in parliament. It served to reinforce his distrust of politicians and parliamentary procedure. He would later say that the loss of Nice made him a foreigner in his own country.

The Nice Committee then worked out a new scheme. Knowing that all French and Sardinian troops were to be withdrawn from Nice during the plebiscite, they planned for Garibaldi and his men to raid Nice after the polls closed. They would seize the ballot boxes and burn all the ballots, thus forcing the authorities to hold a second plebiscite sometime later.[4] The delay would enable Garibaldi to campaign in Nice against cession to France and thus counter the effect of all the pro-French propaganda being levelled at the inhabitants of that province.

Having obtained a ship, Garibaldi and the Nice Committee began preparations for the raid; but the day before it was supposed to take place, Garibaldi was persuaded to abandon the plan by a group of his friends led by Francesco Crispi. Crispi, a Sicilian lawyer, had come to Genoa to persuade him to turn to Sicily instead, where a revolution had broken out against Bourbon rule. The thought of such an undertaking appealed to Garibaldi: the champion of the oppressed leading a volunteer army for the liberation of Sicily! Crispi succeeded in convincing Garibaldi to invade Sicily rather than the ballot box in Nice.

The controversial plebiscites for cession to France were therefore held as scheduled in both Nice and Savoy. The voters were to deposit ballots marked either "yes" or "no" in the ballot boxes. A young Englishman named Laurence Oliphant, who had gone to Nice to observe the plebiscite, reported that he hadn't seen any "no" ballots at the polling station. Oliphant was also allowed to vote, though his name was not on the official voters' register.[5] The vote was 25,943 in favor of annexation and 260 against, with 4,743 abstentions. In Savoy, the vote was 130,533 for annexation and 235 against, with 4,610 abstentions.* Nice and Savoy henceforth belonged to France.

The results of the plebiscites were severely criticised as "patently fraudulent." It was also alleged that (as Oliphant observed), in some districts, no means existed for voting "no." "Yes" ballots, on the other hand, were readily available everywhere. Some districts even reported that more than 100 percent of their registered voters had voted "yes."[6] Despite the criticism, the plebiscite results were allowed to stand.

In retrospect, France gained two very valuable pieces of real estate—Nice and Savoy. The former, ideally located on the scenic Riviera coast, remains the perennial playground of the rich and famous. It is also a favorite setting for motion pictures like *To Catch a Thief* and *The Barefoot Contessa*. The town of Nice, or Nizza, as it is called in Italian, is the "Queen City" of the Rivera and hosts one of the largest Mardi Gras festivals in Europe. It is also a culinary center famous for its Nicoise cuisine.

The *Nizzardi*, or local inhabitants of Nice, are proud of their Italian heritage and continue to speak an old Genoese dialect called *Nizzard*. They also cherish the memory of Nizza's legendary native son—Giuseppe Garibaldi.

Savoy, or "Savoia" as the Italians call it, was also the ancestral home of Italy's royal family—the House of Savoy. The province once formed part of the heartland of the Kingdom of Savoy, which

---

* Figures given in Ridley's *Garibaldi*, pp. 432-433.

later became the Kingdom of Sardinia. Following its cession in 1860, it was divided into two provinces of France—Savoie and Haute-Savoie. The two comprise a region of lush green valleys and high mountains whose slopes are dotted with ancient forts and castles. In earlier centuries, these fortified edifices served as bastions guarding the passes leading into Italy. Today, this region of snow-capped mountains is famous for its ski resorts and ranks as a premier destination for winter sports enthusiasts.

In ceding Nice and Savoy to France, Cavour dispossessed the Italian nation of two monumental landmarks—the ancestral home of its royal family, and the birthplace of its national hero. Nevertheless, Nice and Savoy continue to have a hallowed place in Italian history and folklore. And to this day, many Italians still question the wisdom and validity of the agreement that gave these two provinces to France. It's true that France helped to liberate Lombardy from Austria in the War of 1859. But it is also true that France, though she reneged on her promise to liberate Venetia, demanded *both* Nice and Savoy from the old Kingdom of Sardinia. Although France failed to fulfill part of the agreement, she still took her full share of the spoils.

History has proven that a unified Italy could defeat Austria, as it did in World War I. It is also true that regions of Italian ethnicity, such as Venetia, Trento, and Trieste, were all liberated in due course. So it could be argued that, if Cavour had been more patient, Italy would eventually have gained the regions in contention without France's assistance.

42

The Expedition of the Thousand

THE ISLAND OF SICILY, part of the Kingdom of Naples, had long been a smoldering hotbed of revolutionary activity. For more than five centuries its people had lived under a feudalistic system imposed on them by foreign rulers. Attempts at rebellion or reform had all failed miserably, and the oppression continued. The island was not affected by the Industrial Revolution or by any of the scientific advances of the 19th century. Extreme poverty was common in urban centers like Palermo, Catania, and Messina. In the countryside, illiterate peasants worked the land for the ruling nobility. A virtual class warfare existed between rich and poor.

In this harsh social environment, a secret society known as the *Mafia* exercised a more effective control over the population than did the local constabulary. Originally organized during the uprising of the Vespers against the French in the thirteenth century, this clandestine organization operated as a mutual protection society, employing murder and intimidation to eliminate those who opposed it. According to Sicilian folklore, the term *Mafia* stems from the incident in Palermo that triggered the Vespers' Rebellion in 1282. A French officer was said to have violated a Sicilian girl, causing her father to rush to the main square, shouting: "*Ma fia! Ma fia!*" (My daughter! My daughter!). The incident aroused such indignation that a revolt broke out amid cries of "Death to the French!" The rebellion swept across Sicily and resulted in the massacring of more than 8,000 Frenchmen on the island. A notable by-product of the rebellion was the formation of a secret society for the purpose of protecting the honor of Sicilian women, and though its original purpose was a noble one, later generations saw its transformation into a powerful criminal organization.

Although the Vespers' Rebellion helped to end French domination of Sicily, control of the island passed to the Spanish Aragonese in 1291 and in turn to the Spanish Bourbons in 1738. For the next 122 years, Sicily was to languish under Bourbon rule, its people virtually bound to the land like medieval serfs. Vocal dissidents were arrested, imprisoned, and tortured. Isolated uprisings were brutally put down and followed by savage repression. During such an uprising, Ferdinand II earned the sobriquet "King Bomba" for his continued bombardment of Messina after the city had already surrendered to him. Yet despite the repression that followed these failed uprisings, the flame of liberty continued to burn in the Sicilian soul.

In 1851, William Ewart Gladstone, then a member of the British parliament, estimated the number of prisoners in Neapolitan jails at 20,000. This figure did not include the thousands of others under house arrest and forbidden to leave their homes without police permission.[1] Gladstone, who vacationed in Naples in 1850, had received permission from the Neapolitan government to visit several prisons near Naples. What he saw was horrifying—prisoners chained together, incarcerated under the most deplorable conditions, and guards who took pleasure in torturing them.

Such was Gladstone's indignation over Neapolitan prison conditions that he denounced the governing regime as the "negation of God erected into a system of government."[2] The British press joined in the criticism, referring to the Bourbon ruler of Naples as "a king of torture chambers and prisons." More than anything else, Gladstone's criticisms helped turn public opinion against the Bourbon regime in Naples. Gladstone later went on to become one of England's greatest prime ministers.

Over the years, various attempts to overthrow Bourbon rule occurred, the two most famous being the expedition of the Bandiera brothers and the uprising led by Carlo Pisacone. These early attempts at liberation had, however, failed to gain the support of the Sicilian people, and both had been crushed by a Bourbonist army that numbered 140,000.[3] This army was one of the best dressed, best drilled, and best equipped in Europe; but, behind the facade of fancy uniforms, parade drills, and crack regiments used to maintain the status quo, lay an impoverished land teeming with discontent. Sicily was a power keg waiting to explode.

In May 1859, the notorious King Bomba died, leaving his twenty-three-year-old son to succeed him as King Francis II. Known as "Franceschello," he made some feeble attempts at reform that proved unfeasible, which he in any event soon abandoned. In the end, Franceschello demonstrated that he was almost as unscrupulous a tyrant as his father in the arbitrary use of power. The only opposition to his rule came from the Muratists, who had intended to call Lucien Murat to the throne, and from Sicilian separatists, who wanted to free the island of Bourbon rule.

Since the Peace of Villafranca (1859) made no mention of southern Italy, Sicilians pinned their hopes for liberation on revolutionary leaders like Garibaldi. As we have seen, when a delegation of Sicilians, led by Francesco Crispi, sought to convince him to invade the island with an army of volunteers, Garibaldi himself had serious doubts about the outcome. Moreover, the Sardinian prime minister, Cavour, afraid of antaginizing France and Austria, was opposed to it.

Despite Cavour's misgivings, Garibaldi and his associates, Bixio, Medici, Türr, and Crispi, nevertheless agreed to undertake the invasion of Sicily. On April 15, 1860, Garibaldi took up residence in the house of a friend named Augusto Vecchi,[4] whose villa was located in the suburban town of Quarto, outside Genoa. From this seashore town, preparations for the expedition got underway. With the permission of the Sardinian government, Garibaldi collected and stored a large quantity of guns in the local armory and quickly began recruiting an expeditionary force. He had soon put together an army of red-shirted volunteers, most of whom were from northern Italy. They came from all rungs of the social ladder—aristocrats, professionals, artisans, common laborers, even criminals. Among them were idealists and intellectuals as well as adventurers and roughnecks, but all were patriots. The oldest had fought under Napoleon I; the youngest, Giuseppe Marchetti, was only eleven years old. Twelve of these volunteers later rose to the rank of general in the regular Italian army, and two—Crispi and Cairoli—became prime ministers of Italy.

A number of foreigners also appeared among the volunteers, including Hugh Forbes, Aleksandr Milbitz, Lajos Tukory, and Stefan Türr, all of whom had previously served under Garibaldi. There was also one woman—Crispi's wife, Rosalie Montmasson, who later gained great admiration for nursing the wounded. Other notables among the volunteers included the artist Gerolamo Induno, and Giorgio Manin, the son of Daniele Manin, who had been the leader of the Venetian Republic in 1848–49.[5]

In the meantime, foreign governments had become aware of Garibaldi's plans and formally protested to the Sardinian government. The avalanche of diplomatic protests so alarmed Cavour that he tried to sabotage the expedition by denying Garibaldi's men access to the rifles stored in the armory. Despite this underhandedness, Garibaldi succeeded in obtaining a thousand outdated rifles from the National Society. In addition, Colonel Colt sent Garibaldi a hundred of the famous Colt pistols from the United States.[6] Funds for the expedition trickled in from many sources, but the monies only amounted to a total of 155,000 lire, approximately $31,000.[7]

Amid rumors that Cavour was planning Garibaldi's arrest, a sense of urgency began to permeate the invasion preparations. On the night of May 4, Nino Bixio and thirty men, pistols in hand, seized two vessels belonging to the Rubattino Steamship Company of Genoa. They were aided by Giovanni Fauche, a company director, who gave Bixio instructions for taking over the ships and sailing them out of the harbor. Fauche was to pay dearly for aiding the expedition—he was fired by the steamship company for his complicity in the theft of the two ships, the *Piedmonte* and the *Lombardo*. Fauche then joined Garibaldi in Sicily and saw to the organization of the fleet there. Later, after the unification of Italy, the steamship company took all the credit for providing the ships.[8] Fauche died impoverished in a public hospital in Venice, an unsung hero of the Risorgimento.

While Bixio and his men carried out their act of piracy, Garibaldi was assembling his volunteer force on the rocky shore of the Mediterranean. There were tearful goodbyes with loved ones as the men boarded the fishing boats that would carry them out to the two steamships seized by Bixio. Their departure from shore was hampered by a rough sea. Garibaldi, who had asked for a head-count, was surprised to learn that the volunteers totaled more than a thousand—1,049, to be exact. Out of this total number, 349 of the volunteers sailed with him on the *Piedmonte*; the remainder accompanied Bixio on the *Lombardo*. Garibaldi's force, or *The Thousand* as they came to be called, set out during the night of May 5, 1860. Left behind in Genoa were Medici, Cosenz, and Bertani, each with orders to organize an expeditionary force.

Departure of Garibaldi and his followers on the night of May 5, 1860

No sooner had the two steamers carrying the invasion force left Quarto when Garibaldi noticed that the ammunition for the rifles had somehow been left back on the shore. There was no time for turning back, and it was decided to land somewhere down the coast and try to secure ammunition there. It was a daring improvisation, but it worked. Landing a small detachment of men at Talamone, they bluffed the local commandant, Colonel Giorgini, into believing that they had authority from the king to collect a supply of ammunition. Giorgini not only handed over the ammunition but also gave them a cannon. Giorgini was later court martialled for his gullibility and sent to prison. He was released when Garibaldi's expedition appeared to have succeeded.[9]

Before leaving Talamone, Garibaldi dispatched a volunteer force of sixty men under the command of Callimaco Zambianci to invade the Papal States. This move was intended as a diversion, to deceive the enemy about his intended destination—Sicily. The plan failed miserably when none of the local inhabitants rose in support. Zambianci and his men were captured and imprisoned. All this served to convince Cavour that Garibaldi was irresponsible, and that Sardinia's interests would be best served if the expedition failed.[10]

Both Cavour and Victor Emmanuel remained skeptical about the feasibility and the outcome of the expedition. The king went so far as to comment to the French Ambassador about the possibility of a failed expedition. He reportedly said: "Of course, it would be a great misfortune, but if the Neapolitan cruisers were to capture and hang my poor Garibaldi, he would have brought this sad fate upon himself. It would simplify things a good deal. What a fine monument we would erect to him!"[11]

Cavour imagined himself to be in a no-lose situation: if

Garibaldi failed, Sardinia would be rid of a "troublesome fellow"; if he succeeded, the Sardinian government would stand to benefit tremendously.[12] No matter what the outcome, Cavour himself expected to come out of it smelling like a rose.

Garibaldi and his supporters were confident that the expedition to Sicily would succeed against all odds. The general feeling among Italians was that Garibaldi would come through victoriously, as he had done many times before. This attitude also prevailed in Britain and the United States where his expedition aroused great interest and gained much support.

43

The Landing at Marsala: May 11, 1860

ON MAY 11, GARIBALDI'S INVASION FORCE arrived off Marsala at the western tip of Sicily. Two British warships were already in the harbor, having come there to protect the interests of the British community engaged in the wine trade. The British ships made no attempt to interfere with the landing. Garibaldi docked the *Piedmonte* without difficulty and began disembarking his men, but the *Lombardo* ran aground about three hundred feet from the beach. As the small boats were being lowered into the water to bring the men ashore, two Neapolitan warships suddenly appeared and opened fire on the Red Shirts attempting to disembark. They were forced to disengage when the two British warships passed in the line of fire between them and the port. By the time the Neapolitans were able to resume firing, all the Red Shirts had reached shore safely, either in small boats or by swimming the distance to shore. The Neapolitans wound up bombarding two empty ships.

Moving quickly, the Red Shirts occupied Marsala without resistance. A small party seized the telegraph office and found a scribbled message that had just been sent to the Neapolitan authorities in Trapani. It read: *Two steamers have arrived in the harbor and are landing armed men.* One of the Red Shirts grabbed the key and sent a second message: *Sorry, I am mistaken, the two vessels are merchantmen from Girgenti with cargoes of sulphur.* The authorities in Trapani telegraphed back: *Imbecile!*[1] The Red Shirts then cut the telegraph lines.

In the meantime, Crispi took charge of the political situation. He summoned a meeting of the town council of Marsala and persuaded the members to sign a proclamation declaring the end of Bourbon rule over Sicily. He also invited Garibaldi to take control as Dictator in the name of Victor Emmanuel, King of Italy. Garibaldi accepted the invitation and was so proclaimed amid the cheering of his men.

Using the dictatorial powers given him, Garibaldi requisitioned food, blankets, and what little cash he could find in the city. He gave strict orders against looting, and he even shot a man who was caught stealing fruit from an orchard.[2] He issued a decree ending the Bourbon tax on salt and pasta, and made a pledge to break up the large landed estates. At that early stage of the invasion, most of the local inhabitants did not take him seriously and couldn't yet determine whether he was a liberator or just another invader come to exploit them. Most of them chose to remain on the sidelines, at least until they were certain that Garibaldi was what he claimed to be.

From Marsala, the Red Shirts set out for Salemi, some twenty miles to the east on the road to Palermo. There, they received an enthusiastic welcome from the townspeople and came into contact with partisan bands who were also battling the Bourbons and whose help was to prove invaluable to Garibaldi during his campaign to liberate the island.

Garibaldi also found some unexpected allies in the local clergy. In Sicily, the clergy were themselves an oppressed class, because many of them favored social reforms. One of these, a Franciscan monk named Fra Giovanni Pantaleo, joined the ranks of The Thousand and remained at Garibaldi's side throughout the campaign. Garibaldi called him "the new Ugo Bassi,"[3] and at the end of the campaign Fra Pantaleo was to have the honor of conducting the thanksgiving mass at the cathedral in Naples. Another priest named Gasparo Salvo had secretly buried two cannon with the idea of using them in a future revolution.[4] He dug them up and presented them to a grateful Garibaldi. The cannon were outdated but could still be fired.

Bracing to challenge the invaders was the 140,000-man Neapolitan army, 25,000 of whom were already in Sicily. Besides a fleet patrolling the waters around Sicily, the Neapolitans had a superiority in cavalry and artillery. Against this formidable force, Garibaldi pinned his hopes for victory on the Sicilian people, whom he felt would rise up to support him. Accordingly, he dispatched small units called "Sicilian action squads" to stir up peasants' revolts in the interior. They were aided in their efforts by many of the clergy, who had good rapport with the people and helped win them over to the revolution.[5] From this time onward, the ranks of the Garibaldini would be swelled by groups of volunteers.

King Francis II of Naples had 20,000 soldiers stationed in

Palermo, the capital of Sicily. Three thousand of these were sent out under General Landi to crush Garibaldi's invasion force. They met at Calatafimi, near the site of the ancient Greek temples at Segesta. Landi had positioned his troops on the terraced slopes overlooking the road to Palermo; and when the Garibaldini approached from the west, he ordered his troops to open fire. For Garibaldi, there was no turning back. He knew that the outcome of the battle would determine whether or not the Sicilian people followed him. He had to prove his invincibility, and he was determined to do it at Calatafimi.

44

Liberation of Sicily

CALATAFIMI PRESENTED A DO-OR-DIE SITUATION to Garibaldi. He faced an enemy that outnumbered him by almost three to one, held a superior position, and was armed with better rifles. He knew that a victory was essential for the morale of his men, and that a defeat would mean the end of the campaign. But mainly, Calatafimi presented Garibaldi with an opportunity to prove his invincibility.

The two armies clashed briefly outside the town, with the Neapolitans retreating to fixed positions on a hilltop. Garibaldi ordered his men to advance toward the enemy positions with fixed bayonets. Up the slope they went in the face of intense fire, carrying a banner on which Italy was represented in the form of a beautiful woman flanked by gold and silver trophies. The banner had been given to Garibaldi by the Italian residents of Valparaiso in South America in 1855.[1]

Astride a white horse he had named "Marsala," Garibaldi led his men up the terraced hillside, recklessly exposing himself to enemy fire. In doing so, he displayed a bravado that seemed to lend him the aura of invincibility he was trying to project. Following him, the Red Shirts pressed on up the slope, taking six separate terraces at the point of the bayonet. They fought with a determination seldom seen before in Italian military history. Relentlessly they pushed up the slope, finally reaching the highest terrace just below the summit. At that point, Garibaldi ordered his men to pause for a few minutes. The angle of the ground above the terrace gave them some cover from the Neapolitan troops entrenched on top of the hill. Garibaldi sat down on a rock and calmly lit up a cigar. After a brief smoke, he summoned Bixio to his side and spoke these immortal words: "Here we make Italy or die trying."[2] Then, mounting his horse, he drew his sword and ordered a final charge to reach the summit. The Red Shirts charged the enemy positions, bayonets glistening in the midday sun. Fierce hand-to-hand combat ensued, with the Red Shirts driving the Neapolitan troops off the crest of the hill and into headlong retreat. It was a victory for sheer courage.

The action at Calatafimi attracted attention around the world, turning Garibaldi into a heroic figure of monumental proportions. He had gained the respect and admiration of the Sicilian people, and he now issued a general call for all Sicilians to take up arms against the Bourbonist regime and its supporters. Action squads sprang up all over Sicily as bonfires were lit on hilltops to spread the news of insurrection. Meanwhile, volunteers started pouring into Garibaldi's camp, swelling his forces to more than 3,700 men.

General Giuseppe Garibaldi on the cover of Harper's Weekly, *June 9, 1860*

After the victory, Garibaldi was greeted ecstatically in the villages through which he passed. The people acclaimed him as a liberator and kneeled to kiss his hands and garments.

He advanced cautiously toward Palermo, marching at nighttime along difficult hill paths. Though he succeeded in concealing his whereabouts from the enemy, a war correspondent for the *London Times* apparently had no difficulty locating his camp in the mountains south of Palermo. The British correspondent described the Red Shirts' camp life in these terms:

> *They were all collected around a common nucleus—a smoking kettle with the larger part of a calf in it, and a liberal allowance of onions, a basket with heaps of fresh bread, and a barrel containing Marsala [wine]. Everyone helped himself in the most communistic manner, using fingers and knife, and drinking out of a solitary tin pot . . . and with all those grand Sicilian mountains, forming a background such as no picture can produce.*[3]

For three days the Garibaldini had to live and sleep in the open, sometimes drenched by torrential rains. To many, the capture of Palermo seemed like an impossible task. More than 20,000 troops under General Lanza were concentrated around the city, and the Neapolitan fleet was anchored in the harbor, ready to lend support to the ground troops. Another large Neapolitan force was stationed at Messina, to the east of Palermo. Despite the overwhelming odds against him, Garibaldi believed that he could capture the city if the civilian population rose up in insurrection. He was about to carry out the greatest strategic triumph of his career.

He planned a maneuver that military historians have since come to refer to as "the diversion of Corleone."[4] The plan was to lure part of the Neapolitan army away from Palermo by creating the impression that the Garibaldini were withdrawing into the interior. The strategy worked perfectly. Garibaldi approached Palermo from the west, and then suddenly swung to the south, disappearing into the mountains as if he was retreating towards the center of Sicily. After marching southward some twenty miles, he turned sharply to the northeast while a pursuing Neapolitan force under Colonel von Mechel went searching for him as far south as the town of Corleone. A small force of Garibaldini, led by Vincenzo Orsini, continued to lead von Mechel on a wild-goose chase. The well-executed diversion baffled the Neapolitan high command and enabled Garibaldi to approach Palermo unnoticed from the southeast.

On May 26, the word was quietly passed around the streets and houses of Palermo that Garibaldi would enter the city that night. Sure enough, as darkness fell over the city, the Red Shirts came down from the mountains and attacked the sentries guarding a stone bridge called Ponte dell Ammiraglio. After a half-hour battle, Garibaldi's lancers, led by Captain Francesco Nullo, charged across the bridge and entered Palermo through Porta Termini. By the morning of May 27, after several hours of fighting, most of Palermo was in the hands of the Garibaldini. The prison was captured and the prisoners released. Church bells rang, signaling the townspeople to emerge and help the liberators. Barricades sprang up everywhere.

As the Red Shirts advanced, the defending Neapolitan forces retreated to the vicinity of the royal palace and the cathedral. After regrouping near the cathedral, they counterattacked along the Toledo, the wide street now called Corso Vittorio Emanuele. Any civilians encountered on the street were shot by the Neapolitans on the rationale that they might be revolutionaries. Meanwhile, in retaliation, thirty men accused of being police spies were hanged by the revolutionaries.[5] Atrocities were committed by both sides, and seldom was any quarter given. During the day's action, Bixio was wounded but continued to lead his unit until he was ordered by Garibaldi to report to the hospital.

As the fighting intensified, General Lanza ordered a naval bombardment of Palermo by the offshore warships. That bombardment continued for three days and nights killing over three hundred civilians and wounding five hundred more.[6] Cannon shells hit churches and convents, which had been converted into hospitals and shelters, sometimes burying the patients and staff in the rubble. Yet, although the bombardment inflicted heavy casualties and flattened whole areas of the city, it also served to further arouse the townspeople's spirit of resistance. The men joined in the street fighting. The women helped by throwing mattresses and furniture from the windows to provide the materials for the barricades. They poured boiling water on the Neapolitan troops who ventured into the narrow alleyways, and, at night, they placed lights in their windows to show that they were siding with the revolutionaries in the streets.

Meanwhile, the Garibaldini crept ever closer to the royal palace as their snipers pinned down the enemy troops holed up there. Other Neapolitan strong points, such as the San Antonio Barracks, the Porta Maqueda, and the Convent of the Annuziata, fell to the Garibaldini after fierce hand-to-hand combat. The fighting left the streets littered with corpses. Even the air smelled of death.

By May 30, the Neapolitans only held the area around the palace and the cathedral, along with the harbor fortress of Castelamare, prompting Lanza to ask Garibaldi for a truce. He wrote a letter addressed to "His Excellency, General Garibaldi," requesting a meeting on board a British warship anchored in the harbor. Lanza's forces were facing serious shortages of food and medical supplies, and his wounded were suffering greatly.

That afternoon, Garibaldi dressed in his Sardinian general's uniform and, accompanied by Crispi, came aboard the HMS *Hannibal* to meet General Letezia of the Neapolitan army. British Admiral Mundy was present, as were the commanders of the French, American, and Sardinian naval squadrons at Palermo. An armistice was discussed, and it was agreed that the Neapolitan army was to evacuate Palermo and set sail for Naples. One week later (on June 7), the main body of the Neapolitan army in Sicily marched down the Toledo to the harbor and left by ship. Following their evacuation, the only Neapolitan forces remaining in Sicily were the 18,000 troops in the northeast corner of the island, around the fortress city of Messina.

The unbelievable had happened—a volunteer force of a thousand men had defeated a professional army of 25,000 who could be reinforced by sea. Garibaldi now had an opportunity to actually rule over a province and to initiate needed reforms. He retained the title of Dictator and decreed certain reforms, but he left the details of managing the government to Crispi, his secretary of state. Crispi had an intimate knowledge of the Sicilian people, and he knew how to deal with the politicians who still hoped to limit the scope of the expedition.

In the meantime, Mazzini, the spiritual leader of the Risorgimento, remained in hiding in Genoa while the people rallied behind Garibaldi and the national cause. Thousands of Italians, mainly from the northern cities, volunteered to serve under Garibaldi in Sicily. Others, rich and poor, sent money to support his expedition. Everywhere in Italy, Garibaldi's name was on the people's lips.

Cavour, who had previously opposed Garibaldi's expedition to Sicily, tried to seize the benefits of Garibaldi's victories for the Kingdom of Sardinia. He quickly dispatched a commissioner to annex Sicily to Sardinia and even agreed to supply money and munitions for Garibaldi's expedition.[7] Medici and Cosenz, whom Garibaldi had left behind in Genoa, were allowed to organize their expeditions openly. On June 10, Medici sailed for Sicily with 2,500 reinforcements for Garibaldi; three weeks later, Cosenz sailed with an additional 1,500 men.[8] Cavour was thus able to claim the credit for sending reinforcements to Garibaldi.

Garibaldi, however, while thankful for these reinforcements, was not ready to place Sicily under a Sardinian commissioner who might not allow the revolution to proceed further. He intended to remain Dictator for as long as possible—possibly until he had liberated Naples and Rome—unwilling to relinquish his power until he could proclaim Victor Emmanuel king of a united Italy. After that, he reasoned, the Sardinian government was welcome to disavow him if he failed in his mission.

45

The Dictatorship

GARIBALDI HAD BECOME A GREAT HERO to the Sicilian people, and as Dictator he was determined to use his power to improve their lot. He initiated a land reform program through which the large estates would be divided up and the land redistributed among the peasantry, who, he believed, in their extreme poverty were entitled to a share of the land.

In a further attempt to end Sicily's feudal image, he outlawed the *baciamento*, the custom requiring a tenant to kiss the hand of his landlord. He also discontinued the use of the term *Your Excellency* when addressing a person of rank, himself included.[1] These measures helped him gain the support of common people who, for centuries, had lived under the yoke of the landed aristocracy.

Hoping to stimulate the island's economy, Garibaldi abolished tariffs and restrictions on exports and imports. He also eliminated the Bourbon tax on salt and pasta, measures that pleased Sicilian merchants. He tried to help the homeless street urchins of Palermo by setting up a Garibaldi foundling home, where they could learn the rudiments of good citizenship. The home was administered and conducted along military lines by Alberto Mario, with Garibaldi himself often coming in to give the youngsters lessons in patriotism.[2] As happy as the boys were in the foundling home, many later left to join the ranks of the Red Shirts and die in battle.

Despite his ongoing feud with the papal authority, Garibaldi wisely respected Sicilian religious traditions. While attending Mass on Ascension Day in the town of Alcamo, he received the Crusaders Cross as he knelt before the main altar.[3] And, when he attended a celebration Mass in the Cathedral of Palermo, he sat in the royal chair, a place formerly reserved for the Bourbon rulers of Sicily. On the feast day of Santa Rosalia, patroness of Palermo, he respectfully made a pilgrimage to her grotto. He even made a goodwill tour of the local convents, asking if they needed provisions. In return, the grateful nuns sent him gifts of handmade embroideries.[4]

Through these acts, Garibaldi demonstrated that he was a religious man at heart, and that he would support devout priests who were dedicated to serving the spiritual needs of the people rather than their own materialistic aims. From his good relations with the Sicilian clergy, one can surmise that his hostility toward the church hierarchy was not directed at the faith itself but at those who used religion as an instrument for suppressing freedom. Thus, at least in Sicily, Garibaldi stood as champion of the people and as a defender of the faith.

Priests and monks joined the populace in praising the liberator,

Entrance to Grotto of Santa Rosalia on Mount Pelligrino, near Palermo

and the Archbishop of Palermo even consented to bless the troops. In a letter to a friend named Ruggiero Settimo, Garibaldi wrote: "This brave people is free. Joy is written on every face, the country echos with the glad cries of the liberated."[5] The Dictator granted audiences to virtually anyone who came to him, aristocrat or peasant. Formalities were pushed aside and all petitions and requests given equal treatment and consideration.

In the summer evenings, the terrace roof of the palace was used as a rendevous for the Garibaldini officers, the ladies of Palermo, and foreign diplomats and representatives. There was exciting conversation and eager questioning whenever the talk turned to the battles and adventures that had hitherto brought them all together. All spoke confidently of Garibaldi's ability to liberate Naples, Rome, and Venice in the near future. The whole setting— the place, the time, the events—produced a sort of delirious ecstasy that has not been recaptured in the subsequent history of

Palermo.

By then, Garibaldi had become a fatherlike figure to the Sicilian people. However, despite his tremendous popularity, some of his measures were failing miserably. His attempt to collect taxes, and his introduction of military conscription in Sicily, were both very unpopular. He also failed to stamp out corruption in the civil service. Captain C.S. Forbes, a retired British naval officer who visited Sicily during the summer of 1860, commented that the lesser officials in Garibaldi's government "would do nothing unless they were first offered bribes."[6]

Meanwhile, there was turbulence in rural areas, where angry peasants rose up against the landowners. The cry of "Long live Garibaldi" was succeeded by "Death to the aristocracy!" In some villages, the anger of a people who had been exploited for centuries erupted with volcanic fury. The landed gentry were brutally murdered, and their mansions looted—a horrifying scene largely reminiscent of the French Revolution and the Reign of Terror.

As the violence spread, Garibaldi made every effort to suppress crime and maintain order. He forbade the illegal seizure of property and imposed the death penalty for murder, kidnapping, and theft. In early August, he dispatched Bixio with a detachment of troops to suppress an uprising in the town of Bronte, near Mount Etna. There, an unruly mob led by Niccolo Lombardo had murdered local notables and looted their houses. Bixio, moving quickly, restored order and arrested many of the perpetrators. Seven of those arrested were tried by court martial on charges of murder and arson. They were found guilty, and five, including Lombardo, were sentenced to death. Before the execution, one of Lombardo's relatives asked permission to give the prisoner some eggs for his last meal. Bixio denied the request, telling the relative that

Lombardo didn't need any eggs, because he would be shot in the head the next morning.[7] He *was* shot, on schedule, along with the others—without breakfast. The affair served as a warning to the rest of the island.

Although Bixio had acted on his own authority, Garibaldi supported his actions when questioned about the matter. He believed that crime and violence had to be suppressed in order to avoid rural anarchy. His firmness in maintaining law and order won him the loyalty of Sicilian landowners who were increasingly fearful for their lives. Nevertheless, Bixio's behavior in suppressing the uprising at Bronte was widely criticised in the foreign press.

While this happened, Garibaldi's forces were being swelled by reinforcements and volunteers. Medici and Cosenz had already arrived in Sicily with 4,000 reinforcements. These troops were now joined by foreign volunteers attracted to the cause of liberty personified in Garibaldi. Various legions were formed to accommodate the desire of these foreigners to serve in the same fighting unit with their compatriots. An English Legion was organized under the command of Colonel John Dunne, who had served with the British army in India and the Crimea. Dunne seemed to have the ability to inspire courage and discipline in untrained volunteers. French volunteers, led by Lieutenants Paul de Flotte and Philippe Bordone, formed a French Legion, which eventually numbered about five hundred men. De Flotte was later killed in Calabria, but Bordone would go on to serve under Garibaldi in future campaigns. A Hungarian Legion was also formed under the command of Major Adolph Mogyorody. In addition to those who served in the various foreign legions, many foreign volunteers served in the regular Garibaldini units.

A combination of Swiss and German volunteers constituted

what came to be known as the Foreign Legion. It consisted of about a hundred men, most of whom had served in the Neapolitan army and then changed sides. Although some of the Garibaldini questioned their loyalty, the foreign legionnaires soon gained the respect of their comrades by their valor in battle. Their commander, Adolph Wolff, was a disciplinarian who made the Foreign Legion into an effective military unit. The Legion would distinguish itself throughout the campaign to liberate southern Italy. Later, Wolff fought under Garibaldi during the campaign of 1866 and even took part in several attempted republican revolutions. But the truth about him emerged in 1870, when France was defeated by Prussia in the Franco-Prussian War and it was revealed that Wolff had been a secret agent in the hire of Emperor Napoleon III of France for the past twenty years.[8] What a shocker!

Other notables who joined the expedition were Colonel Hugh Forbes, who had served under Garibaldi during the retreat from Rome in 1849, and Jessie White Mario, an Englishwoman who had married one of Garibaldi's officers. Jessie Mario was a former medical student who was interested in humanitarian causes and worked with Dr. Pietro Ripari in organizing and running the hospital service, enlisting the aid of the Ladies' Garibaldi Benevolent Association. She was also instrumental in getting medical supplies from Britain and later became known as "the Florence Nightingale of the Red Shirts."[9]

Also joining Garibaldi was the celebrated French novelist Alexandre Dumas. He came to Sicily on his private yacht, accompanied by a beautiful girl dressed as a midshipman. He was later to write a romanticized biography of Garibaldi and a history of the Expedition of the Thousand in which he himself figured heroically. In reality, however, Dumas seemed laughable to the Red

Shirts—he and his girlfriend following the campaign from aboard a luxurious yacht well-stocked with champagne.

The Red Shirt camp certainly had its share of theatrics. In addition to the flamboyant Dumas, Garibaldi was soon joined by the eccentric Countess Maria della Torre. She had met him in London during his 1854 visit and fallen in love with him. Nothing had come of the affair, but she insisted on joining his expedition in Sicily. She appeared in camp wearing a red shirt, riding boots with spurs, and sporting a large plumed hat. As if her getup wasn't enough to draw attention, she carried a large sword that clanked in its scabbard whenever she moved about. Succeeding in her determination to accompany Garibaldi into battle, she soon collapsed from exhaustion and was hospitalized. Shortly afterwards, she was committed to an insane asylum.[10]

Besides this influx of volunteers, Garibaldi's expedition also got some needed financial aid when it captured the mint in Palermo. There, the Red Shirts seized a huge cache of ready money the Neapolitan government had called in for re-coinage.[11] In addition to this lucky find, the Sardinian government began to release some of the funds promised for the cost of the expedition. Garibaldi's victories in Sicily also stimulated an increase in financial contributions from other countries, including the United States. The City of New York contributed $100,000; the State of California sent $3,000 and four cannon,[12] each of which bore the inscription *To Italy from her sons in California.*

46

Battle of Milazzo

THE SURRENDER OF THE NEAPOLITAN FORCES at Palermo enabled Garibaldi to occupy all of Sicily except for the northeast corner around the town of Messina. Messina's strategic location on the strait that separates Sicily from continental Italy made it the next objective of his campaign.

With the addition of various new volunteer units, Garibaldi's army had by July 1860 grown to a fighting force of about 20,000. The force originally known as The Thousand, was now restructured to form four divisions, as though they were additions to the existing fourteen of the regular Italian army. Designated the "Southern Army," they comprised the 15th Division under Türr, the 16th under Cosenz, the 17th under Medici, and the 18th under Bixio.[1]

On July 14, Garibaldi's Southern Army began advancing toward the Neapolitan defense perimeter protecting the Strait of Messina, particularly the fortress town of Milazzo. Medici's division set out from Palermo along the coast road leading to Milazzo while the troops led by Türr and by Bixio headed south into the interior of Sicily to liberate the towns still held by Neapolitan garrisons. After completing their missions, they were to meet at Punta del Faro on the Strait of Messina, their next strategic objective being the invasion of the Italian mainland.

Near Milazzo on the north coast, Medici encountered a Neapolitan force led by Colonel Bosco, and fierce fighting ensued. Bosco was a tough professional soldier who believed that he could defeat the insurgents, but when Garibaldi arrived with reinforcements for Medici, Bosco was forced to fall back toward Milazzo. The town sits in the shadow of a fortress of the same name that dominates a promontory jutting out into the sea and can only be approached by land through the town. Garrisoned by a force of about a thousand men, its ramparts were ringed with forty cannon. Another four hundred troops guarded the northern tip of the peninsula against a landing from the sea. Along the southern edge of the promontory, Bosco positioned 2,500 of his best troops, and eight cannon, in a semicircle stretching for two miles. They were protected on both flanks by the sea and supported by a squadron of cavalry Bosco held in reserve.

On July 20, the Garibaldini approached these positions from the south. They had to advance through fields covered with prickly pear trees and thickets of cane so tall they almost concealed the armies from each other.[2] Thick hedges of cactus, or high stone walls, marked the boundaries of each field. It was here in these fields, under a blazing sun, that Garibaldi and Bosco clashed in deadly combat. The battle raged with an intensity that seemed to rival the summer heat. Although the combatants suffered from thirst and fatigue, they continued to fight on through the heat of the day. Both sides hung on grimly. No one surrendered. Hundreds fell—brought down by enemy fire or bayoneted to death. Others collapsed from exhaustion in the heat. The cries of the wounded could be heard everywhere.

Garibaldi himself led several charges, his battlefield heroics setting an example for the young volunteers under his command: During a Neapolitan cavalry attack, he stood in front of his men and cut down the leading horsemen with his sword. In the same action, his young aide-de-camp, Giuseppe Missori, shot down several other horsemen with his pistol.[3] These acts of bravado spurred the volunteers to greater feats of valor.

Garibaldi noticed a former Palermo street urchin courageously battling the enemy. The youngster had volunteered to join the Garibaldini; and for his valor in battle, Garibaldi promoted him to the rank of sergeant. The boy was twelve years old.[4]

After eight hours of intense hand-to-hand combat, the Garibaldini cracked the Neapolitan defense perimeter and captured Milazzo. The inhabitants had already taken refuge in the thick olive groves covering the nearby hills. The defending Neapolitan troops retreated into the fortress only to discover that, while they had plenty of ammunition, little food or water remained. When the troops were put on half-rations, they threatened to mutiny. This prompted Colonel Bosco to telegraph a message to headquarters at Messina, detailing his precarious position and requesting food and reinforcements from the garrison there. But the Neapolitans in Messina would not march to relieve Bosco for fear that Türr's column would advance northward from

Catania to attack the exposed town. Instead, the Neapolitan high command chose to surrender Milazzo to Garibaldi, provided that the garrison be allowed to evacuate by sea. Both sides agreed to a treaty of capitulation by which the Neapolitan troops could march out with their weapons and embark for Naples.

On July 25, then, over the objections of the fiery Bosco, the Neapolitan garrison surrendered the fortress and marched out with the honors of war. At the end of the column walked Colonel Bosco, who had once bragged that he would re-enter Palermo "riding on Medici's horse." Instead, he left Milazzo on foot, amid the jeers of a townspeople freed at last from the enforcer of Bourbon tyranny.[5] He and his men sailed away aboard the Neapolitan warships that had arrived off the coast.

It soon became known that Bosco had *not* in fact acted honorably regarding the terms of the capitulation treaty. When the Garibaldini took possession of the fortress, they discovered that most of the cannon had been spiked, and that the horses and mules which were to be turned over to them had been slaughtered. They also uncovered a delayed fuse hidden under a pile of straw and a trail of gunpowder leading to the powder magazine—set up to blow the fortress and its new occupants sky high.[6] Evidently, Bosco had intended to leave Milazzo with a bang!

All told, the Garibaldini had suffered 750 casualties, including two hundred killed, a high price to pay for their legacy of invincibility.[7] Conditions for the wounded in the hospitals were horrible. The surgical instruments were inadequate, and there were no anaesthetics. The Englishwoman Jessie White Mario set an example for courage and compassion as she cared tirelessly for the wounded. During an operation on a twelve-year-old boy, she held the patient on her lap while his arm was being amputated. She was to attend to the wounded throughout the campaign and, for her unselfish devotion to duty, held in the highest esteem by the Red Shirts, who referred to her as "that excellent creature of the Lord."[8]

Although the Neapolitan forces suffered only two hundred casualties in all, their morale was shattered by the defeat. The towns of Siracusa and Ragusa fell to Garibaldi without a fight, leaving him in command of almost all of Sicily by August 1, 1860.* The question then arose: Could his Red Shirts successfully cross the Strait of Messina and invade the mainland?

---

* The citadel at Messina continued to hold out until March 12, 1861, when, after a heavy bombardment, it finally surrendered to the Italian army under the command of General Cialdini.

47

The Road to Naples

By August 1860, the Strait of Messina, patrolled by about ten warships under the command of the Neapolitan Admiral Salazar, had become the last obstacle to the invasion of the Italian mainland. Defending Calabria on the mainland side of the Strait were about 17,000 Neapolitan troops with more than a hundred cannon. Strong points included the fortress at Reggio and the artillery batteries at Villa San Giovanni, Alta Fiumara, Torre Cavallo, and Castello di Scilla. Transporting an army of more than 10,000 men across the Strait, under the guns of hostile forts and a vigilant navy, seemed an almost impossible task.

In addition, there was genuine concern over the possibility of French and British intervention to stop Garibaldi. It was known that Napoleon III wished to preserve the Bourbon regime in Naples as a "constitutional state under French direction." In order to achieve this, he proposed that the British and French fleets patrol the Strait of Messina to prevent any crossing by the Red Shirts. The British, however, rejected the French proposal, commenting that the Neapolitans themselves should decide on whether to accept or reject Garibaldi.[1] Since France was not prepared to interfere alone, the threat of foreign intervention on behalf of the Bourbons was greatly diminished.

Complicating matters even more, the Sardinian government itself was opposed to Garibaldi crossing to the mainland. Prime Minister Cavour had become increasingly alarmed by Garibaldi's popularity among the masses and by the presence of radical elements in his new government in Sicily. In an attempt to seize control of the situation, he sent his friend, Giuseppe La Farina, to Sicily to push for the immediate annexation of the island to the Kingdom of Sardinia. La Farina, an exiled Sicilian, had served as secretary of the National Society and developed close ties with Cavour. However, he was not on good terms with either Garibaldi or Francesco Crispi, the newly appointed secretary of state for Sicily. Crispi was among those whom Cavour considered the most dangerous.

La Farina's arrival in Palermo triggered the revival of old animosities. He quarreled with Crispi over the question of immediate annexation and proceeded to level a barrage of criticism against the Dictatorship. In his report to Cavour, he described the situation in Palermo as "a mixture of wonder and horror," claiming that though the Sicilian people loved Garibaldi as their liberator, they hated his administration. La Farina accused Garibaldi's government of "administrative and financial incompetence," and he called for Crispi's dismissal and the immediate annexation of Sicily by Sardinia. When Garibaldi refused to go along with these demands,

La Farina organized demonstrations against the Dictatorship, hoping to disrupt preparations for the invasion of the mainland.[2]

At this time, a sinister plot to assassinate Garibaldi came to light. Sicilian police arrested two secret agents in the hire of the Bourbon regime in Naples. The two had slipped into Palermo with the intention of assassinating Garibaldi "by the knife or by poison."[3] One, Giacomo Griscelli, turned out to be a double agent acting for Cavour. Both Griscelli and his associate, Totti, confessed both these roles to the police.

There is little doubt that Griscelli and Totti had been hired by the Bourbons to murder Garibaldi. But how does Cavour fit in? The answer may be found in a letter written by the Sardinian fleet commander, Admiral Persano, to Garibaldi on July 7, 1860. Persano's letter implies the two agents were being paid by Cavour to murder Garibaldi and make it look as if the Bourbonists were behind it.[4] Persano evidently wrote the letter to Garibaldi because he had been ordered by the Sardinian government to intervene in the matter on behalf of the two conspirators. The whole affair remained shrouded in mystery, and in the end, Griscelli and Totti were spared from execution.

All of this tended to convince Garibaldi that Cavour was behind the assassination plot, and that La Farina, his principal agent in Sicily, was also involved in the conspiracy. Consequently, he ordered the expulsion of La Farina from the Island. The emissary was arrested at his home in Palermo and forcibly placed on board a Sardinian vessel along with the two hired assassins. The three were then shipped back to their mentor—Camillo di Cavour! As a further insult to La Farina, his name appeared alongside those of Griscelli and Totti in the official notice of their deportation for subversive activity.[5]

These events help to explain the great animosity between Garibaldi and Cavour. They also explain why Cavour refused to visit Naples when Victor Emmanuel took possession of the city later that year. Previously, he had always accompanied the king on such occasions. He excused himself on the grounds the Red Shirts held him in "extreme dislike."[6] Did he so fear the Red Shirts, or was he unable to face Garibaldi after he had paid two assassins to murder him?

In any case, the degrading manner in which he deported La Farina should not be construed to blur Garibaldi's benevolent image. He took no other action against La Farina, or for that matter, against Griscelli and Totti. A less magnanimous leader would have hanged all three.

Their expulsion served to diffuse the tense political situation in Palermo, thus enabling Garibaldi to get on with the task of liberating Sicily. As for Cavour, he set his mind on one vindictive objective—to stop Garibaldi!

In yet another attempt to thwart Garibaldi's campaign, Cavour deterred an expeditionary force, led by Dr. Agostino Bertani, from invading the Papal States. The force of 6,000 men was to attack from the north, capture Rome, and then advance southward to join forces with Garibaldi. Cavour was concerned that an invasion of the Papal States would lead to conflict with France, so he compelled Bertani to divert his force to Sicily by sea.[7] He was thus able to sabotage Garibaldi's plan for opening a second front in his campaign to liberate southern Italy.

Behind the scenes, Cavour was also advising King Francis II to grant a constitution to the Neapolitans before the Red Shirts invaded the mainland—a move intended to gain popular support for Francescello and diminish Garibaldi's revolutionary appeal.

Cavour also suggested that the Bourbon ruler form an alliance with Victor Emmanuel and that the two kingdoms work together for Italian independence.[8] This would finesse Garibaldi out of the picture. When Francescello balked at the idea, Cavour came up with another scheme for annexing the Kingdom of Naples without Garibaldi's help: He would have the Sardinian fleet prevent Garibaldi from crossing to the mainland, while his agents instigated a revolution in Naples and seized power before Garibaldi's arrival.[9]

These intrigues were later revealed in Cavour's correspondence with Costantino Nigra, the Sardinian Ambassador to France. In July 1860, Cavour warned:

> We must stop Garibaldi from conquering Naples and try to bring about the annexation of Sicily as soon as possible. . . . It is of the greatest interest to us and I will say for Europe, that if the Bourbons have to fall, they should not fall through the action of Garibaldi. The annexation of Sicily is a way of annulling Garibaldi.[10]

As it turned out, the revolution in Naples failed to materialize, and the Sardinian fleet did not blockade Garibaldi. Cavour shifted his position on the matter when he realized it would be advantageous for him to support the Red Shirts' march on Naples. Even he wanted to receive some of the credit for the success of Garibaldi's expedition.

A series of rumors about diplomatic double-dealings began to circulate in some of the foreign offices. The French government was alarmed by rumors that Garibaldi was secretly negotiating a deal with the British to make Sicily a protectorate of Britain. Hadn't Garibaldi, they reasoned, landed at Marsala under the protection of British warships? One French newspaper even went so far as to accuse him of being a British agent.

For their part, the British worried that Cavour was negotiating another secret agreement with Napoleon III. This time, rumor had it, France would allow Victor Emmanuel II to annex Sicily and Naples in return for the cession of Genoa and the island of Sardinia to France. Cavour denied the idea, but then, hadn't he also denied the secret cession of Nice and Savoy to France?

The Mazzinians attempted to capitalize on British fears by circulating the draft of a secret treaty between Cavour and Napoleon III, under which Genoa was to be ceded to France in exchange for allowing Victor Emmanuel II to annex Sicily. The mysterious document aroused Garibaldi's indignation and raised a chorus of denials from both the Sardinian and the French governments. When its authenticity could not be established, it was generally agreed that the document was a Mazzinian forgery.[11]

Not wishing to be left out of the diplomatic drama, Victor Emmanuel, who was in the habit of carrying on his own secret diplomacy, now saw an opportunity to facilitate Garibaldi's advance on Naples despite foreign pressure against it. He issued two contradictory letters to him—one ordering him to halt his advance, the other directing him to disregard the first letter and march on Naples. The contents of the first letter were made public in order to calm the fears of France and Austria; the existence of the second letter remained a secret until its discovery in 1909, some fifty years later (it was found among the papers of Count Litta-Modignani, the king's orderly).[12]

This deception apparently worked. European leaders believed that the Sardinian government was not supporting the red-shirted revolutionaries, thus enabling the Pope and the King of Naples to feel more secure in their realms. In the meantime, Garibaldi pushed ahead with his plan for crossing the Strait of Messina and landing in Calabria. He assembled his men on the east coast of Sicily below Messina and began requisitioning boats to ferry them across. On the night of August 8, he sent a force of two hundred Garibaldini across the Strait in twelve small boats. Led by Giuseppe Missori and Alberto Mario, their purpose was to land on the coast of Calabria and establish a beachhead so that he could make the crossing with the main force. Upon landing, the small band of Red Shirts was fired upon by Neapolitan warships and forced to retreat inland to the mountains of Aspromonte. They were to hide in those forbidding mountains until he arrived with reinforcements.

In an attempt to deceive the enemy, Garibaldi then ordered several of his requisitioned ships to sail westward around Sicily in a counterclockwise direction. This movement of vessels away from the vicinity of the Strait baffled the enemy, though the Neapolitan fleet continued to shadow them in the hope of locating the assembly point for Garibaldi's invasion force. It turned out to be another wild-goose chase, with the Neapolitan navy pursuing empty ships bound for nowhere. Meanwhile, Garibaldi and Bixio, with a force of 3,600 men, quietly boarded two steamers and set sail for the mainland. The crossing was made during the night of August 18, 1860, and was not intercepted by the Neapolitans. At dawn, the Garibaldini landed in Calabria near the little town of Melito.[13]

When news of this reached Neapolitan military headquarters at Reggio, the commander, Colonel Dusmet, led his troops out of the city to intercept Garibaldi. The two armies clashed along the coastal road; Dusmet was killed and his troops driven back into Reggio. Garibaldi advanced on the city and proceeded to bombard it with captured artillery pieces, forcing the terrified Neapolitan garrison to surrender and handing the Garibaldini a major victory. Since their landing on the mainland, they had suffered 147 casualties, but they had captured the city of Reggio and seized thirty-eight cannon and 2,000 rifles.*

Moving quickly, Garibaldi advanced northward toward Villa San Giovanni, the port opposite Messina on the Strait. Another force of 1,500 Red Shirts, under General Cosenz, landed on the coast above the city and began marching southward on the town. Trapped between the two advancing columns of Red Shirts stood 6,000 Neapolitan troops under the command of General Brigante. In the battle that followed, Brigante suffered heavy casualties and was forced to retreat inland, away from the port at Villa San Giovanni. This allowed the main body of Garibaldini to cross to the mainland and begin their triumphant march northward. The march to Naples was an unchecked advance of more than two hundred miles in the heat of summer.

During this advance, the problem of food supply was quickly solved by the friendly Calabrian peasantry. Despite their great poverty, the peasants unselfishly offered to share their meager provisions with the Garibaldini. Some stood by the roadside and offered the produce from their gardens. Others emerged from their cottages with cooked food and fresh bread for the troops. Farmers came in from the fields and placed baskets of fruits and olives along the line of march. All seemed imbued with a strong sense of duty—to aid their liberators. At Monteleone, Garibaldi and his men were treated to a feast by the jubilant townspeople. At Catanzaro, the citizenry proclaimed Garibaldi Dictator even

---

*These figures may be found in Viotti's *Garibaldi, The Revolutionary and His Men*, p. 117.

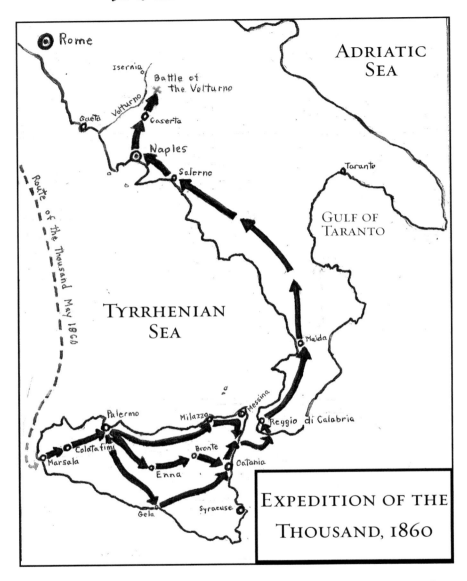

though the town was still occupied by Neapolitan troops! Further north, revolts against Bourbon rule broke out in Lucania and Puglia, where guerrilla bands were being organized to fight for Garibaldi.

Royalist resistence crumbled before Garibaldi's advance. By

the end of August, more than 10,000 Neapolitan troops, including General Ghio, had surrendered to him. Because his men were unable to guard the thousands of enemy soldiers who surrendered, Garibaldi offered them the choice of either joining his army or surrendering their weapons and going home. Nearly all chose to return home.[14] For them, the war was over.

Garibaldi was still in Calabria when he learned of Cavour's plan to instigate a revolution in Naples. Though the attempt failed miserably, Garibaldi feared that Cavour might make another attempt to impede his march northward and decided to quicken his advance. He pressed forward along the Tyrrhenian coast, riding in an open carriage and accompanied by a cavalry unit mounted on captured horses. He was also surrounded by foreign journalists and friends, including Jessie White Mario and Evelyn Ashley of the British Foreign Office. Colonel John Peard rode ahead with a detachment of legionnaires, announcing Garibaldi's arrival in each district. This had a demoralizing effect on the Neapolitan troops, causing many of them to desert and go home.

Meanwhile in Naples, King Francis II and his ministers watched in dismay as the situation continued to deteriorate. After Garibaldi's victory at Palermo, the Bourbon king had granted a constitution, but it had come too late to gain the support of the populace. In reality, power in Naples was now largely in the hands of Liborio Romano, the chief of police. In addition to this office, Romano also controlled the secret society known as the *Camorra*,[15] the Neapolitan counterpart of the Sicilian *Mafia*, which had considerable influence over events in the city. In June 1860, Romano had been appointed minister of the interior by King Francis, thus formally bestowing upon him the power he already exercised in practice.

On August 23, he was visited by Alexandre Dumas, who had just arrived on his yacht from Palermo and who advised Romano to join Garibaldi and thus facilitate the liberation of Naples. Romano accepted the proposal and was told by Dumas not to show his hand until Garibaldi was about to enter the city.[16] Francis II suspected Romano's treachery but was powerless to act against him. The king's power rested in his army and in the more prosperous peasantry living in the northern part of his kingdom. Francis did not wish to turn Naples into a battleground like Palermo, so he abandoned her and retreated to the fortress of Gaeta with his royal entourage. There, he would rebuild his shattered army and prepare for a counteroffensive against Garibaldi. With this plan in mind, he left Naples on the evening of September 5. He never saw the city again.

48

Defeat of the Bourbons

THE SUDDEN DEPARTURE FROM NAPLES of King Francis II only facilitated Garibaldi's advance northward. On September 5, 1860, the same day Francescello left Naples, Garibaldi reached Salerno, where 20,000 people came out to cheer him. Such was the people's exuberance that they danced in the streets throughout the night. During the festivities, Garibaldi received a telegram from Liborio Romano, the Neapolitan minister of the interior. The telegram read:

> *To the invincible General Garibaldi, Dictator of the Two Sicilies:*
> *Naples awaits your arrival with the greatest impatience to salute you as the redeemer of Italy and to place in your hands the power of the State and her own destinies. . . . I await your further orders and am*

with unlimited respect for you, invincible Dictator.
Liborio Romano, Minister of the Interior and Police[1]

The next day, a delegation led by the mayor of Naples came to Salerno to meet with Garibaldi. They were afraid that the situation in Naples would soon become chaotic because of the absence of any sort of authority. They urged Garibaldi to come to Naples immediately and take command of the government. This move was opposed by his general staff; for them, it would be dangerous for him to enter Naples before the troops had occupied the city. But Garibaldi himself was too impatient to wait for his troops, and he immediately set out for Naples in a special train accompanied by only a handful of his men.

On September 7, he entered Naples to the thunderous cheers of a liberated populace. Wild celebrations broke out everywhere despite the fact that royalist troops still garrisoned the city's forts. The royalists' military presence did not deter him. He rode through the city in an open carriage, passing in full view of the royalist garrison manning Fort Carmine—and instead of firing on him, they saluted him.[2] Seemingly, his many victories had given him an aura of invincibility.

After passing beneath the charged cannon of Fort Carmine, Garibaldi's carriage reached the harbor front, where a multitude of Neapolitans were waiting to cheer him. His drive along the quayside created a spectacle reminiscent of the triumphal parades of ancient Rome. The sidewalks were crammed with as many people as could find standing room. Above the street, others cheered and waved from the windows and balconies of every building. And on the bay, where many ships were anchored, every deck swarmed with cheering sailors waiting to get a glimpse of the pirate turned national hero. Some sailors even climbed the masts to get a better view.

After riding through a sea of waving arms, fluttering handkerchiefs, and saluting royalist soldiers, Garibaldi reached his destination, the Foresteria, an annex of the royal palace used for the entertainment of court guests. A crowd surged around him, cheering and trying to touch him. Even the official reception committee was swept up in the general outpouring of adoration. Repeatedly, the crowd echoed the cry: "*Viva Garibaldi!*"

Addressing the crowd from a balcony, he thanked the people of Naples for the welcome, and told them to celebrate the beginning of a new era in which the people of Italy "passed from the yoke of servitude to the rank of a free nation."[3] During this speech, he first made the gesture that came to be known as the "Garibaldi sign"— holding up the right hand with only the forefinger extended upward to signify One Italy.[4] The ships in the harbor fired off their guns in salute and raised the red, white, and green tricolor with the emblem of the House of Savoy. It was Garibaldi's finest hour.

While the Neapolitans were giving him the greatest ovation of his life, the royalist garrison began marching out of Naples to join King Francis II at Gaeta, some forty miles to the north. They were joined by other royalist units retreating northward from Calabria. These troops would later fight with valor in the defense of Gaeta, and demonstrate how a losing cause could be defended with dignity and honor.

The next day Garibaldi went to the cathedral to attend a thanksgiving service for the deliverance of the city, the Mass being celebrated by the soldier-priest Fra Pantaleo. Garibaldi also took care to pay his respects at the shrine of Saint Gennaro, the city's patron saint. The shrine possesses two small vessels containing the crystalized blood of that early Christian martyr. Tradition has it that Saint Gennaro's blood miraculously liquifies on the anniversary of his martyrdom in the month of September, signifying that the city will be spared from any upheaval that year. When the Saint's blood fails to liquify, Neapolitans consider it a bad omen— a sign that some catastrophe will strike their beloved city. Luckily for Garibaldi, he had the satisfaction of learning that the blood of Saint Gennaro had in fact liquified,[5] lending further credence to the belief that he had saved the city from impending disaster.

With, then, the blessings of the Saint and of the Neapolitan civic leaders, Garibaldi assumed the Dictatorship of Naples and formed a new government. He appointed General Enrico Cosenz minister of war, and Giuseppe Sirtori as pro-dictator in his absence. He alarmed Cavour by appointing Dr. Agostino Bertani, a Mazzinian, to the important position of secretary of state, and by keeping Liborio Romano, a former Bourbonist, as minister of the interior and chief of police. General Stefan Türr became the miliary commander of Naples, and the Frenchman Alexandre Dumas was appointed director of excavations at Pompeii. Dumas' appointment aroused some ridicule because of his reputation as a playboy and spendthrift.[6]

Garibaldi's first act as Dictator was to hand over control of the Neapolitan fleet, at anchor in Naples harbor, to Admiral Persano of the Royal Sardinian Navy—an extremely generous gift from someone Cavour had once described as "that cabin boy from Nice."[7] The fleet, which consisted of ninety ships and more then 7,000 sailors, was larger than the Sardinian navy, and Garibaldi's largesse only served to weaken his position as Dictator. Furthermore, the navy would have proved invaluable in any campaign against the Papal States. There is no doubt that, if Garibaldi had retained control of this navy, he would have been treated quite differently by King Victor Emmanuel and the Sardinian government.

It was a different situation with his ground forces. The ranks of the Southern Army had grown with the enlistment of 20,000 new recruits, thus bringing its total strength to more than 43,000.[8] However, most of the new recruits were national guardsmen who remained on duty in their home towns. The actual fighting force consisted of about 25,000, their firepower enhanced by cannon and other equipment abandoned by the retreating royalist forces.

Meanwhile, in the region around Naples, many of Francis II's former subjects continued to remain loyal to the Bourbon cause. Together with dispersed troops from the defeated Neapolitan army, they began to organize a resistance movement against Garibaldi, especially around the city of Isernia on the Volturno River. Francis II, who had taken refuge in Gaeta, refused to abdicate his throne, and he even expressed the intention of recapturing Naples. Meanwhile, his field marshal, Giosue Vitucci, was massing a royalist army of 50,000 men north of Naples for one last decisive battle against Garibaldi. It became known as the Battle of the Volturno.

49

Battle of the Volturno: Autumn 1860

While he consolidated his position in Naples, Garibaldi also prepared for a last decisive battle against the Bourbon king, Francis II, who had retreated a short distance to the north of the city. He also announced his intention of continuing the war until Rome and the Papal States were liberated. This announcement drew a stern warning from the British, who by then wanted to maintain peace in the Mediterranean region. The warning only served to anger Garibaldi, who said that "Rome was an Italian city and that no foreign power had any right to keep him out of it."[1] This attitude apparently caused him to lose the support of the British government in any attempt to capture Rome. In the meantime, Garibaldi denied Cavour's demand for the immediate annexation of the conquered territories to the Kingdom of

Sardinia.

Cavour now saw an opportunity to recapture the initiative from Garibaldi and the revolutionaries. Suspecting that Garibaldi would use his authority as Dictator of the Two Sicilies to mount an attack on the Papal States, he met with French Emperor Napoleon III at the latter's new summer home at Chambery in the province of Savoy. There, he succeeded in convincing the emperor that the only way to prevent Garibaldi from attacking Rome was for the Royal Sardinian Army to march through the Papal States and invade the Kingdom of Naples from the north. This would have the effect of blunting Garibaldi's advance northward, thus preventing him from achieving the ultimate victory—the capture of Rome.

Cavour got his way, and in early September, a Sardinian army of 33,000 men under the command of Generals Fanti and Cialdini invaded the Papal States from the north. The Papal troops put up a brave resistence, but they were defeated at Castelfidardo. Soon afterward, the fortress at Ancona also surrendered, thus enabling the Sardinians to continue their advance southward through the provinces of Marche and Umbria. Rome, however, was bypassed, leaving the pope untouched and thus satisfying the French. Napoleon III could rest easier, knowing that he did not have to dispatch additional French troops to protect the Holy See.

At about the same time, another of Cavour's underhanded dealings came to light. French diplomatic correspondence revealed that Napoleon III had given his approval to Cavour's plan only after being told that the Sardinians were marching south "to combat the influence of Garibaldi" and "to prevent the revolution from spreading into northern Italy."[2] This startling revelation lent further credence to the belief that Cavour's objective was to subvert the revolution personified by Garibaldi.

Meanwhile, Garibaldi had determined to advance north to Gaeta and defeat Francis II once and for all. For this purpose he established his headquarters at the royal palace at Caserta and prepared to conduct a campaign against the royalist army massing near the Volturno River. His plans were disrupted when a dispute developed between DePretis and Crispi in Sicily. DePretis, the pro-dictator of Sicily, favored *immediate* annexation to the Kingdom of Sardinia; Crispi, the secretary of state, was opposed to it. In an attempt to remedy the situation, Garibaldi made a quick visit to Palermo. During his brief stay, he appointed Antonio Mordini as pro-dictator, replacing DePretis. Mordini was more radical than DePretis, and, like Garibaldi and Crispi, he was opposed to immediate annexation. Having made the change, Garibaldi returned to Naples.

During his five-day absence, preparations had been completed for a decisive battle against the royalist army, and a force of 7,000 men under General Stefan Türr set out to probe royalist positions around the Volturno. After minor skirmishes, Türr concluded that the royalists were testing his strength in preparation for a general offensive. He therefore decided to jump the gun and attack them first, though Medici's division had not yet reached the front to support him. Crossing the Volturno, Türr captured the town of Caiazzo and continued on toward the fortress town of Capua, leaving behind three hundred men to defend Caiazzo.

At Capua, the Garibaldini ran into stiff resistance from the royalist defenders and were repulsed with heavy losses. Türr, afraid of being cut off, ordered a general retreat and fell back toward the Volturno. Meanwhile, the Garibaldini defending the town of Caiazzo continued to hold their position while Türr completed his pull-back. They fought on with great heroism until finally being overcome by superior forces. Few of them were taken prisoner. The royalists had won their first battle. Thus, during Garibaldi's brief absence, the Red Shirts had received their first setback of the campaign.[3]

Surprisingly, Field Marshal Ritucci did not press home his advantage following the victory. The royalist army did nothing for a week while Garibaldi, who had just returned from Palermo, advanced toward the Volturno with the remainder of the Southern Army of 25,000. Though outnumbered two-to-one by royalist forces, he remained confident of success.

For their part, the royalist troops were inspired by the appearance at the front of King Francis II and his two brothers, the Count of Trapani and the Count of Caserta. Marshal Ritucci deployed his force of about 50,000 in a twenty-mile-wide semicircle around the town of Caserta. This created a rather wide front for the number of troops involved. Garibaldi positioned his troops in a more compact formation covering a distance of twelve miles. This would make it easier for him to shift his reserves from one sector of the front to another. The left wing of the formation was anchored by a force of 7,000 Garibaldini under the command of Medici. On the right wing, Bixio, with 5,000 troops, held the town of Maddaloni, and a small detachment under Bronzetti held Castel Morrone on the extreme right. Garibaldi and Türr were positioned in the center of the line, at Caserta, with the remaining 13,000 Garibaldini.*

By the end of September, both sides were ready for battle—the well-drilled professional army of the Bourbon king, and Garibaldi's red-shirted volunteers. At stake was control of a kingdom and the

---

* Figures from Jasper Ridley's *Garibaldi*, p. 497.

potential of a unified Italy. For the Bourbons, losing the battle would mean the end of their rule over southern Italy. For the Red Shirts, a defeat meant the end of the national movement personified by Garibaldi. The fate of Italy would soon be decided, and an eerie feeling seemed to permeate the already tense atmosphere.

On the night of September 30, Garibaldi was visiting an outpost near the village of Sant'Angelo when he saw a rocket fired into the sky behind the enemy lines. Believing it the signal for an enemy attack, he alerted all his commanders. While making his rounds, he came upon one of his soldiers, poorly equipped and dressed in rags. The man's plight was such that he was contemplating giving up the struggle and returning home. Garibaldi noticed the look of despair on his face and dismounted to talk to him. Laying his hand on the man's shoulder, he said: "Courage; courage! We are going to fight for our country."[4] These simple words seemed to work like magic. The dejected soldier immediately steeled himself for the upcoming battle.

Sure enough, the next morning (October 1) the royalists launched a massive attack. Advancing through a dense fog, they struck both of Garibaldi's flanks with the objective of breaking through to Caserta. Marshal Ritucci sent 8,000 men against Bixio and Bronzetti on the right. Exhibiting great tenacity, Bixio was able to hold his position at Maddaloni, though some of the new recruits lost their nerve and ran. At Castel Morrone, Bronzetti and his small force held out for four hours until they were overwhelmed by the enemy. He and his men fought bravely to the last, displaying a courage reminiscent of those brave Texans who died at the Alamo in 1836. In doing so, they prevented some 5,000 royalist troops from joining the battle against Bixio.

On the left wing, Medici held out against an attacking force of

16,000 royalists led by General Alfan de Rivera. Backed up by heavy cannon fire, the royalists attacked both the outpost at Sant'Angelo and the town of Santa Maria, where Medici had his headquarters. As the situation worsened, Garibaldi went there to take personal command of the situation. On the way, he was ambushed by the enemy near Sant'Angelo. Surrounded by royalist troops, he leaped from his carriage with saber drawn and led his companions in a desperate charge. When the enemy discovered whom they had ambushed, they fled.[5]

Garibaldi's appearance at the front helped to stabilize the situation; as the royalist attack fizzled, he ordered Medici to counterattack. All day, he remained in Medici's sector of the battlefield, leading various units into the battle. He paused only for a few minutes to eat a bunch of grapes handed to him by Jessie White Mario, who had been placed in charge of the front-line hospital. Later that day, Garibaldi's position was overrun by two squadrons of royalist cavalry. He quickly ordered his men to lie down in an embankment and fire their weapons as the enemy horsemen galloped over them. The unexpected volley frightened the horses and shattered the formation.[6]

By late afternoon, the advancing Red Shirts had driven the royalists from their remaining outposts in that sector of the front, which included the Convent of the Capuchines, one of the main royalist strong points. As the Red Shirts swept ahead, royalist resistence seemed to dissolve before them. Royalist troops retreated to the fortress of Capua, where the Red Shirt advance ended, concluding the day's action on the left flank.

Meanwhile, on the right, Nino Bixio continued to hold out against tremendous enemy pressure. The royalists had already captured the outpost of Castel Morrone, killing Bronzetti and wiping

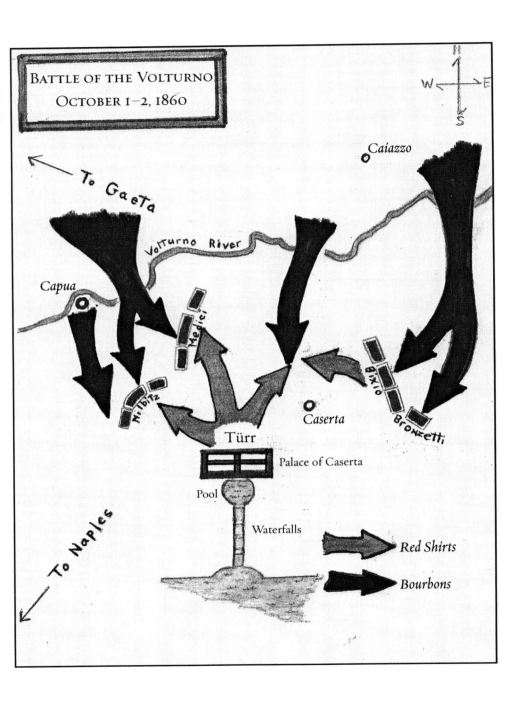

BATTLE OF THE VOLTURNO
OCTOBER 1–2, 1860

Caiazzo

To Gaeta

Volturno River

Capua

Medici

Milbitz

Bixio

Bronzetti

Caserta

Türr

Palace of Caserta

Pool

Waterfalls

To Naples

Red Shirts

Bourbons

out the 280 defenders. This setback forced Bixio to fall back to new defensive positions in order to avoid being cut off from the rest of Garibaldi's army. Fortunately, he was soon reinforced by the arrival of reserve units under the command of Colonel Giuseppe Dezza and Major Menotti Garibaldi, the general's son. Dezza and Menotti joined Bixio in a frontal attack that, after a series of bloody charges, dislodged the enemy from its forward positions and forced Marshal Ritucci to order a general retreat in that sector.

But while this action was under way, a royalist column of 3,000 troops under Colonel Perrone had broken through the Garibaldini defense lines and was rapidly advancing toward Garibaldi's head-quarters at Caserta. Perrone's advance posed a serious threat behind the Garibaldini lines. Türr's reserve force prepared to defend Caserta, as Medici and Bixio were now ordered by Garibaldi to converge on the enemy column from both sides. Perrone's force was soon surrounded, but continued to do battle. On the morning of October 2, Garibaldi himself led the attack which won the battle and forced the enemy to surrender.[7]

This victory concluded the engagement known as the Battle of the Volturno. It was Garibaldi's most significant success on the battlefield because it liberated almost all of southern Italy from Bourbon rule. The Garibaldini suffered 1,634 casualties at the Volturno, along with 389 men captured or missing. Royalist losses amounted to 1,128 killed and wounded, and another 2,163 captured.* King Francis II had fled with his courtiers to the safety of the fortress of Gaeta, which still remained in Bourbon hands, along with Capua and the fortress of Messina in Sicily. Garibaldi issued

---

*These figures are given in Andrea Viotti's *Garibaldi, The Revolutionary and His Men*, p. 129.

a proclamation thanking the men of the Southern Army who had fought with such valor to uphold the "martial honor of their compatriots." He also expressed his sorrow over the battle "in which Italians fought Italians."[8]

The Battle of the Volturno meant the end of the Kingdom of the Two Sicilies and marked one of the high points of the Risorgimento. Garibaldi's resounding victory was one of his great feats of war and ranks with San Antonio, Montevideo, Calatafimi, Palermo, and Milazzo. It showed that he had mastered the art of European warfare and proved that he could command a large army with success. His sound strategy, and his inspirational presence on the battlefield, helped carry the day against a numerically superior enemy. No doubt remained about his abilities as a military commander.

Garibaldi had originally intended to cross the Volturno and capture Capua, but King Victor Emmanuel put a damper on that plan, issuing specific orders that Garibaldi desist from further attack on the Bourbons.[9] Apparently, the capture of Capua and Gaeta was to be reserved for the glory of the Royal Sardinian Army, not the Red Shirts. In that way, the Sardinians could claim some of the credit for defeating the Bourbons.

Meanwhile, the Royal Sardinian Army was continuing its march southward through the Papal States, and on October 9 Victor Emmanuel officially announced that he was taking possession of *his* Neapolitan provinces. Garibaldi was well aware of the Sardinian government's intention to annex southern Italy. But he did not know that Prime Minister Cavour had instructed Generals Cialdini and Fanti "to hurl the Garibaldini into the sea" if they should resist.[10]

The prospect of civil war suddenly loomed very real as Victor

Emmanuel's army advanced toward Naples. Garibaldi realized that the days of his Dictatorship were coming to an end, and that he had to make one last great decision: Should he allow a plebiscite for the annexation of the conquered territories by the Kingdom of Sardinia—or should he order elections for a constituent assembly in preparation for establishing a republic in southern Italy? Everyone anxiously awaited the Dictator's decision.

50

End of the Dictatorship

GARIBALDI'S DICTATORSHIP WAS A NOVELTY FOR NAPLES, a city with a long history of rule by foreign tyrants. His brief tenure there, though somewhat turbulent, represents a colorful chapter in the Risorgimento. With a population of about half a million, Naples was the largest city in Italy at the time. As we have seen, Neapolitan civic leaders welcomed Garibaldi as a liberator, the populace embraced him, and the Bourbon garrison saluted him as he rode into the city on September 7, 1860. Even the blood of Saint Gennaro miraculously liquified in seeming approval of his victory.

It was a historic moment when Garibaldi addressed the cheering crowd from a balcony and declared that Italy was one nation. For the first time in their long history, the people of Naples felt a breath of freedom. Garibaldi immediately used his power to initiate much-needed reforms, introducing bold legislation for free education, land reform, unemployment compensation, and railroad construction, as well as a price freeze on goods sold in stores, in order to prevent price gouging by local merchants. These measures had been uniformly criticized by Cavour and the Sardinian cabinet as the first steps down the road to Socialism.

Cavour was also clamoring for Garibaldi's resignation as Dictator of the Two Sicilies. He believed that Garibaldi was under the influence of Mazzini, and that allowing him to continue would give the republican faction an advantage over the monarchists. Garibaldi, who had tried to maintain a bipartisan administration by appointing members of both factions to positions in his government, was confident that they could work together and eventually reach an accord on the type of government for a unified Italy. But this would prove to be no easy task.

Cavour and his agents continued to press for the immediate annexation of the conquered territories as a means of ending Garibaldi's rule and bringing these territories under Sardinian control. Garibaldi favored postponing annexation until he had liberated Rome and the Papal States. As the rift between the two leaders widened, Garibaldi wrote a letter to Victor Emmanuel, urging him to dismiss Cavour as prime minister. The letter only served to anger the king, who dryly replied that he could not dismiss Cavour "at the moment."[1]

Garibaldi's letter had in fact forced Victor Emmanuel to show his hand. All along, the latter had contrived to use Garibaldi as a ploy against the Sardinian government. Though publicly distancing himself, the king had secretly been going behind the backs of his own ministers and encouraging Garibaldi's clandestine undertakings. For the monarch, it was a no-lose situation without risk: If Garibaldi succeeded, Victor Emmanuel stood to gain in power and prestige; if he failed, the king would deny any responsibility. This arrangement, however, was about to explode in his face. Cavour, perfectly aware of the king's complicity in Garibaldi's expedition to Sicily and eager to stay on as prime minister, threatened to expose the two-faced policy.

Victor Emmanuel was thus faced with a knotty choice—side with Garibaldi and dismiss Cavour, or go along with Cavour and get rid of Garibaldi. He chose his prime minister, who had the support of parliament, and ordered Garibaldi, with whom he had recently been on friendly terms, to "proclaim the annexation at once, or else resign."[2]

In Naples, Garibaldi found himself in a quandary. All attempts to determine the form of government a united Italy would adopt had failed because of partisan disagreements. The republicans in his administration wanted to elect a constituent assembly, which would then decide on the question of annexation. They were being led by Francesco Crispi, the newly appointed secretary of state for Naples. But the principle of an elected assembly was opposed by the monarchists led by Giorgio Pallavicino, the newly appointed pro-dictator in Naples. He demanded that a plebiscite be held for immediate annexation by the Kingdom of Sardinia. These differences soon developed into a struggle between Revolutionary Italy and the Italy of the Establishment, with each faction determined to have its way. While the wrangling continued in Naples, the Royal Sardinian Army continued its steady march southward toward the city. Garibaldi would have to decide whether to go along with the republicans and the promise of a constituent assembly, or throw in with the monarchists and annexation. With the specter of civil war looming tensely in the background, he knew he had to move cautiously. Sardinia would have the support of France and Austria in a civil war, and all he had achieved would be wiped away if he went to war and lost.

After some indecision, he called a cabinet meeting to decide on the issue. The meeting was held on October 2, and, by a 3–2 vote, it decided to hold elections for a constituent assembly.[3] Garibaldi then signed a decree authorizing the elections and setting November 11 as the date for convening the assembly.

Reaction to the plan was swift in coming. Pallavicino, the pro-dictator, resigned in protest. Monarchist demonstrators took to the streets, demanding a plebiscite, and placards were posted around the city urging the people to vote "Sí" for annexation by the Kingdom of Sardinia. Garibaldi was presented with a petition signed by thousands of Neapolitans who favored a plebiscite and opposed a constituent assembly.

Garibaldi, who had never wished to rule against the will of the people and was taken aback by the scale of the opposition, summoned a meeting of his advisors to re-assess the situation and devise a viable resolution. Pallavicino was among those present. Garibaldi had refused to accept his resignation, because he felt that Pallavicino's cooperation was essential for a successful transition process. During the meeting, each faction presented its case. Garibaldi sat silently at the head of the table, pretending to be listening to the rhetoric while he examined the signatures on the petitions. When the matter was finally put to a vote, the result (by a 5–2 vote) still favored a constituent assembly. Pallavicino refused to accept the decision and was unwilling to participate in any transitional process unless the plan for the assembly was scrapped. The republican faction, however, insisted that the vote for the assembly be allowed to stand; the monarchists demanded that it be rescinded. Neither side would back down as Crispi and Pallavicino engaged in heated debate. This came to an abrupt end when General Türr entered the room and presented Garibaldi with yet another petition for a plebiscite, which most noticeably contained the signatures of thousands of his own Red Shirts. The impact on the gathering was tremendous. When the commotion subsided, Garibaldi realized that the moment of truth had arrived.

After a few moments of silence, he rose from his chair, held up the petitions, and said, "If this is the desire of the Neapolitan people, it must be satisfied." Turning to Pallavicino, he added, "*Caro Giorgio*, we need you here still."[4] Pallavicino appeared somewhat stunned by Garibaldi's turnabout. No one in the room made any comment. Garibaldi then cancelled the elections for the assembly and instead ordered a plebiscite to be held on October 21. The republicans angrily left, refusing to shake hands with Pallavicino. This didn't seem to perturb him; he had won his case.

Garibaldi, however, had made no decision regarding Sicily. He intended to leave that decision to Antonio Mordini, his pro-dictator in Palermo. As it happened, Mordini had had every intention of complying with Garibaldi's decision to form a constituent assembly and had issued a similar decree for elections in Sicily. Upon learning that Garibaldi had reversed himself, Mordini cabled for instructions. Garibaldi told him to use his own discretion; and Mordini, who wanted a uniform policy for both the mainland and Sicily, then revoked his earlier decree for elections and ordered that a plebiscite be held instead.

The decision to hold a plebiscite was heralded by the local authorities in Naples and Palermo. Middle-class citizens throughout the south looked upon it as a positive step toward freedom and unity. Many of them believed that annexation by the Kingdom of Sardinia was the best security against the return of the Bourbons and their tyranny. The plebiscite, held on October 21, 1860, asked the electorate to vote "yes" or "no" to the following proposition: "The people wish for an Italy, one and indivisible, with Victor Emmanuel as Constitutional King and his legitimate descendants after him."[5]

On the mainland, the tally was 1,302,064 in favor and 10,312 against, with a large percentage of the electorate abstaining. In Sicily, the people voted 432,053 to 667 in favor of annexation.* Admiral Mundy, the British fleet commander who observed the voting, commented that it took a brave man to vote "no."[6] The vote nevertheless reflected the nationalistic trend of the time: In the Papal States, both Umbria and Marche also voted overwhelmingly in favor of annexation.

Garibaldi was to stay on as Dictator until Victor Emmanuel reached Naples. Hearing news of the king's approach on October 25, Garibaldi rode north with his army early the next morning to meet His Majesty. The two armies made contact near the village of Marganello, some thirty miles north of Naples. Garibaldi and his staff stationed themselves in front of a roadside tavern called Taverna della Catena and awaited the arrival of their new sovereign.

The Garibaldini lined both sides of the road as the Royal Sardinian Army approached, resplendently dressed in their bright blue uniforms. Generals Cialdini and Della Rocca, who were riding at the head of the column, came over to Garibaldi and shook his hand. However, after this warm initial greeting, unit after unit of Royal troops marched past him without saluting—a clear demon-

---

*These voting figures may be found in Trevelyan's *Garibaldi and the Making of Italy*, p. 266.

stration of their contempt for the red-shirted Garibaldini.[7]

Someone shouted: "The king! The king is coming!" Soon, Victor Emmanuel himself came riding up, immaculately dressed in a uniform bedecked with medals. As he approached, Garibaldi took off his hat and shouted, "Saluto il primo Re d'Italia" (I salute the first King of Italy.) The king extended his hand to Garibaldi, and the two men clasped hands for more than a minute. The king asked, "How are you, dear Garibaldi?"

Garibaldi replied, "Well, your Majesty. And you?"

"Excellent," replied the king.[8]

The king and Garibaldi then rode together for several miles, followed by their retinues, with the royal army troops and the Red Shirts riding two abreast, side by side. The mood was one of "cool politeness" as the two armies marched together along the road leading to Teano. The whole event was later to hold a hallowed place in Italian history and folklore. As they rode together, the king informed Garibaldi that he himself would take command of the military operations against the Bourbons, and that the Red Shirts would be held in reserve. Garibaldi felt the decision would have a demoralizing effect on his troops, but he accepted the order and placed his men at the king's disposal. He would, however, take precautions not to let his troops know that he was no longer in command. He and his Red Shirts were thus denied the opportunity for a final victory over King Francis II of Naples.

Eventually, the column came to a fork in the road, and as no invitation had been extended to accompany the king any farther, Garibaldi and his men veered off to the left and took the road to Calvi. The king and his army continued toward Teano, where the royal cooks were preparing a sumptuous meal for His Majesty and his entourage. Garibaldi and his men stopped at a farm near Calvi

Garibaldi welcoming Victor Emmanuel II as King of Italy

for a very modest meal of bread and cheese, with water that had such a foul taste Garibaldi spit it out, declaring, "There must be a dead animal in that well!"[9] Otherwise, he said little and appeared to be pondering the events of the day. He was to spend the night in a barn, sleeping on a pile of straw—an accommodation hardly befitting a man who had just unified a nation!

The next day, worn out physically, he returned to his headquarters at the Palace of Caserta, where he was visited by General Della Rocca of the Royal Sardinian Army. Della Rocca found him lying in bed in a little room over the palace guardhouse.[10] Della Rocca expressed his personal gratitude to Garibaldi for all that he had accomplished. He also had praise for Cosenz and Sirtori, two of the Red Shirt officers who had been assigned to his command. Garibaldi was most appreciative of Della Rocca's visit, which showed that at least some royal army officers had respect for him and his men.

The Royal Palace at Caserta

In the meanwhile, Victor Emmanuel had made a brief visit to the town of Sant'Angelo, where he was greeted by General Medici and his men. The king had hoped to find Garibaldi but was disappointed to learn that he was convalescing in Caserta. As things turned out, this visit to the base at Sant'Angelo would constitute the monarch's only attempt to show personal gratitude to the Red Shirt rank-and-file. He made no effort to visit those who lay wounded in the surrounding hospitals, and his officers continued to snub Garibaldi's men.

The worst affront occurred when the king was scheduled to review the Red Shirts' farewell dress parade at Caserta. Most of Garibaldi's army assembled on the palace parade ground to await the arrival of their sovereign. They were filled with a great pride for their newborn nation. They waited for more than six hours in a steady rain, only to learn from a messenger that the king wasn't coming.[11] No explanation or apology was offered, and the reason for the king's absence remained uncertain.

Rumor had it that he was flirting with a woman in Capua at the time of the parade.[12] The story, however, was never verified. Another rumor had the king shunning the parade because he was afraid of being abducted by the Red Shirts. Apparently, someone had overheard a number of overzealous Red Shirts talking about doing so, and holding him prisoner until he agreed to go to war against Austria. This story has also received little credence.

The general consensus among historical writers has been that the king was persuaded by his staff to mete out a public snub to Garibaldi and his Red Shirts. Monarchists would deny this, but regardless of any rationale to the contrary, the king's demeanor reflected the monarchy's disdain for the red-shirted volunteers who had shed so much of their blood for the liberation of Italy. Garibaldi greatly resented the incident but refrained from public comment at the time. Later, however, the whole affair was magnified in the press.

The fortress at Capua surrendered to the Royal Sardinian Army in early November, and Gaeta eventually capitulated in February of the following year. In the world press, the Sardinians received the credit for both these victories. Garibaldi and his Red Shirts remained in the background and were repeatedly slighted by the officers and officials of the king's entourage. Luigi Farini, the newly appointed governor, refused even to talk to Garibaldi, or to shake hands when they met. He also angered the Red Shirts by banning the *Garibaldini Hymn* from being played in Naples.[13] Tensions remained high, as Garibaldi blamed Cavour for all the hostility against the Red Shirts.

His accusation proved unfounded. Cavour was actually prepared to give Garibaldi and his men the recognition that they deserved. He had already persuaded the parliament in Torino to pass a unanimous resolution of congratulations to Garibaldi. He had also written a memorandum on October 8, stating that "Mazzini and his followers should be swept away, but the government must show magnanimity to Garibaldi's Army."[14] There still remains some uncertainty over whether this was a genuine government attempt at reconciliation with Garibaldi, or a thin-veiled facade to conceal its actual feelings toward the Red Shirts. It remains the case that the royal army brass continued to harbor resentment toward Garibaldi and his Red Shirts.

Victor Emmanuel had planned to enter Naples with Garibaldi riding beside him. Garibaldi himself didn't care for the idea, considering it an attempt to make use of his popularity for the king's own advantage. But for the sake of maintaining unity, he agreed to accept the invitation. Thus, on November 7, 1860, the people of Naples were treated to the rare spectacle of Garibaldi and the king riding through the streets of the city, side by side, in an open carriage. The crowds were noticeably less enthusiastic than they had been when Garibaldi liberated the city a few months earlier. Garibaldi also accompanied the king to a religious service in the cathedral, and then to a reception at Naples' royal palace. But he declined to attend a gala performance at the opera, where he was to sit with the king in the royal box.[15]

The next day, in a ceremony held in the royal palace, Garibaldi formally resigned the Dictatorship, transferring all power to Victor Emmanuel and his government. This was followed by a private meeting at which the king sought to shower Garibaldi with gifts and honors for his service to the crown. He appointed Garibaldi a major general in the royal army and offered him the title of Prince of Calatafimi. He also offered to give him a castle, a yacht, and a generous pension, and to grant an estate to Menotti, nominate Ricciotti as a royal aide-de-camp, and provide Teresita with a dowry when she married. Furthermore, he would confer upon Garibaldi the decoration of the Collar of the Annunciation, which entitled him to be regarded as cousin to the king.[16] Important issues such as the liberation of Rome and the status of the rank-and-file of the Red Shirts, however, weren't even touched upon by the king during the course of the conversation.

To the king's astonishment, Garibaldi refused all these gifts and honors; crumpling up the notice of his commission, he told the king that he had not undertaken the task of liberating southern Italy in order to receive material rewards. He felt that there was still much to be done regarding unification, and that it was essential to preserve his reputation as a person free from governmental influence. The king's ego suffered a severe blow and, for once, he felt what it was like to be snubbed.

Having settled matters with his king, the only thing left for Garibaldi to do was to pack his personal effects and say his good-byes. He briefly visited with Mazzini, who had slipped into Naples after the liberation, and with Admiral Mundy, whose naval squadron was anchored in the harbor. In his last official capacity, he gave his farewell message to the Red Shirts, urging them to put all differences aside and close ranks behind King Victor Emmanuel. Thus ended the Expedition of the Thousand.

Over the years, Garibaldi and his Red Shirts have been immortalized in literature, their deeds enshrined in history. Artists have romanticized them on canvas, and film makers have glorified them on the screen. Later generations have looked upon them as the embodiment of the spirit of the Risorgimento. Seldom, however, does anyone bother to ask: "What became of them?"

Garibaldi himself left Naples by steamship before dawn on November 9. He purposely chose an early departure to avoid any demonstration of support aimed at embarrassing the new government. Only his son, Menotti, and a few friends sailed with him, and the only items he took on board were a bag of seed for his garden, some coffee and sugar, and a year's supply of macaroni.[17] As he sailed out of the harbor, the British naval squadron fired a salvo in salute; the Sardinian ships did not. It certainly wasn't a send-off befitting the man who had just liberated half of Italy from foreign rule. But none of this mattered to Garibaldi. For the first time in many months, he felt free from the pressures of public life. Now, with a few belongings and some seed for his garden, he was returning to Caprera to live the life of a simple farmer.

The Sardinian army was to enjoy the dubious honor of capturing Gaeta and sending Francis II into exile. The Red Shirts took no part in this final surrender, and it became obvious that the government had no use for these volunteer troops. The task of disbanding the Southern Army became a government priority. A special committee was appointed to determine which of the Garibaldini qualified for induction into the new Italian army. The military hierarchy could not accept the idea of filling the ranks of the regular army with former revolutionaries. The result was that many of the Garibaldini were rejected and dismissed outright. Those who did join had to settle for a lower army rank than the one they had previously earned with the Red Shirts.[18]

Even more demeaning to the Garibaldini was the government's lenient policy of admission for the officers and men who had served in the Neapolitan army under the Bourbons. In many cases, the Garibaldini were passed over in favor of the soldiers whom they had defeated a few months earlier. Only 1,584 of the Garibaldini were taken into the regular army, most of these members of the original *Thousand*. Included among them were some of Garibaldi's leading officers. Bixio, Medici, Cosenz, Türr, and eight others were made generals in the Italian army. Several were later elected to parliament. Türr was chosen to be Victor Emmanuel's aide-de-camp. Critics of the government claimed that the appointment of Garibaldi's generals to high positions in the Italian army was simply a trick to separate them from Garibaldi while buying their support for the government. This criticism may have had some validity.

In Naples, most of Garibaldi's laws and reforms were rescinded by a newly appointed administration led by Luigi Farini. The land reform measures Garibaldi had proposed were tossed aside, his public works' contracts invalidated, his political appointments nullified. The social and educational reforms he had initiated were neglected. Soon, there were demonstrations and revolts in open defiance of the new government. Once again there was a serious threat to Italian unity; only this time, the threat came from within.

51

Garibaldi on Caprera: 1860–1861

GARIBALDI'S HEROICS during the Expedition of the Thousand
had forever enshrined him in the hearts and minds of the Italian
people. The bold venture had toppled a repressive regime and
helped create a unified nation whose boundaries extended from
the Alps to the western tip of Sicily. More importantly, the Italian
people had regained their national identity, which had remained
obscure for 1,500 years, since the fall of ancient Rome in 476 A.D.
And the man who had made it happen had retired to the solitude
of his farm on Caprera. It wasn't a proper ending for such a story.

Retirement to Caprera, in fact, actually increased Garibaldi's
fame and enhanced his image as a romantic figure. Journalists portrayed him as a legendary hero on a lonely island. He was likened
to the ancient Roman hero Cincinnatus, who was summoned from

his farm to assume the Dictatorship in a time of crisis and then, having resolved that crisis, relinquished his power and returned to his farm.

Caprera, however, rapidly grew less lonely, because Garibaldi's presence turned the island into a tourist attraction. After November 1860, it was constantly being visited by dignitaries, journalists, poets, and authors, as well as by ordinary sightseers. Some came in their private yachts; others arrived on the mailboat, which stopped at the nearby island of La Maddalena each Friday. Some of these visitors to Caprera in the early 1860s left vivid descriptions of Garibaldi. One commented that he looked "as happy as a school boy home for the holidays."[1] Another, upon seeing Garibaldi's simple lifestyle, described him as "the archetype of the common man."[2] Italian visitors recognized him as a great patriot and called him "*il padre d'Italia*"[3] (the Father of Italy). The U.S. ambassador to Italy, George Perkins Marsh, wrote that, "although Garibaldi is a solitary and private individual, he is at this moment, in and of himself, one of the great Powers of the world."[4] It was Marsh who first made the analogy between Garibaldi and Cincinnatus.

Garibaldi himself seemed to enjoy the notoriety. People no longer saw him as a pirate or someone with a price on his head. He was sought after by diplomatic envoys as well as fans and enthusiasts of every description. Many of these well-wishers wanted autographs or some souvenir of their visit to Caprera. An Englishwoman even managed to acquire his general's uniform. Garibaldi had given it to one of his hired hands, and when the woman found the man wearing it while digging potatoes, she promptly purchased it from him as a memento.[5]

In order to accommodate the many visitors, a hotel was soon

opened on nearby La Maddalena. From there, one could rent a boat for the crossing to Caprera or simply gaze across the narrow channel, hoping to get a glimpse of the great man working his farm. The list of visitors included Alexandre Dumas, Jesse White Mario, Baroness Maria von Schwartz, Sir Charles McGrigor, John McAdam, and Felix Morrand, all of whom later wrote about Garibaldi's life on the island.

Situated in the archipelago of Maddalena, Caprera lies between Sardinia and Corsica. It is about four miles long and three miles wide, with a rocky, indented shoreline and no natural harbor. Originally, the island was inhabited by a few shepherds and some wild goats, and it is from the latter that it derives its name. Caprera means "place of the goats." Much of the island consisted of barren rock, with patches of shrubs and rough bramble growing on the ledges and in the cracks of the rocks, the only source of drinking water being a spring located near the center of the island. It was on this barren, windswept island that GAribaldi had chosen to settle down and try his hand at farming.

In 1855, as mentioned earlier, he had been able to purchase half the island with money left to him by his brother Felice. The rest belonged to a grouchy Englishman named Collins, who quarreled with Garibaldi whenever the livestock wandered onto his half of the land. One of these quarrels had gotten so heated that Garibaldi challenged him to a duel. But cooler heads had prevailed, and the duel never took place. The two at last had reconciled and been able to live peacefully as neighbors. Years later, after Collins died, some of Garibaldi's English admirers were able to raise enough money to buy the Collins property and present it to Garibaldi as a gift—a gift he readily accepted.

So he now owned the entire island outright. He had built his house there years earlier, with the help of his son Menotti and several of his old companions-in-arms, living in tents during the construction. They'd used local granite and some wood shipped over from Nice. An expert stone mason had been brought in to supervise the job, as Garibaldi was not skilled in the trade. He had, thus, been relegated to carrying the stones to the construction site. Once the stone work was completed, the house was stuccoed over, and then whitewashed.

Garibaldi's white house, or *casa bianca*, as it came to be called, was a one-story structure with four rooms and a flat roof to catch the rain water. A separate little outhouse was constructed a few yards from the main house.

Garibaldi had been offered a large estate, a huge pension, and a princely title by King Victor Emmanuel. He and his family could have lived a life of leisure, pampered and catered to, like nobility. Instead, he chose the more difficult calling of farmer. He planted a large vegetable garden and, wherever he could find enough soil, grapevines and fruit trees. He dug wells and brought in a steam engine to pump water. Later, he built a windmill and a small observation tower.

In the beginning, food was not so plentiful; meals consisted mainly of fried local fish or roasted wild fowl. There were also milk and cheese, dried vegetables and figs. Flour, wine, and olive oil had to be brought over from the mainland. Over time, conditions improved. Food became more plentiful, and the size of his herds increased. By 1862, two years after his retirement, Garibaldi was listed as owning thirty head of cattle, a hundred goats, and a hundred sheep.[6]

As the farm became more productive, dining at Caprera became a main event. The entire household, including the hired

help, all sat at the same long table. Garibaldi believed that if someone was good enough to work for him, he was good enough to eat
with him.[7] Friends and dignitaries visited Caprera and dined with
him too, but received no special treatment. Most were astonished
to see hired help sitting at the table. The food was brought in on
large platters and served family-style. Garibaldi, as family patri-
arch, always sat at the head of the table. He served himself and
those seated next to him, and passed along the platters so that
other guests could serve themselves.

From all accounts, the food by then was excellent—pasta, fried
fish or roast meats, and an assortment of salads garnished with
herbs and served with olive oil. Wine appeared at every meal,
though Garibaldi himself always drank water or cold milk. A
choice of coffee and tea completed the repast. After dinner,
Garibaldi usually lit up a cigar and engaged in lively conversation
with his guests. Sometimes, people sang, with Garibaldi's daughter
Teresita providing piano accompaniment. Everyone present,
including Garibaldi himself, joined in the renditions of patriotic
songs. Teresita, who always livened up the place, would sometimes
dance with Garibaldi to the cheers of the guests. She had grown
into a beautiful girl, and at age sixteen she was engaged to marry
Major Stefano Canzio, one of the young officers of Garibaldi's Red
Shirts. King Victor Emmanuel was to send her diamonds as a wedding gift.

Garibaldi usually excused himself and retired to his room
around 10 p.m. That room contained a four-poster metal bed, a
few chairs, and a table covered with books and papers. On the
walls hung relics of various campaigns—guns, swords, and banners.
He also had pictures of his mother; his daughter Rosita, who had
died in infancy; and some of his officers who had been killed in bat-

tle. A clothesline containing a couple of red shirts, which he washed himself, hung across the room. Garibaldi usually slept for five hours, arising at 3 A.M. He spent most of the morning working on correspondence, often dictating letters. He had a number of personal secretaries, including Agostino Vecchi, Giuseppe Guerzoni, and Giovanni Basso. Vecchi had served under him during the Battle of Rome in 1849; Guerzoni and Basso had accompanied him on The Expedition of the Thousand.

Garibaldi received a great deal of mail. This included invitations from various towns in Italy, all eager to claim him as an honorary citizen, some, strangely enough, the same municipalities which had closed their gates to him during his retreat from Rome. There were also appeals for support from charitable foundations and from various nationalistic organizations. Manufacturers sent letters asking permission to use his name in advertisements. Activists solicited his opinion on new causes, such as disarmament, international arbitration, and women's rights. Foreign diplomats sent letters regarding international affairs.

About half of his correspondence, however, came from Englishwomen who looked upon him as a romantic hero in a far-away place. Apparently, distance gave him an aura of enchantment. These female admirers expressed their devotion to him and usually asked for a lock of his hair. As he couldn't accommodate all his admirers, he favored some with a handwritten note of appreciation for their devotion.[8] Included among these female devotees were Emma Roberts, to whom he had been engaged, the Baroness von Schwartz, the Duchess of Sutherland, Florence Nightingale, and the wife of British MP Charles Seeley.

Upon finishing with the correspondence, Garibaldi went out to work in the fields. He believed in the virtues of physical labor—

breaking stones, building walls, herding sheep, and tending his garden. Around the outside of his house he maintained a manicured bed of red carnations. He was also known to be fond of animals. Once, when a young lamb strayed from the fold, he went searching for it in the rain until nightfall, eventually returning home carrying the lamb in his arms.[9] His favorite animal, however, was Marsala, the white mare he had ridden across southern Italy during the Expedition of the Thousand.

While on Caprera, Garibaldi continued to maintain a keen interest in world affairs, especially the events of the American Civil War. He strongly supported the anti-slavery cause in the United States and favored the Northern side in the war. In 1861, not long after the outbreak of hostilities, the American press began praising Garibaldi for his role in the Risorgimento and hinting that he might now return to America. This helped fuel rumors that he would accept an invitation from President Lincoln to fight for the Union cause. For decades, Americans had been following Garibaldi's daring exploits, first in South America and then in Italy. Many were intrigued by the very thought of him in an American uniform, especially at a time when the Union army was reeling from its defeat by Confederate forces at the first Battle of Bull Run. President Lincoln was searching for a capable general who could lead the Union forces to a desperately needed victory, and some in his administration believed Garibaldi was that man. Hadn't he conquered the Kingdom of the Two Sicilies with a thousand volunteers?

The assignment for contacting Garibaldi was awarded to James W. Quiggle, the U.S. consul in Antwerp. On June 8, 1861, Quiggle wrote to Garibaldi, inviting him to take a command in the Union army. "If you do," he wrote, "the name of LaFayette will not surpass yours."[10]   In his letter, he also referred to Garibaldi as "the Washington of Italy." It was a flattering offer, but Garibaldi declined it, citing the need for his services in the continuing struggle for Italian unification. Nevertheless, the U.S. government remained eager to enlist Garibaldi in the Union cause. Secretary of State William Seward contacted Henry Sanford, the U.S. ambassador to Belgium, and directed him to travel personally to Caprera to secure Garibaldi's services.

Meanwhile, the New York Tribune had reported on August 11, 1861, that Garibaldi had agreed to serve in the Union army with the rank of Major General.[11] When the U.S. government would neither confirm nor deny the report, rumors persisted, and the public's interest in the matter increased.

In September 1861, Sanford traveled to Caprera to meet with Garibaldi in person. He carried a letter from King Victor Emmanuel granting Garibaldi permission to accept the U.S. government's offer. Garibaldi said that he would only accept it on two conditions: that he be appointed commander-in-chief of the Union army, and that he be given the power to abolish slavery. Sanford explained that this was impossible under the United States Constitution. But he did offer him the rank of major general and "an independent command of sufficient importance to be worthy of his abilities and fame." He urged him to accept the offer, if he felt that the Union cause was sufficiently worthy of his support. Garibaldi, however, refused to accept the offer, pointing out that Lincoln had not yet abolished slavery, and that the war was actually being fought over such issues as states' rights and trade protection.[12] He believed that these issues were of interest only to Americans, not the rest of the world. Under the circumstances, Sanford realized that he would be unable to secure Garibaldi's services, and he rescinded the offer.

A year later, Lincoln issued the Emancipation Proclamation, abolishing slavery in the Confederate states. Historians see the proclamation as a war measure aimed at gaining the support of four million freed blacks in these states. By freeing the slaves, Lincoln also hoped to gain the support of the European powers and thus lessen the danger of foreign intervention on the side of the Confederacy. In the Spring of 1865, after the North emerged victorious and the slaves were in fact freed in the rebellious states, a constitutional amendment was passed abolishing slavery throughout the United States. As it turned out, Garibaldi had passed up an opportunity to engage in another war of liberation, leading some historians to suggest that, if he had accepted Lincoln's offer, he would have been an even greater hero in the world's eyes today.

52

The Return of Garibaldi: Spring 1861

In February 1861, Victor Emmanuel assumed the title King of Italy over a realm more than five times larger than his original kingdom. He ruled more than 22 million people, of whom nine million had been given to him by Garibaldi in the former Kingdom of Naples.

His new subjects in the South were, however, causing trouble for the governor of Naples, Luigi Farini. Secret agents sent by the former king, Francis II, to organize revolts among the peasants had succeeded in stirring up a guerrilla movement against the authorities. Farini tried to suppress the uprisings by summary executions on a large scale. The policy only served to arouse more resentment against the new Italian government.

From the remoteness of Caprera, Garibaldi continued to monitor the situation on the Italian mainland. He was aware of the widespread discontent in the south, and he placed the blame for the unrest on the incompetence of the Farini administration. He was also critical of the Italian government for the unfair treatment meted out to his Red Shirts. Of the 43,000 men who had served under him during the liberation of southern Italy, less than four percent had been absorbed into the regular Italian army, the remainder were dismissed without recognition or compensation for their services. Garibaldi felt that he and his men had been betrayed by Cavour and the government, and he was determined to do something about it.

After the annexation of the newly liberated territories, parliamentary elections were held, and Garibaldi was elected as an MP from Naples. But he did not take his seat when the Italian parliament convened in Torino early in 1861, causing some to conclude that he preferred to be a voice in the wilderness. In April, however, he suddenly journeyed to Torino, his purpose shrouded in mystery. At that time the government was debating how to reorganize the army. The issue was whether or not the government should maintain a volunteer corps distinct from the regular army. Garibaldi was in favor of such a separate volunteer army; Cavour opposed the idea on the grounds that it was a scheme to maintain a private army for Garibaldi. He suspected that such a force would be used to wage war against foreign powers without the consent of the Italian government. It therefore appeared that he and Garibaldi were again headed on a collision course.

Garibaldi's arrival in Torino caused both excitement and apprehension. Though he refused to comment to the press, it soon became apparent that he had come to address parliament, and that the whole affair had been orchestrated for the purpose of enhancing the Garibaldi mystique. Tensions mounted as hundreds of red-shirted Garibaldini crammed into the public galleries of the parliament hall, buzzing with excitement, almost as though they were attending a reunion. In actuality, they had come from all parts of Italy to hear their invincible leader. On the floor of the chamber, MPs sat at their benches in nervous anticipation. The atmosphere was electric. Everyone awaited the arrival of their Cincinnatus.

Then, just as the commotion subsided, Garibaldi suddenly entered the chamber. He made his way to a seat at a bench on the extreme left, his blazing red shirt contrasting sharply with the black coats of the other MPs. The crowds in the public galleries gave him a tremendous ovation, rising to their feet and applauding for almost five minutes, ignoring all attempts to call them to order. They were joined in their applause by a group of MPs, led by Francesco Crispi, who rose in their places. The others remained seated in icy silence. When the applause finally diminished, Garibaldi rose to address the chamber.

After acknowledging the presence of various dignitaries, he spoke in favor of maintaining a separate volunteer army. He then turned to level an attack against Cavour for his devious political intrigues during the campaign to liberate the south. He accused Cavour of having provoked civil war when he sent the royal army south to block the further advance of the Red Shirts northward. Unfortunately for Cavour, the French government had recently made public some diplomatic correspondence revealing how Cavour had secretly obtained Napoleon III's permission for the Royal Sardinian Army to march south through the Papal States. Apparently, Napoleon had been duped into thinking that the Sardinians were doing so to frustrate the revolution as personified in Garibaldi. It even emerged that Cavour had instructed General

Manfredo Fanti, the commander of the Sardinian army, to use force if necessary, and that the Red Shirts might have to be "exterminated to the last man."[1] *This* was the type of backroom politician Garibaldi had come to denounce before Parliament.

Although the attack drew angry protests from the government benches, Garibaldi calmly continued with his speech, accusing Cavour of having planned to wage a war pitting brother against brother. This remark caused a loud uproar in the chamber. Cavour leaped to his feet, shouting, "It is not true!" and demanded that Garibaldi withdraw the accusation. Garibaldi stood his ground, waiting for the noise to subside. Pointing a finger at Cavour, he repeated the accusation: "You were planning to wage a fratricidal war!" "The effect was tremendous," wrote an observer, "all the deputies leaped from their seats shouting and gesticulating." Hell broke loose as a group of opposition MPs tried to rush Cavour. When Cavour's friends attempted to block their path, a wild melee broke out. What followed resembled a scene out of a Wild West movie, not the halls of parliament. There was punching and shoving, with tables being overturned and some of the MPs knocked to the floor. It took twenty minutes for the police to restore order in the chamber. Garibaldi remained calm throughout all the action, receiving congratulations from Crispi and his group. Meanwhile, Cavour's friends crowded around him to express their sympathies. Other MPs gathered in clusters to discuss the situation. Colonel John Dunne, an Englishman who had served under Garibaldi in Sicily and happened to be there, commented that there was little doubt that Cavour's government had treated the volunteers in a "beastly manner."[2] Apparently, many of the Red Shirts sitting in the gallery believed that Garibaldi's attack on Cavour was justified.

When the session resumed, Cavour, who was visibly shaken,

rose to speak. In a somewhat shaky voice, he said that he regretted the quarrel that had arisen between him and Garibaldi. He proceeded to explain why the proposal for the maintenance of a separate volunteer army was impractical. He was applauded by many of the MPs but by few spectators in the gallery. Cavour was followed at the podium by General Nino Bixio, who appealed for unity and asked everyone to treat the incident as though it had never occurred. His speech had a calming effect on the chamber.

Garibaldi addressed Parliament again. Many expected a reconciliatory speech, but he repeated his attack on Cavour and called once again for the establishment of a separate volunteer army. When he finished speaking, he left the chamber, followed by the Red Shirts, who poured out of the public galleries. They went into the streets, praising Garibaldi as they escorted him back to his hotel. However, Garibaldi had offended many MPs by refusing any attempt at reconciliation, and his proposal for a separate volunteer army was voted down in Parliament by a vote of 194 to 79, with 5 abstentions.[3]

A few days later, he was bitterly attacked in a letter written to the press by General Enrico Cialdini. In the letter, Cialdini accused Garibaldi of having ordered his men to receive the royal army with bullets.[4] Garibaldi replied by repudiating the charges and challenging Cialdini to a duel; but before the duel could take place, the king intervened. He invited Garibaldi, Cialdini, and Cavour to the palace and asked them to shake hands and be friends. They agreed to do so, and at least on the surface their parting was friendly. Evidence later showed that Cialdini's accusation was unfounded.

After his return to Caprera on May 1, Garibaldi received a very friendly letter from Cavour informing him of impending talks with the Hungarian revolutionary leader Lajos Kossuth. In a reply dated May 18, Garibaldi complimented Cavour on his "superior capacity and firm will to affect the good of the country."[5]

Nineteen days later, on June 6, Cavour died of a high fever. His family announced that he had received the sacrament of Extreme Unction from a local priest and had died with the "comforts of religion."[6] He was only fifty years old, and his supporters, who had no knowledge of Garibaldi's last letter to Cavour, claimed that his death was brought about by Garibaldi's vicious attack on him in Parliament.

King Victor Emmanuel visits the dying Cavour

In Torino, there was an official day of mourning; shops were closed and the streets virtually deserted. Parliament was suspended for three days. Among government officials, there was a sense of irreplaceable loss. Former Prime Minister Rattazzi called Cavour's death "a national disaster." General LaMarmora praised Cavour for his "extraordinary courage and intellectual gifts." The newspaper *L'Opinione* eulogized the deceased leader as a person whose "authority and prestige" had contributed much toward the success of the Risorgimento.

Vatican officials were infuriated over the fact that Cavour, a non-practicing Catholic, had received last rites and a Catholic burial. Church leaders denied the validity of the last rites given to a person who reportedly had not confessed or retracted "the evil he had done to the Church."[7] It had been he who, in 1860, ordered the invasion of the Papal States, which had resulted in the annihilation of the papal forces at Ancona. Father Giacomo da Poirino, the priest who had administered the last rites, was summoned to Rome, reprimanded by the pope, and suspended from his priestly duties. He subsequently died in obscurity.

In Berlin, prices on the stock exchange fell sharply on fears that Cavour's death might trigger another crisis in Italy. In Paris, Napoleon III had misgivings about a proposed plan to gradually withdraw French troops from Rome. In Britain, the reaction to Cavour's death was mixed. Prime Minister Palmerston acclaimed Cavour as "one of the most distinguished patriots who have adorned the history of any country." Sir James Hudson, British ambassador to Italy, described Cavour as "the warmest, most constant and most genial of friends." British publications mostly gave Cavour favorable treatment, describing him as "the most remarkable man of our generation" and "the foremost statesmen in Europe."

Not all Britishers shared these views about Cavour. The Catholic historian Lord Acton described Cavour's life as "a triumph of unscrupulous statesmanship." Catholic MPs in the British parliament denounced Cavour as "a man who had violated every law, human and divine," and Benjamin Disraeli, a future prime minister, considered him "utterly unscrupulous."[8]

In retrospect, it cannot be denied that Cavour's diplomatic wizardry contributed greatly to the success of the Risorgimento. However, his diplomatic double-dealings caused many rulers and statesmen to hold him in abhorrence. There were also various factions in Italy, namely the Garibaldini and the Mazzinians, who held Cavour in disdain. For the most part, they failed to recognize his ability as a political strategist and looked upon him as a conniving manipulator. Twentieth-century historians have come to acknowledge the importance of his role in the national movement, and today he is widely acclaimed as "the brains of Italian unification."

At the time of Cavour's death in 1861, only the region of Latium around Rome, and the Austrian provinces of Venetia and Tyrol, remained to be liberated and joined to the Kingdom of Italy. Italian government leaders realized that the nation was not strong enough to defeat Austria in a war. They also knew that any attempt to liberate Rome would be checked by French military intervention. For the time being, therefore, plans for Italian unification had to remain on hold.

Meanwhile, on Caprera, Garibaldi made no secret of his intention to liberate Rome and Venetia. Foreign agents spread rumors about preparations for another expedition, and there was speculation in the press about where Garibaldi would strike next. Adding to the intrigue, Garibaldi went to Torino in December 1861 for a private audience with the king, following which he traveled to Genoa, where he presided over a gathering of all the democratic nationalistic groups in Italy. Though it had no legal standing and had been convened at the behest of private individuals, it marked the first time that a political party convention had ever been held on Italian soil. Delegates gave speeches on important issues facing the nation and voted on resolutions urging government action on these matters.

Garibaldi then toured northern Italy, visiting Milan and several other cities in the Po Valley. Everywhere he was greeted with the greatest enthusiasm by the population, and in every town he gave a speech from the balcony of the town hall. He would shout out rhetorical questions, and the crowds would shout back the expected answers—a method of oratory later adopted by Benito Mussolini in imitation of him. (Mussolini also adopted the black shirt and the Fascist salute in imitation of the red shirt and the Garibaldi salute. Mussolini took the title of *Duce* as well—a name that the Red Shirts had used when referring to Garibaldi.)

Everywhere, Garibaldi called on the people to form rifle clubs, where they would meet on Sundays and practice shooting.[9] This would enable Italy to have a popular militia of trained riflemen to supplement the army in case of war. Thousands of men answered the call and formed such clubs. The rifles were supplied by the Garibaldi Rifle Fund, with the consent of the Italian government. These activities aroused concern among the political leaders of Europe, who sensed that he was dragging the Italian government toward an armed conflict with its neighbors, and thus endangering the peace of the continent.

Garibaldi journeyed to Lake Maggiore to visit Signora Cairoli, a widow whose five sons had fought with the Red Shirts. Four of them had been killed in battle. After paying his respects to her, he went on to address a number of meetings in some neighboring towns. On June 8, he appeared in Locarno, Switzerland, in response to an invitation from the working men of that city. Speaking before members of the various local trade unions, he described Switzerland as a "land of freedom" and thanked the Swiss for having granted him refuge after his retreat from the Austrians in the War of 1848.[10] Before returning to Caprera, he again visited Lake Maggiore, where this time he met with a government agent named Plezza. What the two discussed is uncertain, but it is believed that Plezza gave Garibaldi a vague promise of government support for some new undertaking. Afterwards, Garibaldi returned to Caprera; but the question now arose: How long would he remain there before embarking on another venture?

53

The March on Rome: Summer 1862

DURING SPRING 1862, THERE WAS MUCH SPECULATION in the European press over where Garibaldi would strike next--the Tyrol, Montenegro, Dalmatia, Greece? Leaders became alarmed as rumors circulated about possible nationalist revolutions in the Austrian Empire or the Balkans. During this time, Garibaldi remained quiet and said nothing. Then, on June 27, he suddenly departed by steamer for Sicily, saying only that he was "going into the unknown." Although the purpose of his mission was shrouded in secrecy, it apparently had the tacit approval of King Victor Emmanuel and the new prime minister, Urbano Rattazzi.

Sicily had seen considerable discontent since its liberation, and a movement was developing for that island's independence. This led some to believe that Garibaldi would use his popularity with the Sicilians to calm their anger. It was feasible, because many Sicilians believed that the new government had failed to carry out the reforms started during the Dictatorship. Now, the former Dictator was returning for the first time since his resignation. European leaders viewed the visit with a sense of apprehension.

Garibaldi's reception in Palermo was even more enthusiastic than the one he had received in Milan the previous summer. He was warmly welcomed by his old friend Giorgio Pallavicino, the newly appointed governor. Pallavicino, who had served under Garibaldi during the Dictatorship of 1860, escorted his former leader to the palace, where he was to stay as an honored guest. The Great Liberator had finally returned to the land that he freed from the tyranny of the Bourbons.

From Palermo, Garibaldi embarked on a tour of old battle-fields, recalling the glorious days of the Expedition of the Thousand. Everywhere he was greeted with shouts of "*Viva Garibaldi!*" For three weeks he traveled around the island, addressing cheering crowds and calling for the liberation of Rome. In a speech at Marsala, he aroused nationalistic fervor by denouncing Napoleon III of France as a "thief, robber, and usurper," and telling him to get out of Rome. The crowd shouted back: "Rome is ours!"[1] Garibaldi's purpose in coming to Sicily was finally beginning to emerge.

At the end of the tour, he attended a special Mass in Palermo's cathedral. The place was packed. The sermon was given by Fra Pantaleo, who had served as the Red Shirts' chaplain during the campaign to liberate southern Italy. His sermon focused on the liberation of Rome and; when it ended, he summoned Garibaldi to come to the front. He did, raised his hand toward the altar, and took the oath: "Rome or death."[2] Thereupon, the entire congregation echoed the oath throughout the church: "Rome or death."

By then, it was obvious to the world that he had come to gain Sicilian support for a march on Rome. His statements caused alarm in European capitals. In neighboring France, preparations got underway to stop him. Napoleon III, in a strongly worded statement, said that "a nation like France does not give way to the threats of a Garibaldi."[3] Once again, the threat of war loomed over the Eternal City.

But Garibaldi had by then come to believe that the entire island was ready to join with him in a march on Rome. In no time he had 3,000 volunteers, all of them caught up in the frenzied excitement of the moment. All the red flannel on the market was quickly bought up as volunteers flocked to his banner. The new recruits assembled at a camp outside Palermo, where they were issued guns and ammunition. Local officials made no attempt to stop them, even when the volunteers broke camp and began their march eastward across Sicily. Evidently, the Red Shirts had been guaranteed free passage across the island. Anyone barring their path was shown a mysterious document stamped with a large red seal and, as if like magic, permitted them to pass through unhindered.[4] Upon reaching Catania, Garibaldi purchased additional supplies, paying for them in cash, all the while proclaiming his loyalty to King Victor Emmanuel.

The king's involvement in this venture is in fact debatable. Tradition has it that Garibaldi set out on the mission with the approval of both the king and Prime Minister Rattazzi. The king even admitted that Garibaldi was carrying out his orders "to a certain extent."[5] The plan appears to have been quite simple: Garibaldi was to recruit a volunteer army in southern Italy and then march on Rome. He did not know that the Royal Italian

Army, with the expected approval of Napoleon III, was to invade the Papal States under the pretext of protecting the pope from the Red Shirts—a time-tested piece of chicanery. But Napoleon III would not be fooled a second time and refused to go along with the scheme. The king and Prime Minister Rattazzi were thus left to waddle in their own muck and, rather than risk war with France, they decided to sacrifice Garibaldi.

To distance himself, the king issued a proclamation stating that his government would not permit any individual, however eminent, to defy the law and conduct warlike operations against a foreign power. He said that anyone who formed a private army without royal authority was guilty of high treason. This warning would go unheeded. Garibaldi proceeded with his military preparations, believing that Victor Emmanuel did not mean what he said and that the Italian army would not attempt to stop him. His failure to appreciate his actual position would have disastrous consequences.

Despite the ominous warnings, Garibaldi moved ahead with his plan to march on Rome. Under the noses of the local officials, he was able to commandeer two ships in Catania harbor and embark with his men. They crossed the Strait without any interference. Once again he landed at Melito, and once again he had to encounter a royal garrison at Reggio, Calabria. But this time, he retreated into the mountains of Aspromonte, determined to avoid doing battle with the Royal Italian Army. This strategic decision illustrates the great difference between this campaign and the Expedition of the Thousand in 1860. Then, the Neapolitan army had lacked the will to fight against fellow Italians; this time it was the Red Shirts who refused to do battle with the Italian army. And this time, the local peasants did not supply the invading force with provisions, as they had done in 1860. Unaccustomed to living off the land, the volunteers suffered from hunger and fatigue. They were soon reduced to eating raw vegetables stolen from the fields, causing the local peasantry to look upon them as bandits![6]

Government leaders, at this moment, displayed a lack of backbone. In an attempt to redeem themselves, they dispatched a military force to stop Garibaldi, led by the one man that they felt could beat him— General Enrico Cialdini. He and the regular army had been waiting for a chance to measure themselves against Garibaldi and his Red Shirts. Their opportunity approached quickly. Landing at Reggio, Cialdini ordered his units "to pursue Garibaldi, attack him if he sought to escape, and destroy him if he accepted battle."[7]

On August 29, Garibaldi thus encountered the Italian army in the mountains of Aspromonte. From his position on a mountaintop, he was able to observe the royal troops with his telescope as they began their uphill advance. Neither he nor his men expected to be fired upon by the royal troops, and he had given orders not to shoot—he had no intention of firing on his own countrymen. What he hoped to do was to make friendly contact with the royal troops and win them over to his side. However, the royal troops opened fire as they advanced, not allowing him the opportunity. As he stood in front of his Red Shirts, urging them not to return the fire, he was hit twice—once in the right ankle, and once in the left thigh. Still standing, he again called on them not to fire. Most of his men obeyed the order, but those commanded by his son, Menotti, returned the fire. Seven royal army soldiers and five volunteers were killed during the brief exchange of gunfire.

Felled by his wounds, Garibaldi propped himself against a tree and lit a cigar. He ordered his men to release a captured royal army officer and send him back to his commander with an offer of a truce. This was done, and shortly afterwards, the commander himself came to Garibaldi. Addressing him with the utmost respect, he asked for his surrender. Garibaldi, not seeing himself as a rebel, agreed to do so and handed over his battle sword. He was carried down the mountainside on a stretcher to an Italian gunboat anchored in the port of Scilla. It was a long painful journey down, with only a short rest at a herdsman's hut. Garibaldi was then strapped up and hoisted aboard the gunboat by a rope. As he was being pulled up, he saluted General Cialdini, who was watching from the ship's bridge. Cialdini did not return the salute.[8] It was a clear indication that the hero had fallen from grace.

In his report, Cialdini referred to the action at Aspromonte as "a fierce combat," when in actuality, it had been a one-sided engagement that only lasted a few minutes. The wounded Garibaldi was taken to La Spezia and imprisoned in the fortress of Varignano. The volunteers who had served under him were interned in prisoner-of-war camps. Meanwhile, the victorious royal army troops were rewarded with seventy-six medals for bravery. Many were given promotions; the colonel in charge was made a general.

However, the rest of Italy was not proud of the episode. Demonstrations broke out in protest to the government's treatment of Garibaldi and his men. The actions of government leaders were scrutinized by the press, and Prime Minister Rattazzi was forced to resign under a barrage of criticism. At first, the government intended to put Garibaldi on trial for high treason, but it began to have second thoughts. Rattazzi, and other leaders, worried that a public trial might reveal embarrassing evidence about their collusion in the aborted expedition. It was being rumored that the Red Shirts were in possession of "a certain piece of paper" that could compromise the government.[9] Evidently, it could have been used to implicate the king as well, and the king dared not risk exposure. The whole matter was suddenly dropped and a royal pardon was granted Garibaldi and the prisoners of Aspromonte. The pardon, however, excluded those soldiers who had deserted from the Royal Italian Army to serve under him. They were sentenced to death.

Garibaldi was released from Varignano Prison on October 22, 1862, carried out on a special adjustable bed that had been sent by friends in England. From Varignano, he was taken to the house of a friend in La Spezia, where doctors could attend to him more easily. The wound he received had caused a compound fracture of the right ankle, and the various surgeons who had examined him could not locate the bullet because of the excessive swelling. Several considered amputating the foot, but the general consensus was that this would not be necessary. Finally, after much probing, the bullet was located and extracted from the wound by the famous Italian specialist Dr. Zanetti. It had been lodged there for eighty-seven days. Jessie White Mario, who assisted in the operation, later described how Garibaldi clenched her hand and bit on a cigar while the operation was being performed without anaesthesia. When Zanetti extracted the bullet and held it up to view, there was great jubilation. The bullet was given to Garibaldi's son Menotti, who refused to sell it to collectors, even though they offered to purchase it for large sums of money. The bloodstained sheets, however, were quickly gathered up and torn into strips for distribution as treasured mementos.[10]

Though the operation was successful, Garibaldi had to endure excruciating pain for a prolonged period of time, and, according to Jessie White Mario, he bore it with "angelic patience."[11] The news of his suffering spread throughout the world, arousing much sympathy for the wounded hero and his cause. There was a constant parade of visitors, some of whom succeeded in gaining entrance to the prison while others were turned away.

Many of the visitors were female admirers who came from other countries. The incomparable Jessie White Mario was already there to nurse him. Speranza von Schwartz offered to cook for him, only to be spurned by his family. Even his lawful wife, Giuseppina Raimondi, wrote a letter asking that she be permitted to come to him, but to no avail. Many ardent followers headed for Varignano to ask for a lock of his hair, their requests going unheeded. Get-well letters poured in from around the world, virtually all of them going unanswered. In actuality, Garibaldi's heroic struggle in the cause of Italian unity had made him one of the most famous public figures in the whole world. He was now more than a hero; he was a martyr.

Following a period of convalescence at La Spezia and then at Pisa, he returned to Caprera. His wound took a long time to heal, and for more than a year, he could only walk on crutches. During this time, he grew completely disillusioned with politicians and government. Though his sword was returned to him by the Italian government and an amnesty had been granted to his volunteers, Garibaldi remained at odds with the administration. He commented bitterly, "You only gave an amnesty to people you consider guilty; but that guilt lay only in having failed and having compromised the government."[12]

Some twentieth-century scholars have come to blame King Victor Emmanuel and the government for the failure of the expedition to liberate Rome in 1862. They cite the government's unwillingness to make any attempt to stop Garibaldi prior to

Aspromonte as proof of its complicity. Garibaldi apparently had *some* sort of authority from the government to recruit volunteers in Sicily for a march on Rome. Unlike his previous expedition to Sicily, this one had presented no difficulty to him in obtaining weapons and supplies, and the entire enterprise seems to have been well funded. Garibaldi had also paid for everything in ready cash. Could it be that he had in fact been financed by the Italian government? He certainly wasn't robbing banks anymore.

Some even give credence to the Mazzinian theory that King Victor Emmanuel and Prime Minister Rattazzi led Garibaldi on, encouraging him to invade the Papal States in 1862, and then, fearing war with France, betrayed him at the last moment! This theory might also explain why the royal troops tried to shoot him at Aspromonte even though he had ordered his men not to return fire. Could it be that someone in the government wanted him dead because he knew too much? If so, who *was* that someone? These lingering questions have gone unanswered for lack of sufficient evidence, and to this day the whole of the Aspromonte affair remains cloaked in mystery.

54

Garibaldi Visits England: 1864

IN SPRING 1864, ENGLAND WAS BUZZING with excitement—it was learned that the "Hero of Two Worlds" was coming there for a visit. Two years earlier, the tragedy of Aspromonte and Garibaldi's subsequent suffering had aroused so much sympathy in Britain that some of his English friends extended an open invitation to visit England. The visit would be sponsored by various groups and organizations sympathetic to the cause of Italian freedom. Garibaldi, who felt sufficiently recovered from his wound, decided to accept.

On March 19, he and his sons, Menotti and Ricciotti, boarded a British steamship that had been diverted to Caprera to pick them up. Also accompanying Garibaldi were his personal physician, Dr. Basile, and his two secretaries, Basso and Guerzoni. It would be

Garibaldi's fourth and final visit to England.

Although the British press described the visit as a "purely private one," some apprehension existed among government and religious leaders about a possible secret political motive. The Conservative leader Benjamin Disraeli was opposed to the visit, and some MPs considered Garibaldi a demagogue who went around stirring up revolts. Bishop Henry Manning, the leader of Britain's Roman Catholics, warned his flock that Garibaldi was a Socialist "stimulating and assisting the seditious revolutions" that at the time "threatened every government, absolute or constitutional, throughout Europe."[1] Queen Victoria herself strongly disapproved of Garibaldi's visit, though she made no attempt to prevent it.

Despite all the fuss, Garibaldi arrived in Southampton on April 3 to a reception that couldn't be dampened by either controversy or inclement weather. An enormous crowd stood on the quayside, some waving the Italian tricolor. As soon as the ship docked, the crowd surged onto the vessel, virtually trapping Garibaldi in his cabin. Not even in Italy had he been received so enthusiastically. Once he managed to get ashore, he addressed the crowd in English, thanking the British people for their support. It seemed as though the cheering never stopped, even after he left the docks to attend a civic reception given in his honor at the home of the lord mayor.

From Southampton, he was taken to Brook House Manor on the Isle of Wight, where he was to be the guest of the Liberal MP Charles Seely. Seely had always been an ardent admirer of Garibaldi and was one of the principal sponsors of the visit. He graciously welcomed his hero to Brook House and provided him with every comfort. Garibaldi remained there for eight days and, during that time, he was visited by prominent liberals like Lord

Garibaldi lands in Southampton

Garibaldi greeted by Alfred, Lord Tennyson at Farringford Hall
(from the Illustrated London News, *April 23, 1864)*

Shaftesbury and George Holyoake. The latter had been instrumental in collecting subscriptions to help finance Garibaldi's expedition against the King of Naples in 1860.[2]

During his stay, Garibaldi traveled to the nearby town of Freshwater to visit Alfred Tennyson, the poet laureate. Tennyson, who had praised Garibaldi in his poems, now greeted "the warrior of Caprera." It was a case of the author meeting his subject matter in the flesh. After exchanging pleasantries, the two sat down to enjoy a smoke while reciting Italian poetry. Before his departure, Garibaldi planted a memorial tree in Tennyson's garden. Tennyson was so impressed by Garibaldi's "divine simplicity" that he later commented: "What a noble human being. I expected to see a hero, and I was not disappointed."[3]

At the request of Admiral Seymour, Garibaldi visited the British naval base at Portsmouth, touring the harbor in an admiralty yacht as the whole naval squadron fired guns in salute. This kind of reception for a former pirate was highly unusual, especially in England. In fact, the last time that an ex-pirate had received such a tribute had occurred in 1588, when Sir Francis Drake returned home after defeating the Spanish Armada.

On April 11, Garibaldi and his entourage left Southampton for London on a special train. Crowds of people lined the route, waving at their hero as he rode by. At London Station, a military band played the "Garibaldi Hymn" nonstop as he stepped off the train to tumultuous cheering. Numerous speeches followed, all of which welcomed the conquering hero, and when they were finished, Garibaldi was hustled to a waiting carriage. His arrival at Southampton had brought a tidal wave of admirers. What followed next would bring an avalanche!

An estimated half-million Londoners lined the streets to get a glimpse of the "Hero of Two Worlds." No other visitor had ever received such a triumphant welcome. The carriage took six hours to make the five-mile trip from the train station to Stafford House, where Garibaldi had been invited to stay. The police were unable to hold back the vast crowd that surged around the carriage, often bringing it to a halt. It seemed as if every Englishman and woman yearned to see the Italian Robin Hood. The pressure of the crowds against the sides of the coach was so great that the carriage sustained structural damage, causing the doors to fall off their hinges. After struggling to the West End of London, the battered carriage finally reached Stafford House. Garibaldi calmly emerged from the wreck and stepped into "a circle of fair ladies and great statesmen," as the vehicle in which he had come literally fell to pieces in the driveway.[4]

At Stafford House, Garibaldi was greeted by the Duke and Duchess of Sutherland, two of his greatest admirers. That evening, the Sutherlands hosted a gala dinner party in his honor. In attendance were the prime minister, Lord Palmerston, and a host of other titled aristocrats. Throughout the evening, a military band played music for their listening enjoyment. After dinner, the magnificent salons of Stafford House, including the art gallery, were thrown open to the guests. The duchess herself took guests on a tour of the house, even showing them her boudoir. There, to the astonishment of the other guests, Garibaldi daringly lit up a cigar without incurring any objection from the duchess.[5] This incident, when recounted, raised eyebrows all over London—even in Buckingham Palace! Aside from that gaffe, Garibaldi carefully maintained his posture as a modest and courteous guest of honor.

As it turned out, the dinner party at Stafford House was one of the most memorable events of Garibaldi's visit to England. His hosts went to extravagant lengths to put on the lavish party that so impressed him. On earlier visits to England, he had been bored by the long dinner parties at Emma Roberts' house, and he had subsequently broken off their engagement. This time, however, he thoroughly enjoyed playing the hero's role, even if it was under the scrutinizing eyes of the elite upper class. At least on the surface, it appeared as though the zealous revolutionary had won the respect and admiration of the aristocracy.

All this admiration and support caused apprehension among Garibaldi's fellow revolutionaries, especially Giuseppe Mazzini and Alexander Herzen. They were concerned that Garibaldi would fall under the spell of the ruling establishment and thus jeopardize any of his future attempts to incite revolts in other countries. A struggle ensued in which the revolutionaries and the aristocracy both attempted to use Garibaldi's visit to suit their own purposes. Aristocrats like the Duke of Sutherland and Lord Shaftesbury wished to introduce him to London society by honoring him at banquets and receptions in London; the revolutionaries wanted him to make radical speeches at mass demonstrations in northern Britain. Garibaldi himself was willing to deal with both groups but refused to be controlled by either.

For the next two weeks, London was delirious with excitement as the Garibaldi craze swept the city. "Garibaldi biscuits" were sold by vendors, and blouses called "Garibaldies" were a hot item. Shops even advertised a Garibaldi perfume, which was supposed to make you "irresistible."[6] Everyone wanted to cash in on the craze. Continuing on his busy schedule, Garibaldi visited the House of Lords, where he was received with the utmost respect. He made a brief visit to the boy's school at Eton, where he was greeted enthusiastically by the faculty and the entire student body. He was taken to see the opera and cheered by the audience. He had a private talk with Lord Palmerston that lasted over an hour. He dined with chancellor of the exchequer, William Gladstone, and lunched with the foreign minister, Lord James Russell, both of whom advised him not to undertake any venture to liberate Rome or Venice. He even met with the Prince of Wales (the future King Edward VII) despite the queen's strong disapproval. Later, in a letter to the queen, the prince commented that he was very much impressed with Garibaldi and described him as having a "dignified and noble appearance."[7]

The women who met Garibaldi seemed to be dazzled by him. When Florence Nightingale was introduced to him, she "besought him to visit her incognito."[8] Later, she was to write to him on Caprera. The Duchess of Sutherland was so infatuated with him that she sought to accompany him around London, even suggesting that he visit Windsor Castle. Later, she too carried on an intimate correspondence with him. Even the wife of MP Charles Seely fell in love with Garibaldi and wrote him passionate love letters, letters which she dared not let her husband read.

Despite all the adulation, some prominent people disapproved of Garibaldi's visit. Conservative leader Benjamin Disraeli refused all invitations to meet "such a character." Queen Victoria expressed displeasure about the whole matter, declaring that she was "half ashamed of being the head of a nation capable of such follies."[9] The Queen was also critical of the reception given to Garibaldi by her aristocratic friends, especially the Duchess of Sutherland. In her diary, the Queen described the duchess as "foolish" and referred to the cheering crowd as "the lowest riffraff!"[10] From across the Channel, French Emperor Napoleon III angrily protested to the British government about the ostentatious reception given to that "pardoned rebel."[11] In Italy, the government was so taken aback by Garibaldi's reception in England that it cancelled plans for Prince Umberto's forthcoming visit to that country, concerned that the prince's visit would seem anticlimatic.

There was also criticism from the other end of the political spectrum. Karl Marx, the author of *The Communist Manifesto*, described Garibaldi's visit as "a miserable spectacle of imbecility."[12] Friedrich Engels, a close associate of Marx, commented that "this year, April Fools' Day had been extended to cover the whole month."[13] Sir Henry Elliot, the British ambassador to Italy, observed, "The effect of a red rag on a bull has long been known, but the whole British Nation going mad at the sight of a red shirt has even astonished the Italians."[14]

Through all this, Garibaldi played the role of Legendary Hero to perfection. His dignified appearance, and his courteous unassuming manner, put those in his presence at ease. He conversed in a quiet and gentle tone of voice, and seldom spoke about himself. All of this did much to enhance his image among the British and gain their support for the cause of Italian unity. Wherever possible, Garibaldi thanked his hosts for their hospitality. He shook hands, kissed ladies, signed autographs. He posed for portraits, sculptures, and photographs. He even drank beer with workers at a brewery. Thus, his cult drew followers—from the aristocratic ladies who idolized him, to the servants at Stafford House who collected bottles of soapsuds from his washbasin as souvenirs.

But Garibaldi's essential distaste for the artificiality of pomp and ceremony finally surfaced. He shocked his aristocratic hosts by meeting with British trade union leaders. He even had the audacity to attend a trade union rally at the Crystal Palace in Sydenham, some four miles south of London. The great hall was filled to capacity with 30,000 supporters calling for a unified Italy and an independent Poland. Addressing the rally, Garibaldi pledged to continue the struggle for Italian unification and Polish independence. He urged the British people to help him in this struggle.

On April 17, he went to a private dinner attended by prominent revolutionaries, including Mazzini and Alexander Herzen. In a speech, he referred to Mazzini as his "first teacher," and he praised Herzen for his heroic struggle against Russian Czarist tyranny.[15] Afterwards, he visited the homes of two exiled French revolutionaries— Alexandre Ledru-Rollin and Louis Blanc.

These appearances alarmed some European leaders who already suspected that his visit to England was cloaking a secret agenda. A series of diplomatic protests to the British government prompted Prime Minister Palmerston to inquire into these meetings. When Palmerston asked Garibaldi his motive for meeting Mazzini, the latter replied that, if he had found Mazzini in prosperity, he would not have visited him, but that, having found him in adversity, he could not throw him aside.[16] The reply seemed to satisfy Palmerston.

The next few days were busy ones for Garibaldi—one reception after another, and everywhere he was feted as if he were royalty. At the Guildhall, the lord mayor conferred upon him the honor of the Freedom of the City of London. At the Reform Club, Lord Ebury referred to him in a speech as "the instrument of God."[17] At the upscale Fishmongers' Hall, Garibaldi banqueted with a glittering assembly of London socialites. After dinner, he shook hands with literally hundreds of guests until he could no longer stand on his feet. Thereafter, he continued to greet them while seated. One of the guests was the very Maria Ouseley who had been romantically linked with him in Montevideo in the flirtation back then that aroused the jealous wrath of Anita. Lady Ouseley had come to the banquet to see her hero—and had come unescorted.[18] The former lovebirds lingered about together until the party ended.

Meanwhile, British Radicals like Joseph Cowen and John McAdam were eagerly trying to arrange for him to speak at rallies in industrial centers. They disliked the way he had been fenced in and monopolized by the London aristocracy. In order to neutralize that influence, they planned to have Garibaldi visit industrial towns across the country, hoping to thus convert his visit into a popular demonstration against the Conservative establishment. Garibaldi received invitations to visit some fifty British cities, but despite his acceptances, none of those venues were destined to receive him.

Queen Victoria was annoyed at the uncontrolled exuberance exhibited for Garibaldi, and Prime Minister Palmerston was concerned about Garibaldi's relationship with the exiled revolutionary radicals. The visit, which had been billed initially as a purely private one, was becoming a very public one indeed, and both the queen and her first minister were shocked by the latest turn of events. The official response was to judge these further appearances as "an anticlimax and a source of permanent political anxiety."[19] Palmerston determined that Garibaldi's visit should be terminated. The government promptly announced that Garibaldi was cancelling his plans to visit the provinces, and that he would be leaving England for Caprera, on the grounds that the strain of the tour was proving too much for his health.[20] This fabrication failed to convince anyone, especially Garibaldi's personal physician, Dr. Basile.

William Gladstone was given the task of politely informing Garibaldi that his presence was no longer desired. It was not a pleasant assignment—but Gladstone was in fact among those in government who believed Garibaldi had overstayed his visit. With the utmost discretion, he outlined his government's position. Garibaldi got the message; he replied that he would not stay in England as an unwelcome guest, and made preparations to sail for Caprera.

The news of Garibaldi's premature departure stunned the British public. Mazzini and his British friends tried to organize a campaign of protest and accused the British government of forcing Garibaldi to leave England in order to please Napoleon III of France. There was a protest demonstration in London against the expulsion, but it was broken up by the police. Meanwhile, Garibaldi's aristocratic admirers organized a fund to provide him with money, supposedly as a tribute to his achievements. The Duke of Sutherland and Charles Seely each contributed two hundred pounds; Palmerston added a hundred.[21] As the money poured in, the radicals began calling it a bribe; others suggested it was conscience money. Garibaldi in any event refused to accept the gift, and all the money reverted to the donors, save the organizers' expenses.

Before leaving England, Garibaldi kept one last engagement— a visit to his old comrade-in-arms Colonel John Peard, who had fought under him in 1860 during the Expedition of the Thousand. Accompanied by the Duke and Duchess of Sutherland, he found Peard in his home at Penquite in Cornwell. The two spent several hours reminiscing. After a sad farewell on April 28, Garibaldi sailed for Caprera on the Duke of Sutherland's yacht, thus ending his extraordinary visit to Victorian England.

55

Venetia Joins Italy: 1866

THE BRITISH GOVERNMENT REMAINED UNAWARE that Garibaldi was actually quite eager to return to Italy. Toward the end of his visit, he had received a secret message from Victor Emmanuel mentioning something about a forthcoming war of liberation against Austria. The king knew that Garibaldi yearned to command an expedition against Austria—and what better way to draw him away from friends in England?

Victor Emmanuel had another motive for coaxing Garibaldi back. He was a constitutional monarch and, as such, had limited power. He hungered for the power to make policy decisions without having to consult his minsters or parliament. In the past, he had clashed with Cavour over the extent of the sovereign's autonomy, and since Cavour's death, he had dismissed several prime ministers without referring the matter to parliament. These moves could be construed as an attempt to bypass parliament and strengthen the absolute power of the monarchy.

His Majesty had at this juncture contrived a scheme for extending his power beyond the boundaries of Italy—and all without the knowledge of parliament or his ministers. Now, he needed someone capable of carrying out his plan.

In the past, he had discreetly engaged Garibaldi to partake in some hazardous military undertakings. He knew that Garibaldi was a loyal subject who would readily take responsibility for a mission and expect nothing in return. Whenever a mission failed, the king merely disavowed him, as was the case after the engagement at Aspromonte. When Garibaldi was successful, as he had been in the Expedition of the Thousand, the king was cheerfully there to reap the benefits. Now he saw yet another opportunity to use Garibaldi for the benefit of the crown.

He made contact with Garibaldi on Caprera through his shadowy emissary, Colonel Porcelli, who came bearing a secret message, the contents of which still remain unknown. Shortly afterwards, Garibaldi and his lieutenants were summoned to a meeting on the island of Ischia, off the coast of Naples, its purpose shrouded in secrecy. The press reported that he had gone there to take the hot baths for his arthritis.

Although details about the meeting are skimpy, it appears Garibaldi and the others were asked to consider a plan for invading the Balkans and acquiring a throne for Victor Emmanuel's second son, the Duke of Aosta. Understandably, there was disagreement among those present over the justification for such a mission. The scheme would serve the self-interests of the House of Savoy rather than those of Italy, and a heated debate that ensued over the feasibility of the controversial venture prevented the group from reaching a decision.

When details of the meeting were leaked to the press, the king quickly abandoned the project, fearful of being implicated in yet another revolutionary plot. Before the group dispersed, Colonel Porcelli accused Garibaldi's secretary, Giuseppe Guerzoni, of being the source of the leak. The two fought a duel, and Guerzoni shot Porcelli. In doing so, he had defended both his own personal honor and the honor of his leader, Giuseppe Garibaldi.

For the next year and a half, Garibaldi remained on Caprera and worked his farm. It was a struggle to scratch a living out of that rocky, windswept island. Nevertheless, he managed to earn a modest income from the sale of livestock, and his farm had long since produced enough food for his family. He was also presented with a yacht as a gift from his admirers in England. It came in handy for sailing back and forth to La Maddalena and more distant points on the Italian mainland. Later, when he could no longer afford its upkeep, Garibaldi sold the yacht to raise money for his family.

The year 1865 was rather uneventful for Garibaldi. He had his memories and mementos to remind him of past days of glory, but his life lacked a sense of current fulfillment. Eighty percent of all Italian territory had been unified under the House of Savoy, but two major cities had not yet been liberated. Rome was still under papal control, and Venice, with its hinterland extending to the Alps, remained part of the Austrian Empire. In 1864, the Italian government had signed a treaty with Napoleon III under which France agreed to withdraw its troops from Rome in return for Italy's guarantee to respect the frontiers of the papal domains. The Italian government had also agreed to move the capital from Torino to Florence, in order to demonstrate that it had no design on making Rome its capital. To the dismay of Italian nationalists, it began to appear as though the government was perfectly satisfied with the existing frontiers.

Then, suddenly, in Spring 1866, things began to happen. Austria was faced with a challenge from Prussia for the leadership of the German Confederation of States. Otto von Bismarck, the Prussian chancellor, wanted to establish a unified German nation with Prussia as its dominant force. To do so, he realized that Austria would have to be displaced from its position of leadership. War between the two leading German states now seemed inevitable, and in preparation for the upcoming conflict, Bismarck offered to form an alliance with the Kingdom of Italy, promising Venetia in return for Italian assistance in any war with Austria. The Italian government gladly accepted the offer, and an Italian–Prussian Alliance was ratified in April 1866.

The opportunity to liberate Venetia had finally come. King Victor Emmanuel now decided to use Garibaldi again, this time in a war against Austria. He dispatched General Fabrizi to Caprera to offer Garibaldi command of a volunteer army of 35,000 men. Garibaldi, who had been at odds with the government since the encounter at Aspromonte, accepted Fabrizi's offer, commenting: "I forgive wrongs quickly." [1] Wasting no time, the pair sailed together for the mainland that same day, June 10.

Victor Emmanuel's original plan called for Garibaldi to attack the Austrians in the Balkans. Garibaldi was to cross the Adriatic and seize the Dalmatian coast, forcing the Austrians to divert part of their army away from northern Italy. This would facilitate the liberation of Venetia by the Royal Italian Army. However, when hostilities began, the plan was suddenly scrapped, and Garibaldi was sent instead to the Tyrol, near the Alps. He was given command of 10,000 volunteers near Lake Garda and ordered to advance northward into Austrian-held territory. His army quickly grew in numbers as he was joined by many of his former comrades-in-arms. "Be eagles," he told his troops as they advanced northward, capturing a number of important mountain heights.[2] Monte Suello, Caffaro, Forte Ampolla, and Bezzecca all fell to them as they routed an Austrian force of 8,000—an impressive string of victories.

As it turned out, these were the only Italian successes in the entire campaign. The regular Italian army was routed by the Austrians at the Second Battle of Custozza, while the Italian fleet under Admiral Persano was defeated by the Austrian navy off the Dalmatian coast. The outcome of the war was decided at the Battle of Koniggratz in Bohemia, where the Prussians won a decisive victory, enabling them to advance on Vienna and causing the Austrian government to sue for peace.

Before he could advance deeper into Tyrol, Garibaldi received the news that the war was over, and that a treaty was being drawn up. The war had lasted a mere seven weeks, hence the name-- the Seven Weeks War. Prussia had achieved its goal—the leadership of a unified Greater Germany. In his peace terms, Bismarck was lenient with Austria, hoping to preserve her as a future ally in central Europe. Venetia was to be ceded to the Kingdom of Italy, but Austria was to retain Tyrol. The news of the peace terms aroused indignation throughout Italy. The Italians had hoped to liberate *both* Venetia and Tyrol but had to settle for only the former. The Italian government, realizing that Italy could not continue alone in the war against Austria, reluctantly decided to accept the peace terms.

On August 25, Garibaldi received orders to withdraw from

Tyrol; he replied in a one-word telegram to General La Marmora: "*Obbedisco*" (I obey).[3] Evidently this time, he had no intention of continuing the war on his own as he had in 1848, when Charles Albert surrendered to the Austrians. The order to withdraw had so infuriated the Garibaldini that some of them broke their swords or shattered their bayonets in protest.[4] Many believed that they had fought the war in vain.

Venetia was ceded to Italy on October 19, 1866, and a plebiscite was held there to legitimize the cession, in which 647,246 residents cast ballots for union with Italy while only 69 voted against it.* South Tyrol (Trentino-Alto Adige) remained Austrian territory until the end of World War I, when it was finally joined to Italy after three years of bitter fighting and 600,000 casualties.

When Garibaldi visited Venice on February 26, 1867, the entire city turned out to greet him. It was his first time in Venice, and people filled the streets as well as all the boats on the canals in order to glimpse the legendary hero. Not even in Naples had he received such a welcome. In St. Mark's Square, the crowds pressed around him so closely that some officials feared he would be crushed to death. In a rousing speech from the balcony of the Doges' Palace, he told the Venetians that Rome must be liberated, because "Without Rome, Italy cannot be!"[5] The vast crowd responded by echoing the same words: "Without Rome, Italy cannot be!"

---

* These vote totals are given in Jasper Ridley's *Garibaldi*, p. 570.

56

The Defeat at Mentana: 1867

IN THE SUMMER OF 1867, tensions increased between Garibaldi and the Catholic Church as he accused the papacy of being an obstacle to Italian unification. In a speech at the International Congress of Peace held at Geneva in September 1867, he offered a motion calling for the abolition of the papacy and the adoption of a theology based on truth and reason. He also called for an end to wars and for the settlement of international disputes through a congress of democratic nations, an organization similar to today's United Nations.[1] The motion was rejected because many in the congress considered his ideas on religion more radical than those of Martin Luther or John Calvin, and his proposal for an international body to settle world disputes was apparently way ahead of its time.

Pope Pius IX

In Rome, the Church had toughened its stance against Garibaldi and any form of radical change. Pope Pius IX issued an encyclical, *Quanta Cura* (Condemning Current Errors), in which he condemned all beliefs and teachings averse to Catholic Church dogma. The pope specifically singled out Naturalism, Communism, and Socialism as ideologies that attempted to subvert the role of religion in the conduct of human society. These ideologies, in his view, used science or civil law as the basis from which domestic society derived the whole principle of its existence. They treated religion as a nonentity. The pope also rejected such liberal tenets as religious tolerance and freedom of conscience and the press. He asserted that such freedoms would facilitate attacks on religion and thus jeopardize the Church's role in saving men's souls.[2] In short, the encyclical generally condemned the liberal tendencies of the time. It aroused great indignation among Italian liberals, prompting Francesco Crispi to declare, "Christianity must purge itself of the vices of the Church of Rome, or it is doomed to perish."[3]

The situation grew more tense as the Vatican commissioned the formation of the Antibes Legion, a volunteer unit created to protect the papal territory after the withdrawal of French troops. Many of its officers, including the commander, were veterans of the French army. Even more ominous, reports in the press revealed that another French expeditionary force was preparing to move on Rome to protect the pope, should the need arise. Once again, war jitters gripped the population of central Italy.

By the autumn of 1867, it was no secret that Garibaldi was planning an invasion of the papal territory by an army of volunteers. The degree of government complicity in this clandestine operation is hard to establish, but there is no doubt about the involvement of Prime Minister Rattazzi. It appears that he had secretly encouraged Garibaldi to march on Rome and then had second thoughts on the matter. He had Garibaldi arrested instead at Sinalunga, near the frontier of the papal territory. Garibaldi was packed off to Caprera under heavy guard and ordered not to leave. The waters around the island were patrolled by gunboats of the Royal Italian Navy, and the nearby island of La Maddalena was garrisoned by a detachment of royal troops, all with instructions to prevent a crippled old man from leaving his abode. Garibaldi had become a prisoner on his private island.

This did not prevent the Garibaldini on the mainland from mobilizing near the borders of the papal territory. Led by Menotti Garibaldi, Giovanni Acerbi, and Giovanni Nicotera, they crossed that frontier on September 28 and engaged the papal forces in three sectors. All three commanders lacked military ability, however, and the fragmentation of their offensive caused a series of setbacks. Had they consolidated their forces and attacked in mass, they probably would have won a major victory and demoralized the enemy. As it turned out, the outnumbered papal troops fought well and were able to maintain their self-confidence, which was soon bolstered by the arrival at Civitavecchia of another French expeditionary force.

While world attention was focused on these developments in the papal territory, Garibaldi made a daring escape from Caprera. On October 12, a small fishing boat piloted by Stefano Canzio ran the naval blockade to neighboring La Maddalena, where he contacted Mrs. Collins. The widow had been residing there since her husband's death. Canzio left word with her that he would rendevous with Garibaldi five days later at Prandinga, on the northwest coast of Sardinia. Mrs. Collins relayed the message to Garibaldi through his daughter, Teresita. All Garibaldi had to do was get himself to Prandinga.

Canzio later described how Garibaldi, leaving a friend to impersonate him walking around on crutches, slipped through the blockade in a small duck-hunting boat. Under cover of a thick mist, Garibaldi rowed the craft across the narrow channel to La Maddalena, having wrapped rags around the oars to muffle the sound as he paddled. He passed so close to one of the gunboats during the crossing that he could hear the sailors talking on board.

Landing on Mrs. Collins' property, he concealed his boat and remained at her house overnight. He departed the next evening accompanied by two old friends, Susini and Basso. In the darkness, they rode the three miles on horseback across La Maddalena to the little port of Cala Francese. There, they set sail for Sardinia on a fishing boat belonging to a Captain Cuneo (not to be confused with Giovanni Cuneo). Shortly after putting out to sea, the vessel was stopped by a naval patrol boat. Captain Cuneo told the Italian naval officers that he and his crew were on a fishing expedition, and he was granted permission to continue. To avoid suspicion, Cuneo slowly piloted his boat off the islands of the Maddalena archipelago, making it appear he was fishing in those waters. Then, he suddenly turned south and headed for the east coast of Sardinia.

Six hours later, they landed on a desolate beach and spent the night huddled in a cave. The following morning, they obtained horses from a local rancher and rode into Sardinia's forbidding interior. They made their way across the bandit-infested highlands of Gallura and the arid wastes of Terra Nuova, a region virtually uninhabited at the time. Seldom stopping to rest, Garibaldi and his two companions took seventeen hours to reach the western coast of the island, where they met Canzio near the little port of Prandinga. It was a joyous encounter, with everyone present expressing astonishment at Garibaldi's strength and endurance. Meanwhile, the government remained unaware that he had left Caprera. So convincing was the performance of his impersonator that its agents believed Garibaldi was still on his farm.

After a tasty dinner of fried fish, Garibaldi and his companions sailed with Canzio for the Italian mainland—a dangerous crossing because those waters were constantly patrolled by the Italian navy.

Proceeding with caution, Canzio avoided detection by the naval patrol: He knew that, if they were caught, they would be interned and the boat confiscated. Skirting the islands of Montecristo and Elba, they finally reached the small fishing port of Vado on the Tuscan coast, where they commandeered two carriages for the sixty-mile journey to Florence. Garibaldi knew that if he could get there, his friends in parliament would openly support his efforts to liberate the papal territory. Along the way, they were stopped by police conducting a routine road check. Garibaldi, who had his hair dyed black, was not recognized when he gave his name as Joseph Pane, and they were not detained by the police. In fact, the police weren't even aware that he was in Tuscany. By the time news of Garibaldi's escape made the headlines, he was already in the house of a friend in Florence—Francesco Crispi, who was now an MP in the new Italian parliament.[4]

By then, Napoleon III suspected that the Italian government was involved in a scheme to annex the papal territory, and he therefore dispatched the French expeditionary force under General de Failly to the defense of Rome. King Victor Emmanuel, hoping to avoid conflict with the French and trying to cover up his complicity in the matter, disavowed the Garibaldini. At that juncture, he had disavowed them more often than St. Peter had denied Jesus! He placed the blame for the whole matter on a "revolutionary political faction" that had no authorization for such an incursion.[5] Evidently, Prime Minister Rattazzi had let matters go too far, making it impossible to stop the Garibaldini without exposing his own connivance. Rattazzi resigned, remarking that he preferred war against France than against Garibaldi.[6] Sir Henry Elliot, the British ambassador, concluded that the Italian government had shown "a lack of courage in dealing with these schemes" and that "they had not yet discovered the way to meddle with pitch and still keep their fingers clean."[7]

Protest demonstrations against French military intervention were held in Florence and other Italian cities, and Crispi issued a call for volunteers to join Garibaldi in his attempt to liberate Rome. On October 22, Garibaldi addressed a large crowd in front of Crispi's house before joining his men at the papal frontier. On his way, he learned that volunteers fighting under Acerbi and Menotti had linked up near Monte Rotondo, only twelve miles from Rome. He joined them there two days later. He had not been in that area since his retreat from Rome in July 1849.

Once again in command of the Red Shirts, Garibaldi led an attack against the papal garrison at Monte Rotondo, taking the place by storm and capturing three hundred prisoners. He ordered them fed with the only rations available while his own men went hungry. After the prisoners had finished eating, they shouted "Long live Garibaldi."[8] Despite the adulation, Garibaldi was disappointed that he was not being joined by any of the local population. People simply were unprepared to accept the secular rule of the House of Savoy. An insurrection in Rome was suppressed by the Antibes Legion, following some desperate fighting in the Trastevere district. Two notable casualties of the engagement were Enrico and Giovanni Cairoli, whom Garibaldi had sent ahead to support the Roman insurgents but were ambushed by papal troops near the Tiber River. Enrico died in the fighting; Giovanni died later of the wounds he had received. Their deaths brought to four the number of Cairoli brothers who had died for the cause of Italian freedom.

The total strength of Garibaldi's forces in the papal territory stood at about 8,000 men, of whom 6,529 were concentrated around Monte Rotondo.* But low morale contributed to an increasing number of desertions as Garibaldi futilely awaited an enemy attack. On October 28, he learned that the Royal Italian Army had invaded the papal territory on the pretext of maintaining order. King Victor Emmanuel had informed the French ambassador in Florence that he intended to attack the Garibaldini and "massacre them so that not one would be left."[9] Napoleon III would have no part of it and sent the king an ultimatum demanding that he withdraw his troops. The king agreed to do so. Garibaldi resented the attempted intrusion by the Royal army and issued a proclamation on November 1 that read, "I alone am the Roman General with plenary powers from the only legally elected government of the Roman Republic, and I have a right to maintain an army in this territory under my jurisdiction."[10] Garibaldi then marched on Rome.

When the Garibaldini approached Tivoli, they were engaged by 9,000 papal troops under the command of General Hermann Kanzler. Kanzler's troops attacked Garibaldi's right flank, causing his men to take up defensive positions around the town of Mentana. As the papal troops advanced, Garibaldi attempted to rally his men by firing his only two cannon at the enemy. He loaded and fired the cannon himself, and the cannonade apparently achieved its purpose. Through sheer determination, the Garibaldini drove back the attack and appeared to be on the verge of victory. Only the timely arrival of French troops turned the tide of battle in favor of the Papalists. Armed with their new *chassepot* rifles, the French opened a deadly fire that mowed down the charging Red Shirts. The *chassepot* rifle could fire ten times a minute and

---

* For these figures, see Jasper Ridley's *Garibaldi*, p. 587.

had a range twice that of the outdated weapons available to the Garibaldini. Realizing they had no chance against this new weapon, the Garibaldini broke and retreated in disorder. The officers tried to rally the fleeing Red Shirts, but their heroism was not enough. In a last desperate effort, Garibaldi himself rushed to the forefront, waving his sword. He was prepared to charge into the advancing enemy—and almost certain death. He was stopped by Canzio, who seized his horse's reins and shouted: "Who do you want to die for, General? Who *for?*"[11] Canzio then led him away to safety.

Colonel Fabrizi, who was there, later wrote, "Garibaldi appeared to be transformed. . . . I have never seen anyone age so quickly as he did at that moment—gloomy, hoarse, pale; only his eye was still firm and clear."[12] Nightfall saved the Garibaldini from total annihilation. In the engagement, 150 had been killed and 900 taken prisoner. Papal troops had suffered 230 killed, the French 26, with a total of 200 wounded.*

Garibaldi and the remainder of his men retreated to the frontier, where the royal army was waiting to disarm them and place them under arrest. As an elected MP, Garibaldi assumed that no proceedings would be mounted against him, but the new government, led by General Menabrea, had other ideas. He was arrested and once again imprisoned in the fortress of Varignano. Apparently, the new government was hoping that he could be persuaded to incriminate former Prime Minister Rattazzi, but Garibaldi would say nothing. Instead, he accused the government of treachery and claimed that the monarchy had sold him out to the French. Three times he had begun his march on Rome, and each

---

*These casualty figures are given in Jasper Ridley's *Garibaldi*, p. 589.

time the politicos had at first secretly encouraged him and then publicly turned against him. This time, he would not easily forgive.

His imprisonment failed to achieve any purpose. Throughout Italy, there was widespread criticism of the way the government had treated him and his men. Finally, the U.S. ambassador intervened to secure Garibaldi's release from Varignano. Garibaldi, however, had to promise the authorities that he would return to Caprera and not leave the island for six months.[13] The other imprisoned Red Shirts were also released and sent home. Thus was shattered the myth of Garibaldini invincibility.

57

The Army of the Vosges: 1870

AFTER HIS DEFEAT AT MENTANA, Garibaldi didn't leave Caprera for almost three years but for an occasional visit to nearby La Maddalena or Sardinia. He had taken up with his housekeeper, Francesca Armosino, and was raising a second family. Though hobbled by arthritis and old injuries, he continued to work the farm on his better days.

He also tried his hand at writing novels, something that he had always wanted to do. In 1868, he completed *Clelia*, a tragic love story that unfolds against a backdrop of revolutionary activity and church corruption. Although the book received poor reviews, its publication in 1870 earned Garibaldi some much-needed income. Later the same year, he published a second novel, *Cantoni il volontario* (*Cantoni the Volunteer*), which contains few fictional elements and is mainly based on actual events during the period 1848–1849.

In the meantime, events in other parts of Europe were about to transform the political situation in Italy. France and Prussia, the two dominant powers on the continent, fell into a serious dispute over the succession to the Spanish throne. The Prussian prince, Leopold von Hohenzollern, had put forth his candidacy, but France was opposed to any foreign power placing a prince on the throne of Spain. When Napoleon III demanded that the Prussian royal family renounce any present and future claims to the Spanish throne, he received a reply so harsh in tone that it had the effect of waving a red flag in front of a bull. On July 19, 1870, France declared war on Prussia.

As it happened, war with France was precisely what Chancellor Bismarck of Prussia wanted. He could at last employ his nation's military might to secure its position as the greatest single power on the European continent. Most contemporary political observers considered France the aggressor in the Franco-Prussian conflict, though it eventually surfaced that Bismarck had secretly edited the official Prussian reply to the French demand so as to deliberately provoke the French.

The Kingdom of Italy offered to enter the war on France's side, if Napoleon III agreed to the withdrawal of French troops from Rome. Napoleon refused, reaffirming his intention of maintaining the French military presence in Rome. Italy therefore remained neutral in the war. Garibaldi remained silent on the matter, although most of the Garibaldini were sympathetic to the Prussian side. From the beginning, the war went badly for the French as the Prussians won several easy victories. Then on September 1, the Prussians defeated the French at the Battle of Sedan, capturing Napoleon III along with 82,000 French soldiers. Napoleon was forced to abdicate as emperor, ending his nineteen-year reign.

Shortly thereafter, revolution broke out in Paris, and the Third Republic was proclaimed under Leon Gambetta. The new government immediately withdrew the French garrison from Rome, a move which prompted Victor Emmanuel to send Italian troops into Rome under the pretext of preventing a revolt. Over the objections of Pope Pius IX, the Italian army marched into the city after only token resistence from the Swiss Guard. General Bixio commanded one of those army divisions. It was a great event for him, a veteran of Garibaldi's Red Shirts during the battle for Rome in 1849. Garibaldi, however, was prevented by the Italian government from having any share of the credit for the final liberation of the Eternal City. Mazzini had meanwhile traveled from London to Italy as his dream of a united Italy was being realized. He was immediately arrested by Italian police and imprisoned in Gaeta. He was later released and spent the last few months of his life in Italy—a united Italy. Upon learning of Mazzini's death in March 1872, Garibaldi declared, "Let the flag of the thousand wave over the bier of the great Italian!"[1]

In the meantime, the French Republic had rejected Bismarck's harsh peace terms and was prepared to continue the war against Prussia. This served to draw republicans and radicals from around the world to the side of the French Republic. Even Garibaldi emerged from his cocoon on Caprera and wrote an open letter to the Italian press urging support for the French Republic. He then sent a telegram to the French government, offering them his services.

Although that government was hesitant to accept the offer, a number of French patriots were determined to bring Garibaldi to France. They dispatched Phillipe Bordone, a French doctor who had fought with the Red Shirts in Sicily, to escort him to France. Bordone succeeded in his mission, and, on October 7, the two reached Marseilles aboard a French yacht. To his surprise, Garibaldi was treated to a tremendous welcome, with the fortress cannon firing a salvo in salute. This outpouring of adulation underscored, even in France, public appreciation for "the hero of two worlds." A special train took Garibaldi to the city of Tours, where the Republic had established a temporary capital. There, Garibaldi was met by Leon Gambetta, one of the leaders of the French Republic, who had flown there from Paris in an aerostatic balloon.

Despite criticism from some old opponents of Garibaldi, the French government appointed him Commander of the Army of the Vosges, a force consisting of 10,000 irregular French troops called *francs-tireurs*—members of French rifle clubs who were trained to fight as sniper-guerrillas behind enemy lines. They did not wear regular army uniforms, and those who were captured by the Prussians were executed. Garibaldi and his *francs-tireurs* were directed to work closely with General Cambriels' regular French forces, although neither commander ranked above the other.

Moving quickly, Garibaldi established his headquarters at Autun, some seventy miles west of Dijon. There, he gathered around him a corps of international volunteers similar to those he had previously assembled in Uruguay and in Sicily. They came from many different countries and from all walks of life. French critics pointed out that they were fighting, not in patriotic love of France, but for their own concept of an "international democratic republic."[2] In Autun itself, a local magistrate referred to the Army of the Vosges as "a gang of vandals, bandits and ruffians."[3] A French newspaper even described how old Garibaldi looked, with a "white beard and pale face," and how he rode about in a carriage "into which he had to be helped."[4] This type of ridicule was nothing new to Garibaldi. Throughout his career he had fought for allies who gained from his victories but failed to show the slightest gratitude for his efforts. This campaign was to be no exception.

He appointed Colonel Phillipe Bordone as his chief of staff and was joined by his sons, Menotti and Ricciotti, and by his son-in-law Canzio, all of whom were to help in the training of new recruits. Another welcome volunteer was Jessie White Mario, who had come to look after the wounded and to report on the war for the *New York Tribune*.[5] Her arrival in camp was, as always, a morale booster.

Early in November, the Prussians began their push toward Dijon, driving the French army back. The loss of Dijon would have endangered the defense of the entire Vosges sector and allowed the Prussians to advance on Lyons. The French command ordered Garibaldi's army to stop that advance, and the two armies soon clashed. As fighting intensified, a brigade under the command of Ricciotti Garibaldi routed the Prussian troops at Chatillon-sur-Seine. The *francs-tireurs* also beat back an enemy attack at Autun, thus halting the Prussian advance in its tracks. The sector remained rather quiet until January of the following year (1871), when the Army of the Vosges was again ordered to defend Dijon, this time against an advancing Prussian force of 150,000. A massive battle ensued in which Menotti, Ricciotti, and Canzio all distinguished themselves. During the three-day struggle (January 21–23), Garibaldi's forces smashed another determined Prussian attack, inflicting heavy losses on the enemy and capturing the Standard of the 61st Pomeranian Regiment.[6]

Soon after came news that an armistice had been signed on

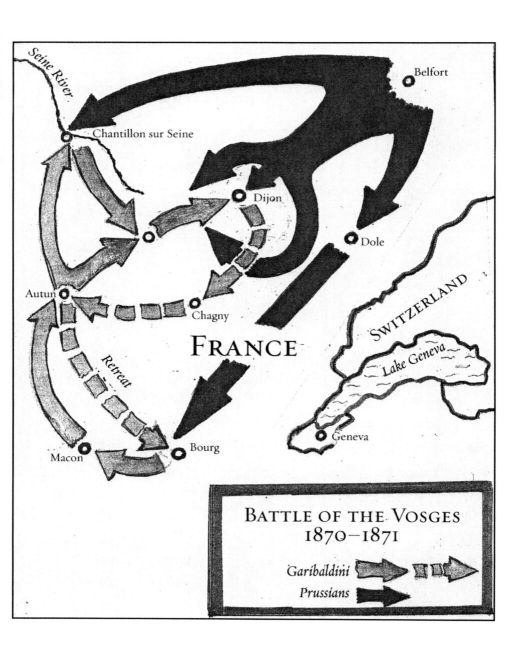

Seine River

Belfort

Chantillon sur Seine

Dijon

Dole

Autun

Chagny

FRANCE

Retreat

SWITZERLAND

Lake Geneva

Macon

Bourg

Geneva

BATTLE OF THE VOSGES
1870–1871

Garibaldini

Prussians

January 29 between the French and Prussian high commands. The French, having surrendered Paris, had agreed to all the Prussian demands. But the armistice agreement *excluded* the Vosges Sector around Dijon. Bismarck, had apparently refused to include Garibaldi's forces in the terms of the armistice, in order to give the Prussian army an opportunity to destroy them. He probably resented the fact that Garibaldi had volunteered to fight on the side of the French.

In Dijon, no one could believe that the French government would sign an armistice that did not apply to one of its fronts. Garibaldi sent a telegram to the government and received a reply that his army had been excluded from the armistice "by mistake."[7] It became painfully clear that the French government had abandoned Garibaldi and his men to their fate. In fact, he hadn't even been informed by his superiors that the armistice didn't apply to his sector. To confirm the betrayal, the Prussians completely encircled Dijon in preparation for a final, punitive battle. Garibaldi, however, wishing to avoid useless bloodshed, chose to retreat from the city. He led his army out of the city on January 31 and miraculously slipped through the Prussian lines without the loss of a single man.[8] It would be his last great military feat.

With the war over, elections were held for the new National Assembly of France. Surprisingly, the electorate returned a majority of the Conservatives and Bonapartists to their old seats. Garibaldi, whose name had been placed on the ballot by his friends, was nevertheless elected deputy in six different Departments of France. He chose to represent Dijon. Immediately, his opponents asserted that he was ineligible for election because he was a foreigner. Radicals, however, claimed that he was indeed eligible because he had been born in the "French town of Nice." Upon hearing of his election, he left his troops in Menotti's charge and traveled by train to Bordeaux, where the newly elected French government was meeting. There, he was greeted by crowds shouting, *"Vive Garibaldi!"* He replied, *"Vive la France!"*

On February 13, he attended the opening session of the Assembly. His entry into the chamber provoked a hostile reception from the Conservative deputies when he refused to remove his famous red hat. He delivered a letter to the president in which he anounced that he had rendered his services to France but now was resigning his seat. When the president read the letter out loud, some deputies protested, claiming that Garibaldi could not resign because, being an alien, he had not been validly elected. When Garibaldi rose to reply, the president told him that he could not speak because he had just resigned his seat. When Garibaldi tried again to reply—amid much shouting and yelling of deputies—the president ordered him to sit down and declared the session closed. Garibaldi silently left the chamber and returned to Caprera the same night.[9]

Three weeks later, another uproar occurred in the Assembly when Victor Hugo criticized that body's refusal to allow Garibaldi to speak. He denounced the Conservative deputies for denying free speech to a man who had come to fight for France. He added that Garibaldi remained the only general in the French army who had not been defeated in the war. Like Garibaldi, Hugo was also shouted down—but before leaving the chamber, he shouted, "Three weeks ago you refused to listen to Garibaldi. Today you refuse to listen to me. I shall go and speak far away from here."[10] Then, he too left.

58

Retirement on Caprera: 1871

GARIBALDI RETURNED TO CAPRERA on February 16, 1871, following an absence of 132 days. Although disappointed with the treatment he had received from the French government, he had no regrets about having served in the cause of France. He wished now to enjoy a peaceful retirement at his island home. He had finally realized that he was getting too old to play soldier.

Meanwhile, political discord in France had brought that nation to the brink of civil war. The French people were seething under the humiliation of the peace treaty imposed on them by the Prussians. Republican factions were fearful that the newly elected Conservative government would try to restore the monarchy, and radical revolutionaries were calling for the workers to overthrow the existing government. All of this helped set the stage for a violent upheaval.

On March 18, radical elements in Paris rebelled against the government and seized control of a large part of the city. The rebels proclaimed the establishment of the *Commune of Paris*, a term recalling the radical municipal government of the city during the time of the Reign of Terror (1793–94). The *Communards*, as they were called, adopted measures calling for the ending of support for religion and the imposing of a moratorium on the payment of debts and rents.

As the crisis worsened, Premier Adolphe Thiers ordered the French army to drive the Communards from the streets of Paris. The Communards wrote to Garibaldi, asking him to be their commander-in-chief, but he declined, citing poor health. The revolt was crushed by the French army following several weeks of savage street fighting, during which the Communards shot the archbishop of Paris and set fire to part of the city. The revolt left 33,000 dead, along with a bitter legacy of class antagonism in France. Although Garibaldi sympathized with the Communards, he did not approve of their tactics, and he condemned their attempt to abolish the private ownership of property. In this respect, he also disagreed with radical political theorists like Karl Marx and Friedrich Engels. Today, the Paris Commune occupies an important place in Marxist-Leninist mythology and is portrayed as an early example of proletarian government.

Garibaldi also returned to his writing. Name recognition alone was sufficient to ensure that his work would continue to be accepted by publishers. Five years had passed since *Clelia* and *Cantori il Voluntario*. His third novel, *I Mille* (*The Thousand*), appeared in 1873. Evidently, he hoped to reach a wider audience through works that glorified the revolution and heroism. He wrote on other subjects as well, such as monarchy, dictatorship, the status of women, capital punishment, and the irrigation of the Tiber Valley.[1] Along with his personal memoirs, these efforts appeared in several different languages and helped him pay off some debts.

He needed the money because he had, once again, become entangled with a woman, settling down with his housekeeper, Francesca Armosino. Initially brought over to Caprera as a nursemaid for Teresita's children, Francesca had soon become the island's mistress. When Garibaldi fell in love with her, his children—Menotti, Teresita, and Ricciotti—had left the island in protest. He and Francesca went on to have three more children—Clelia, Rosa, and Manlio. The middle child had died when Garibaldi was in France fighting the Prussians. She was only seventeen months old, and the second infant daughter of that name to die while Garibaldi was away at war. (The first Rosita, as has been noted, had died in Montevideo while Garibaldi was engaged in the battle for Salto.) Needless to say, the death of each of these infant daughters deeply saddened him.

Despite his firm belief in free enterprise, Garibaldi continued to fare poorly in his business ventures. He had spent much of his own money on devising a plan to divert the water of the Tiber River for purposes of irrigation. The plan proved unfeasible, and nothing came of it. To complicate matters, he had also taken a mortgage on his property in order to help his son Menotti finance a construction project in Rome. That project was also unsuccessful, and Garibaldi found himself unable to repay the loan. In another attempt to raise money, he agreed to sell his yacht, the *Princess Olga*. He stood to make 80,000 lire on the sale, but his agent, Antonio Bo, ran off to America with the money and never returned.[2]

The press, which had so often covered Garibaldi's adventurous undertakings, now seized the opportunity to write about his woes. Articles detailing his financial difficulties began to appear in the newspapers. They aroused public indignation and caused people to wonder how a nation such as Italy could allow its national hero to live his retirement years in poverty. In order to avoid further embarrassment, the government awarded him an annual pension of 50,000 lire—its way of showing gratitude for his service to the nation. Garibaldi, however, declined to accept it, saying that he did not want to become a "prisoner of the government." Admittedly, the cost of freedom is high; but this independent attitude of Garibaldi was to prove detrimental to his family's well being.

Afraid of living in poverty, Francesca urged him to reconsider for the sake of their children. After struggling with his conscience, he finally consented. He later exclaimed, "I never thought I would be reduced to the state of a pensioner!"[3] His family members, however, were elated over the acceptance, for they all stood to benefit monetarily. As it turned out, very little of the money went to Garibaldi himself. Menotti had failed in the construction business and needed 20,000 lire to save him from bankruptcy. Ricciotti had squandered money living *la dolce vita* and been reduced to selling his father's decorations for money.[4] He needed 10,000 lire to pay off his debts. Teresita's husband, Canzio, had been arrested and charged with engaging in revolutionary activity, and funds were needed to cover his legal fees. Garibaldi's mistress, Francesca, badgered him as well into taking out a 10,000-lire life insurance policy, of which Clelia and Manlio were the beneficiaries.* So it

---

*These figures appear in Andrea Viotti's *Garibaldi, The Revolutionary and His Men*, p. 186.

appears inescapable that Garibaldi faced the humiliation of having to accept government money in order to pay off mounting debts *and* maintain peace within the family.

In the meanwhile, Italian politics had become much less exciting than it was during the period of the Risorgimento. There were some occasional problems caused by left-wing agitation, but for the most part affairs ran smoothly in the Kingdom of Italy. Nearly all government leaders during this period were men who had fought under Garibaldi—Francesco Crispi, Benedetto Cairoli, Agostino Depretis, and Antonio Mordini. These old Garibaldini had abandoned some of the revolutionary principles and beliefs for which they had fought, and once they came to power, they actively suppressed all other revolutionary movements.

When elections were held in November 1874, Garibaldi again won parliamentary seats for several constituencies. This time, he went to Rome to take his seat. It was the first time that he had been in the Eternal City since he marched out with his Red Shirts on July 2, 1849, during the last days of the Roman Republic. Upon his arrival at the train station, he was greeted by General Medici and other former Red Shirts now serving in the Italian army. From the station, he was driven by carriage to parliament and, this time, received with prolonged applause from all the deputies. After a brief session, Medici escorted him to the Quirinale Palace, where they were greeted by King Victor Emmanuel himself. It was a heart-warming event for Medici as the king embraced Garibaldi and the two became reconciled. Victor Emmanuel again offered him various gifts and privileges, all of which he politely declined. The two were to remain friends until Victor Emmanuel's death in 1878, upon which he was succeeded by his son, Umberto.

On January 14, 1880, Garibaldi's won his last battle, this time

King Victor Emmanuel II

in the courts, when his previous marriage to Giuseppina Raimondi was annulled on the grounds of nonconsummation. In a land where divorce was illegal, it was a monumental victory for the plaintiff. Twelve days later, on January 26, 1880, he and Francesca Armosino were married in a civil ceremony by the mayor of La Maddalena. The private wedding was attended by members of the family and a few close friends. Among those in attendance were Menotti and his wife Italia, Teresita and her husband Canzio, Clelia, Manlio, and a host of grandchildren. Only Ricciotti and his wife, Constance Hopcraft, were missing. Also present were several relatives of Francesca, who had journeyed from the mainland to Caprera for the wedding. The bride appeared in a white gown with an orange blossom headdress. Garibaldi wore a white poncho, with a scarlet kerchief knotted around his neck. The king sent his congratulations. The marriage ceremony was followed by a feast at which Garibaldi sang some of his favorite songs.[5] The wedding was written up in the press—and since Giuseppina had already remarried, the drama between her and Garibaldi was finally ended.

59

Death of Garibaldi

AFTER 1880, GARIBALDI'S HEALTH declined steadily. His hands and feet were bent by arthritis, and he had difficulty getting around. Often he was confined to bed for weeks at a time. During this period of recurring illness, his wife Francesca took care of him—feeding him, bathing him, and generally taking care of his needs. She exerted every effort to make him comfortable. To help cover expenses, she earned money selling livestock and some of the wine produced on the farm. She also did a thriving business selling locks of her husband's hair to his admirers.

Despite his poor health, Garibaldi traveled to Milan in November 1881 for the unveiling of a war monument commemorating the Garibaldini who had fallen at Mentana in 1867. He was so weak that his speech had to be read for him by his son-in-law,

Stefano Canzio.[1] In April 1882, he traveled to Sicily to attend the celebration marking the 600th anniversary of the rebellion of the Sicilian Vespers. On his way there, he visited Naples for the first time since 1860 and was received with tremendous enthusiasm. He proceeded to Palermo, where the entire city turned out to greet the man who, twenty-two years before, had liberated their island from Bourbon rule.

To the Sicilian people Garibaldi was a larger-than-life figure, but because of his condition, the people were asked not to cheer as he was carried through the streets on a litter. Instead, they stood in deathly silence as they viewed the pale, crippled figure of their hero being carried past them. He had by then entered the Sicilian consciousness as a legendary figure who had freed them from foreign oppressors. During his brief stay in Palermo, he received more than 1,500 telegrams from well-wishers.[2] He sailed away for the last time on April 17, 1882, but he has remained forever an immortal figure in Sicilian folklore.

Shortly after returning to Caprera, Garibaldi fell ill with bronchitis and died at 6:22 P.M. on June 2, 1882. The news of his death made front-page headlines in newspapers around the world. Praise for him was almost universal. Among world leaders, only Queen Victoria made no reference to Garibaldi's death, either in public statements or in her personal diary.

Before his death, Garibaldi had instructed his wife to bedeck him in a red shirt and burn his body on a wooden pyre in the tradition of the ancient Romans. His ashes were then to be placed in the little sepulcher with the remains of his daughters, Anita and the first Rosa (Rosita).[3] He had asked Francesca not to advise the authorities of his death until this had been done. But despite her precautions, the news of his passing away reached the authorities almost immediately, and they demanded that Garibaldi be buried in an official state funeral. There were strong religious objections to cremation, and the very idea of it infuriated his admirers. The matter was discussed at a meeting on Caprera attended by Francesca, Menotti, Teresita, Canzio, Crispi, Alberto Mario, Dr. Albanese, and a friend of Garibaldi's named Fazzini. Francesca and Fazzini argued that Garibaldi's wishes be carried out, and that his corpse be burned. All the others took the view his body belonged to the nation and to his Red Shirts, and that the demand for an official funeral should prevail.

The world, as is so commonly the case, had the last word, and an official funeral took place at Caprera on June 8, 1882. In attendance were Prince Tommaso, representing King Umberto of Italy, the leaders of both houses of Parliament, high-ranking officers of the Italian army and navy, and many veterans of the Garibaldini. The bier was carried by survivors of The Thousand. There was a great thunderstorm during the funeral ceremony, leading some to believe that the elements were protesting against the denial of Garibaldi's wish to be cremated. A more serious disaster occurred during the memorial services for him in Montevideo, where a fire claimed the lives of twenty-seven persons.[4]

Today, his body lies on Caprera beneath a solid block of marble bearing the single word GARIBALDI. Since his burial, an Italian army soldier has perennially stood guard at the site. On Garibaldi's left lie the graves of his daughters Rosa, Anita, and Teresita; on his right are those of his wife Francesca and of Manlio and Clelia. The body of his first wife, Anita, has never been brought to Caprera. As has been mentioned earlier, it was moved from Nice to Rome in 1932 and buried beneath her monument on the Janiculum.

Aside from self-satisfaction and contentment, Garibaldi

received very little for his services to the Kingdom of Italy. Furthermore, almost all of his business ventures ended in failure. His children didn't fare much better in their endeavors. Virtually all of Garibaldi's income was spent on helping them pay off debts and on trying to make Caprera a more productive farm.

Garibaldi bequeathed his house and property to his wife, Francesca, leaving her in possession of the island. This virtually severed the last links between Anita's children and the island. Menotti lived in Rome with his family and entered the Italian army with the rank of general. In 1895, Menotti and Prime Minister Francesco Crispi supported a plan for the conquest of Ethiopia by Italian forces stationed in Eritrea under the command of General Baratieri. Baratieri, who had once served under Garibaldi, was toasted by Menotti as the man who had "renewed in Africa the splendor of Garibaldi's victories!"[5] This turned out to be wishful thinking. Baratieri was disastrously defeated at Aduwa in 1896, causing Crispi's government to fall and Menotti to be censured by court martial. Forty years later, in 1936, Mussolini avenged Italy's defeat at Aduwa by defeating the Ethiopians. It marked the first time in Ethopia's long history that it had ever been conquered by a foreign power.

Teresita Garibaldi Canzio and her family went to live in Genoa, where her husband, General Stefano Canzio, served as governor general. She later led a campaign to free imprisoned revolutionaries who had partaken in a revolt in Milan in 1898. Her appeal to King Umberto eventually got them a royal pardon; they were all released within three years. She died in January 1903, at the age of fifty-eight. Her brother Menotti died seven months later, at the age of sixty-two. Her husband, Stefano Canzio, died in 1904.

Ricciotti Garibaldi lived for a time in America and then in

Melbourne, Australia. Later he moved to Rome and, as head of the Garibaldini, continued his father's tradition of liberating oppressed peoples. In 1897, and again in 1912, he led a volunteer corps of Red Shirts to fight for Greece against the Ottoman Turks. During the fighting in 1912, he was accompanied by his wife, Constance, and their two daughters, Anita and Rosa, who had volunteered as nurses. Ricciotti's force of 2,000 Red Shirts defeated an army of 10,000 Turks at Drisko, affirming once again their invincibility.[6]

In 1914, the Garibaldini again took up arms to fight for France, this time against Germany in World War I. This occurred before Italy joined the Allies in May 1915. The Garibaldini were led by Ricciotti's son, Giuseppe Garibaldi II, also known as "Peppino." Previously, Peppino had fought alongside his father in the Balkans against the Turks in 1897. He had also fought in South Africa on the side of the Boers against the British in 1900, in Mexico with Pancho Villa against Diaz in 1910, and again in Balkans on the side of the Greeks against the Turks in 1912. In the Battle for France in 1914, he was accompanied by his brothers: Ricciotti Jr., Sante, Bruno, Costante, and Ezio. The 3,000 men of the Garibaldi Legion were incorporated into the French Foreign Legion and distinguished themselves against the German army at the Argonne Forest, near Verdun. There, they routed the Germans after fierce hand-to-hand combat—but Bruno and Costante were both killed during the action. Members of the Legion were awarded eleven Legion of Honor crosses and four other military medals for bravery during the action.[7] Ricciotti died in July 1924, at the age of seventy-seven.

Garibaldi's youngest son, Manlio, served in the Italian navy but died in January 1900, when he was only twenty-six years old. His mother, Francesca, died on Caprera in 1923. Garibaldi's youngest daughter, Clelia, who never married, continued to live on Caprera, occasionally granting interviews to journalists and biographers. She contributed many details about her father in her reminiscences about him. After her mother's death, Clelia had a reconciliation with the children of Ricciotti and Teresita. When she died in February 1959, at the age of ninety-one, she left Caprera to Ricciotti's son, General Ezio Garibaldi. Ezio's widow lived there after his death. Today, the island is an Italian national monument.

Garibaldi himself lives on in legend and folklore, and remains an immortal inspiration to the Italian people. He is revered as a great soldier and as a champion of freedom and liberty. *His* was the sword that unified a nation, and *his* is the name that comes first among its heroes.

Epilogue

GARIBALDI'S VISION OF A UNITED ITALY became a reality with the occupation of Rome in 1870. The Italian people had regained their national identity, and the name *Italia* once again appeared on the map of Europe. Garibaldi had retired to his home on Caprera and taken up the simple life of a farmer.

Although the achievement of national unity had virtually ended his active career, he nevertheless remained outspoken on various issues such as maintaining the peace, the death penalty, and women's rights. His mistrust of politicians had left him disillusioned with the government and with those running it. He once said that there were two kinds of people—"the selfish ones who never sacrifice anything for the common good, and the true patriots who freely sacrifice what is most dear to them for the benefit of others. The latter are always misunderstood, insulted and dragged through the dirt, while the former rule the world."

Past experiences in Uruguay and in the Roman Republic had taught him that democracy was not self-executing, and that a strong chief executive or dictator was needed in times of crisis. According to Garibaldi, such leadership was not incompatible with democracy but, rather, essential to its preservation. Italy was to be no exception. Like any other newly emancipated nation, it needed a strong leader, and in his judgment that quality was personified in Victor Emmanuel of Savoy. Garibaldi's loyalty to the king caused him to split with Mazzini. The latter, though he aroused a strong nationalistic sentiment among Italians, had spent most of his adult life in exile or in hiding. Except for his role in the short-lived Roman Republic, he had had little to do with actually putting Italy together. In the end, the combined efforts of Garibaldi, Cavour, and Victor Emmanuel had created the unified country. Though Garibaldi was personally very supportive of the king and the Royal House of Savoy, he believed that the Italian people themselves would ultimately have to decide on the fate of the monarchy.

Victor Emmanuel II of Savoy, the first king of a united Italy, ruled until his death in 1878. He was succeeded by his son, Umberto I, who was reigning at the time of the failed invasion of Abyssinia in 1895. Umberto was assassinated by an anarchist in 1900, whereupon his son, Victor Emmanuel III, ascended to the throne. The latter's reign spanned almost five decades and two world wars. In 1946, after Italy's defeat in World War II, he abdicated in favor of his son, Umberto II, who ruled for barely a month before the Italian people voted in a referendum to abolish the monarchy and establish a republic. Thus ended the rule of the House of Savoy, one of the oldest continuous ruling dynasties in Europe. Umberto II and his family were sent into exile, their vast land holdings all confiscated by the state. In another rebuke, the Italian government passed a constitutional ban prohibiting any male descendants of the House of Savoy from ever returning to

Italy.

Banished from Italy, the royal family lived in Portugal and then Switzerland. Umberto died in 1982 without ever returning to Italy. However, his son, Prince Victor Emmanuel, launched a legal campaign to return to Italy, a land which he hadn't seen since 1946 when he was a child of nine. He brought his case to the European Court of Human Rights, seeking a declaration that he and his male descendants be entitled to return and stay in Italy. The prince and his son, Emmanuel Filiberto, claimed that their banishment was a violation of their human rights, and that it represented a breach of the treaty establishing the European Union. They also argued that the ban was discriminatory in the sense that it applied only to the male descendants of the Royal House of Savoy, and not to the family's female members. In September 2001, the Court declared admissible the application in the case of Victor Emmanuel of Savoy versus Italy, and a hearing was scheduled. Nothing came of it because Victor Emmanuel suddenly decided to drop the case.

At that point, Italy's dynamic prime minister, Silvio Berlusconi, stepped into the picture and urged the passage of a bill lifting the constitutional ban on the return to Italy of the male descendants of the ex-royal family. Despite opposition from Communists and other left-wing diehards, the bill passed both houses of parliament and was subsequently signed by Italian President Carlo Ciampi on October 22, 2002. After fifty-six years of exile, the road was cleared for Prince Victor Emmanuel and his family to return to the land of their forefathers. The prince told reporters that the news was "almost too good to be true."

Victor Emmanuel and his son, Emmanuel Filiberto, pledged their allegiance to the Italian Republic in a signed letter that read: "My son and I guarantee our loyalty to Italy's republican constitution and to our republic's President." In doing so, both father and son renounced any claim to the throne, causing Italian monarchists to turn against them. The Italian Union of Monarchists instead recognized Victor Emmanuel's cousin, Prince Amedeo of Aosta, as the legitimate pretender to the throne. In addition to renouncing any claim to the throne, the Savoy family gave up any claim to royal properties, including the crown jewels. "We have nothing in Italy and we are not asking for anything," said Victor Emmanuel as he stressed his family's desire to be able to return there as ordinary citizens.

Return they did. On March 17, 2003, the ex-royal family flew into Rome's Ciampino military airport. They did not come to meet with Italy's state officials. Instead, Vatican officials whisked them away for an audience with Pope John Paul II. The pope welcomed them warmly and, after some private conversation and an exchange of gifts, encouraged them to "come back as soon as possible."

Before their departure from Rome, the family diverted their motorcade to view the city's historic monuments, some of which they had difficulty recognizing after such a lengthy absence. Of particular interest to them was the Victor Emmanuel Monument, a magnificent white marble edifice named for the prince's great-great-grandfather. Sometimes known as the "wedding cake monument," it had been completed in 1911 to commemorate the fiftieth anniversary of the Kingdom of Italy. Today, it stands as an eternal symbol of that glorious period in Italian history known as the Risorgimento. Prince Victor Emmanuel later said that he felt an "indescribable emotion" at the visit and described it as "a page of history."

Not everyone in Italy was as enthusiastic about the visit as the

The monument to Victor Emmanuel II (the Vittoriano), constructed in 1911

ex-royal family. They were shunned by government leaders, who found it difficult to work up any enthusiasm for the visit. Anti-monarchist demonstrators protested in the streets against their return, and a Communist MP described the event as a "disconcerting leap into the past." Nevertheless, an Italian public opinion poll showed that almost seventy-five percent of those surveyed were in favor of allowing the Savoys back, provided that they did not interfere in politics and made no attempt to reclaim former properties confiscated by the state.

One member of the Savoy family, thirty-year-old Emmanuel Filiberto, has attained celebrity status. The handsome young man, a sports enthusiast, has appeared on TV soccer discussion programs in Switzerland. More recently, he was featured in a television commercial for an Italian olive company that claims eating their olives makes you "feel like a king." The olive ad attracted a lot of attention simply because Emmanuel Filiberto appeared in it.

The young prince created an even greater splash when, on September 25, 2003, he married French actress Clotilde Courau. The lavish fairytale wedding took place in Rome's Basilica of Santa Maria degli Angeli and received extensive media coverage. Around 1,300 invited guests attended. Prince Albert of Monaco, who had first introduced the two, was the best man. Both the bride and groom stressed that they were marrying for love, and that they did not want to be treated as royalty.

Only time will tell if this is really the case or merely another step toward the reclamation of the throne of Italy. Should the latter be the case, the Italian people will again have to decide on the fate of the House of Savoy.

Endnotes

Chapter 1: Young Peppino

1. Denis Mack Smith, *Garibaldi, A Great Life in Brief* (New York, 1956; cited as *Mack Smith, I*), p. 6.
2. John Parris, *The Lion of Caprera* (New York, 1962), p. 16.

Chapter 2: The Merchant Seaman:

1. Jasper Ridley, *Garibaldi* (New York, 1976), pp. 10-11.
2. Giuseppe Garibaldi, *The Life of General Garibaldi* (translation by Theodore Dwight), (New York, 1859) (cited as *Dwight*), pp. 20-21.
3. Parris, p. 19.

Chapter 3: The Revolutionary

1. Ridley, p. 17 (recounted from a story written by Count Gian Rinaldo Carli in 1764).
2. *Mack Smith, I*, p. 8.
3. *Dwight*, p. 21; Parris, pp. 41-43.
4. Parris, pp. 43-44.
5. *Dwight*, pp. 22-23; Parris, p. 45.
6. *Dwight*, p. 22.

Chapter 4: The Exile

1. *Dwight*, p. 23; Parris, p. 47; Ridley, p. 46.
2. Ridley, pp. 47-48.
3. Ridley, p. 49.

Chapter 5: The Corsair

1. Parris, pp. 52, 331, n. 16.
2. *Dwight*, p. 24; Parris, p. 48.
3. Quoted in Parris, p. 49.
4. Ridley, p. 54.
5. *Dwight*, p. 25; Parris, p. 49.
6. Parris, pp. 49-50.
7. *Dwight*, pp. 26-28.
8. *Dwight*, pp. 30-32.

Chapter 6: Gualeguay

1. For the surgery performed on Garibaldi by Dr. del Arco, see *Dwight*, p. 33; Ridley, p. 63.
2. *Dwight*, pp. 33-34; Ridley, p. 64.
3. For Garibaldi's escape and recapture, see *Dwight*, pp. 34-35; Parris, pp. 51-52; Ridley, pp. 66-67.
4. For the torturing of Garibaldi by Colonel Millan, see *Dwight*, pp. 35-36; Parris, p. 52; Ridley, p. 68.
5. *Dwight*, p. 37.

Chapter 7: Río Grande do Sul

1. Anthony Valerio, *Anita Garibaldi* (Westport, CT, 2001), pp. 5, 59; Ridley, pp. 73-74.

Chapter 8: The Río Grande Navy

1. Andrea Viotti, *Garibaldi, The Revolutionary and His Men* (UK, 1979), pp. 20, 22.
2. For Moringue's attack on the

storehouse, see *Dwight*, pp. 44-49.

3. *Dwight*, pp. 38-39; Ridley, p. 71.

4. For Garibaldi's flirtation with Manuela Ferreira, see *Dwight*, pp. 40-42.

5. *Dwight*, pp. 50-51.

Chapter 9: Santa Catarina

1. Elpis Melena, *Garibaldi's Memoirs* (edited by Anthony Campanella, Vol. I (Sarasota, FL, 1981), (cited as *Melena, I*), 30-32; *Dwight*, pp. 52-56; Ridley, pp. 81-82.

2. Ridley, p. 83.

3. *Dwight*, pp. 57-58.

4. Quoted in Parris, p. 56.

5. Quoted in *Mack Smith, I*, p. 16.

6. Quoted in *Melena, I*, p. 34; Parris, p. 54.

7. Quoted in Parris, pp. 53-54.

8. Quoted in Ridley, pp. 89-90.

Chapter 10: Anna Maria Ribeiro de Jesus

1. Ridley, p. 86n.

2. Valerio, pp. 4-5.

3. Valerio, pp. 6-7.

4. Valerio, pp. 7-8; Ridley, p. 87.

5. Parris, pp. 55, 332, n.24; Ridley, p. 92; Valerio, p. 11.

6. Viotti, p. 23.

7. Valerio p. 153.

8. Viotti, p. 23.

9. *Dwight*, pp. 95-96; Ridley, p. 102;

Viotti, p. 24.

10. For a description of Garibaldi's house in Montevideo, see Valerio, p. 68.

11. Quoted in Ridley, p. 89.

Chapter 11: Retreat from Paradise

1. *Dwight*, pp. 216-217; Ridley, pp. 96-97; Valerio, pp. 45-46.

2. Ridley, p. 98.

3. Quoted in *Mack Smith, II*, p. 16.

4. For how Garibaldi saved sixteen prisoners from execution, see Ridley, p. 101.

5. *Dwight*, pp. 93-96; Ridley, pp. 101-102; Valerio, p. 60.

Chapter 12: The Wilderness March: November 1840–January 1841

1. *Dwight*, p. 98.

2. Valerio, pp. 47-48.

3. *Dwight*, pp. 99-105; Ridley, pp. 102-104; Viotti, pp. 23-24; Valerio, pp. 61-63.

Chapter 13: The Road to Montevideo

1. Viotti, pp. 31-32.

2. *Dwight*, pp. 105-106; Ridley, p. 105; Viotti, pp. 63-64.

3. *Dwight*, pp. 106-107; *Mack Smith, I*, p. 20.

4. For Garibaldi's wedding to Anita, see Parris, pp. 57-58; Ridley, p. 105; Valerio, pp. 71-72.

Chapter 14: Uruguay and Civil War

1. For the internal power struggle in Uruguay, see Library of Congress, *Uruguay, A Country Study* (2nd. ed.) (Washington, D.C., 1992) (cited as *Uruguay*), p.4.
2. Parris, p. 59.
3. *Dwight*, p. 112; *Mack Smith, I*, p. 21.
4. Ridley, p. 110.
5. *Dwight*, pp. 113-115; Ridley, pp. 111-113; Parris, p. 60.
6. Ridley, p. 113.
7. *Dwight*, p. 107.

Chapter 15: Juan Manual de Rosas

1. James R. Scobie, *Argentina, A City and a Nation* (2nd ed.), (New York, 1971), p. 78.
2. Scobie, p. 80.
3. Scobie, p. 196.
4. Daniel K. Lewis, *The History of Argentina* (Westport, CT, 2001), p. 202.
5. Ridley, p. 57.
6. Lewis, p. 49.

Chapter 16: The Paraná Expedition: 1842

1. For the engagement at Martín García and the grounding of ships in the shallow channel, see *Dwight*, pp. 116-117; Ridley, pp. 115-116; Viotti, pp. 26-27.
2. Parris, p. 60.
3. Parris, pp. 60-61.
4. *Dwight*, p. 118.
5. For the action around Bajada el Paraná and El Cerrito, see *Dwight*, pp. 118-121; Ridley, pp. 116-117.
6. Viotti, p. 27.
7. Parris, p. 61.
8. For Garibaldi's battle preparations at Costa Brava, see *Dwight*, pp. 121-122; Ridley, pp. 118-119; Viotti, pp 28-29.

Chapter 17: Costa Brava

1. These figures are given in Viotti, p. 28.
2. Ridley, p. 119.
3. *Dwight*, p. 129.
4. For the Battle of Costa Brava, see *Dwight*, pp. 122-129; Ridley, pp. 120-125; Viotti, p. 28.
5. For Admiral Brown's triumphant return to Buenos Aires, see Ridley, pp. 127-128.

Chapter 18: Costa Brava to Montevideo

1. *Dwight*, pp. 129-130.
2. For Garibaldi's love affair with Lucia Esteche, see Ridley, p. 129.
3. Ridley, p. 130.
4. *Dwight*, pp. 131-133; Ridley, pp. 130-131.
5. Parris, p. 61.

Chapter 19: War Comes to Montevideo

1. *Dwight*, p. 140.
2. Parris, pp. 61-62; Ridley, in *Garibaldi*, gives the population of Montevideo as 42,000.
3. Valerio, p. 76.
4. For the formation of the Italian Legion, see Parris, pp. 62-63; Ridley, pp. 134, 136; Viotti, pp. 31-32.
5. Parris, p. 62; Ridley, p. 137.
6. Ridley, p. 137.
7. Viotti, p. 30.
8. For the friction between the French Legion and the Italian Legion, see *Dwight*, pp. 140-142; Parris, p. 62.
9. Ridley, pp. 142-143.
10. Viotti, p. 31.
11. Parris, p. 63.
12. *Mack Smith, I*, p. 25.

Chapter 20: The Red Shirts

1. Ridley, pp. 166-167.
2. Parris, p. 63; *Mack Smith, I*, p. 24; Ridley, p. 178.
3. *Mack Smith, I*, p. 24.
4. Parris, p. 64.
5. For the Legion's action at Tres Cruces, see *Dwight*, pp. 149-150.
6. *Mack Smith, I*, p. 25; Valerio, p. 78.
7. Ridley, pp. 163-164; Valerio, pp. 82-83.
8. For the Maria Ousely affair, see Ridley, pp. 212-213; Valerio, p. 81.

Chapter 21: The Expedition Up The

Uruguay River: 1845

1. Ridley, pp. 161-162.
2. For British and French intervention in the Uruguayan conflict, see Parris, p. 65.
3. For the capture and sacking of Colonia, see *Dwight*, pp. 154-156; Ridley, pp. 179-181.
4. For Garibaldi's rescue of prisoners at Yaquari, see *Dwight*, p. 161; Ridley, p. 183.
5. Ridley, p. 184.
6. For Garibaldi's capture of Gualeguaychú, see *Dwight*, pp. 163-165; Ridley, pp. 185-187.
7. Valerio, p. 87.
8. Ridley, p. 187.
9. *Mack Smith, I*, p. 26.
10. Quoted in Valerio, p. 90.
11. For Urquiza's attack on Salto, see *Dwight*, pp. 178-180; Ridley, pp. 192-193; Viotti, pp. 33-34.

Chapter 22: Battle of San Antonio: 1846

1. For the Battle of San Antonio, see *Dwight*, pp. 185-195; Ridley, pp. 196-198; Viotti, pp. 34-35; Valerio, pp. 92-93.
2. Quoted in Valerio, p. 93.
3. Parris, p. 69; Valerio, p. 90.
4. For Garibaldi's report on the Battle of San Antonio, see Ridley, p. 198.
5. Quoted in Viotti, p. 36.
6. Viotti, p. 36.

7. Ridley, p. 200.

8. Quoted in Viotti, p. 36.

Chapter 23: Politics and Intrigues: 1846–1847

1. For the Battle of Rio Daimán, see *Dwight*, pp. 199-207; Ridley, pp. 208-209.

2. Ridley, p. 209.

3. Valerio, p. 95.

4. Quoted in Viotti, p. 36.

5. Quoted in Viotti, pp. 36-37.

6. Ridley, pp. 213-214.

7. Ridley, p. 217.

8. Ridley, pp. 219-220.

9. Quoted in Ridley, p. 223; *Mack Smith, I*, p. 27.

Chapter 24: The Return to Italy: 1848

1. Parris, p. 68.

2. Quoted in Viotti, p. 37.

3. Ridley, p. 232.

4. Valerio, p. 111.

5. Quoted in Ridley, p. 236.

6. Quoted in Ridley, p. 239.

Chapter 25: The Lake District Campaign: 1848

1. *Mack Smith, I*, pp. 31-32; Ridley, pp. 241-242.

2. Valerio, p. 116.

3. Quoted in Parris, p. 76.

4. Parris, pp. 76-77.

5. Parris, p. 78.

6. Quoted in Parris, p. 80.

Chapter 26: The Roman Republic: 1848–1849

1. Quoted in Parris, p. 83.

2. Parris, p. 85.

3. *Ibid.*

4. Ridley, p. 266.

5. Ridley, p. 268.

6. Parris, p. 88.

7. G.M. Trevelyan, *Garibaldi and the Thousand* (London, 1909) (cited as *Trevelyan, II*), 46; Parris, pp. 82-83.

8. Ridley, p. 273.

9. Parris, pp. 93-94.

10. Viotti, p. 52.

Chapter 27: The Battle of Rome: 1849

1. For the defensive preparations prior to the battle for Rome, see Viotti, pp. 51-52.

2. Parris, p. 95.

3. For the initial French assault on Rome, see *Trevelyan, I*, pp. 128-134; Parris, pp. 94-96; Ridley, pp. 278-280; Viotti, pp. 53-54.

4. For Margaret Fuller's role in caring for the wounded during the battle for Rome, see James Watson, "A Woman Beyond Her Time," *Italy, Italy*, XX (December 2002–January 2003), 48-51.

5. Parris, p. 96.

6. Ridley, pp. 286-287.

7. Ridley, p. 287.

8. For Ferdinand de Lesseps' role in negotiating the fifteen-day cease

fire agreement, see Parris, pp. 97-99; Ridley, pp. 281-282, 290-291.

9. Ridley, p. 291.

10. For a description of the Villa Corsini, see Viotti, p. 60.

11. For examples of valor at the battle of June 3, 1849, see Viotti, pp. 61-63.

12. For the battle of June 3, 1849, see *Trevelyan, I,* pp. 167-193; Ridley, pp. 292-297; Viotti, pp. 60-63.

13. Ridley, p. 291.

Chapter 28: The Fall of the Roman Republic

1. Viotti, p. 65.

2. Quoted in Viotti, p. 65.

3. Parris, p. 102; Ridley, pp. 300-301.

4. Ridley, p. 301.

5. Ridley, p. 303.

6. Quoted in Parris, p. 105.

7. *Trevelyan, I,* pp. 217-226; Viotti, pp. 66-67.

8. Parris, p. 106; *Mack Smith, I,* p. 43; Ridley, p. 306.

9. Quoted in Parris, p. 107.

10. Viotti, p. 68; Valerio, p. 146.

11. *Trevelyan, I,* p. 235.

Chapter 29: The Retreat to San Marino

1. *Trevelyan, I,* p. 243.

2. *Trevelyan, I,* p. 252; *Mack Smith, I,* p. 47; Ridley, p. 311.

3. *Trevelyan, I,* pp. 245-247; Ridley, pp. 311-312; Valerio, p. 152.

4. Ridley, p. 314.

5. *Mack Smith, I,* pp. 46-47.

6. Ridley, p. 314.

7. Ridley, p. 315.

8. Ridley, pp. 316-317.

9. Ridley, pp. 320, 322.

10. *Trevelyan, I,* pp. 264-266.

11. *Trevelyan, I,* p. 266.

12. Quoted in Parris, p. 107.

13. Parris, p. 107.

Chapter 30: Death of Anita

1. *Trevelyan, I,* pp. 285-286; Parris, p. 108; Ridley, p. 328.

2. *Trevelyan, I,* pp. 280-281; Ridley, p. 329.

3. Parris, pp. 108-109.

4. *Trevelyan, I,* pp. 295-299; Parris, pp. 109-110; Ridley, pp. 332-334; Valerio, pp. 167-168.

5. *Trevelyan, I,* p. 299; Parris, p. 110; Ridley, p. 335; Viotti, p. 69; Valerio, pp. 168-169.

6. Quoted in Parris, p. 111.

7. Parris, pp. 111-112.

Chapter 31: Escape Odyssey

1. Parris, pp. 111-112.

2. Parris, p. 112.

3. *Trevelyan, I,* pp. 306-307; Ridley, pp. 336-338.

4. Viotti, p. 69.

5. Ridley, p. 338.

6. Ridley, pp. 338-339; *Mack Smith, I,*

p. 48.

7. Parris, pp. 113-114; Ridley, p. 339.

8. Ridley, p. 340.

9. *Trevelyan, I*, p. 314; Ridley, pp. 342-343.

10. G.M. Trevelyan, *Garibaldi and the Thousand* (London, 1909) (cited as *Trevelyan II*), p. 11.

11. Parris, p. 115; Ridley, p. 347; *Mack Smith, I*, pp. 48-49.

12. *Trevelyan, II*, pp. 11-12; Parris, p. 115; Ridley, pp. 347-348.

13. `Although there is some disagreement among writers as to whether Garibaldi accepted a government pension at this time, it appears safe to say that he did on behalf of his mother and family.

Chapter 32: Exile in New York: 1850—1851

1. *Trevelyan, II*, p. 12.

2. Parris, p. 116.

3. For Garibaldi's stay at Meucci's house, see *Trevelyan, II*, pp. 14-16; *Mack Smith, I*, pp. 50-51; Ridley, pp. 363-365.

4. Ridley, p. 363.

5. *Trevelyan, II*, p. 16.

Chapter 33: Odyssey to the Far East: 1851—1853

1. For Garibaldi's journey to Panama, see *Trevelyan, II*, p. 16; Ridley, p. 366.

2. For Garibaldi's visit to Señora Manuela Saenz, see Ridley, pp. 366-367.

3. Ridley, p. 368.

4. Quoted in Parris, p. 117.

5. For Garibaldi's altercation with Charles Ledo, see Parris, p. 117; *Mack Smith, I*, p. 51.

6. Ridley, p. 371.

7. For Garibaldi's strange dream at sea, see *Trevelyan, II*, pp. 17-18.

8. *Trevelyan, II*, p. 18.

9. Ridley, p. 373.

Chapter 34: New York to Nice: 1854

1. Ridley, p. 374.

2. *Mack Smith, I*, p. 53; Ridley, p. 377.

3. Ridley, pp. 375-376.

4. Ridley, pp. 377-378.

5. *Mack Smith, I*, pp. 53, 60; Parris, 117-118; Ridley, p. 382.

6. *Trevelyan, II*, p. 25.

7. Quoted in Ridley, pp. 386-387, from Garibaldi's letter to *L'Italia del Popolo*, August 4, 1854.

8. *Trevelyan, II*, p. 31.

9. *Mack Smith, I*, p. 58; Ridley, p. 390.

Chapter 35: Private Love Affairs

1. Parris, pp. 19, 328.

2. Ridley, pp. 129, 598.

3. *Mack Smith, I*, p. 53; Parris, p. 117.

4. *Mack Smith, I*, pp. 55, 60; Parris, pp. 117-118; Ridley, pp. 382, 387-388.

5. *Mack Smith, I*, pp. 61, 99.

6. Elpis Melena, *Garibaldi: Recollections of His Public and Private Life* (London, 1887) (cited as "Melena, *Recollections*"), pp. 2-9, 15.

7. Melena, *Recollections*, pp. 22-26; Parris, pp. 118-119, 148, 295-296, 307-308; *Mack Smith, I*, pp. 61-62.

8. Parris, p. 185; Ridley, p. 425.

9. Parris, pp. 167-168; Ridley, pp. 409, 424-425.

10. Parris, pp. 196-197; Ridley, pp. 426-427.

11. Ridley, p. 598.

Chapter 36: Baroness Marie Esperance von Schwartz

1. Melena, *Recollections*, pp. 2-9, 15.

2. Quoted in Parris, p. 120.

3. Parris, p. 139; Ridley, pp. 396, 424-425.

4. Melena, *Recollections*, pp. 35-45; *Mack Smith, I*, pp. 62-63.

5. Melena, *Recollections*, pp. 168-171.

6. Parris, pp. 295, 307; Ridley, pp. 328-329.

7. Melena, *Recollections*, pp. 328-329; Parris, pp. 320-321.

8. Melena, *Recollections*, p. 329.

Chapter 37: War With Austria: 1859

1. *Mack Smith, I*, pp. 68-69.

2. Mack Smith, *Cavour*, (New York, 1985), p. 44.

3. Parris, p. 134.

4. Parris, pp. 134-135; Mack Smith, *Cavour*, pp. 140-142.

5. *Trevelyan, II*, p. 83; Parris, p. 140.

6. *Mack Smith, I*, p. 71.

7. *Mack Smith, I*, p. 72.

8. *Trevelyan, II*, p. 86.

9. For Garibaldi's Lake District Campaign of 1859, see *Trevelyan, II*, pp. 90-109.

10. Parris, pp. 168, 172.

Chapter 38: The Armistice of Villafranca

1. Mack Smith, *Cavour*, p. 174.

2. Parris, p. 174.

3. *Trevelyan, II*, p. 113.

4. Parris, p. 174.

5. Ridley, pp. 409-411.

Chapter 39: Command of Intrigue

1. Parris, p. 176.

2. Parris, p. 188; *Mack Smith, I*, p. 80.

3. *Trevelyan, II*, p. 120; Parris, pp. 180-181; Ridley, p. 418.

4. Ridley, p. 418.

5. *Trevelyan, II*, p. 121.

Chapter 40: Giuseppina Raimondi

1. Parris, pp. 196-197; Ridley, pp. 426-427.

2. *Mack Smith, I*, p. 84.

3. Parris, p. 197.

4. Parris, pp. 197-198.

5. Ridley, p. 428.

6. Parris, p. 199.

7. Quoted in Parris, p. 198; Ridley, p. 429.

Chapter 41: Nice and Savoy

1. Mack Smith, *Cavour*, p. 206.
2. Parris, p. 205.
3. Mack Smith, *Cavour*, p. 204.
4. *Trevelyan, II*, p. 176.
5. Ridley, p. 432.
6. Mack Smith, *Cavour*, pp. 206-207.

Chapter 42: The Expedition of the Thousand

1. *Trevelyan, II*, pp. 45-46.
2. Quoted in *Trevelyan, II*, pp. 52-53.
3. Viotti, p. 94.
4. *Trevelyan, II*, p. 180.
5. Viotti, p. 89.
6. Ridley, p. 436.
7. Viotti, p. 88.
8. *Trevelyan, II*, pp. 120-121.
9. *Trevelyan, II*, pp. 214-215; Viotti, p. 90.
10. Viotti, p. 90.
11. Quoted in Ridley, p. 440.
12. Ridley, p. 441.

Chapter 43: The Landing at Marsala, May 11, 1860

1. Parris, p. 221.
2. Ridley, p. 446.
3. *Trevelyan, II*, p. 250.
4. Viotti, p. 95.
5. *Trevelyan, II*, p. 242.

Chapter 44: Liberation of Sicily

1. Viotti, p. 96.
2. *Trevelyan, II*, p. 258.

3. Ridley, p. 449.
4. Viotti, pp. 99-100.
5. Ridley, p. 450.
6. Viotti, p. 103.
7. G. M. Trevelyan, *Garibaldi and the Making of Italy* (UK, 1911) (cited as *Trevelyan, III*), 34.
8. Viotti, p. 107.

Chapter 45: The Dictatorship

1. *Mack Smith, II*, p. 44.
2. *Trevelyan, III*, p. 64.
3. Parris, pp. 224-225.
4. *Mack Smith, I*, pp. 98-99.
5. *Trevelyan, III*, pp. 58-59.
6. Quoted in Ridley, p. 455.
7. Ridley, p. 475.
8. The formation of the various foreign legions is described in Viotti, p. 111.
9. Viotti, p. 110.
10. *Mack Smith, I*, p. 99.
11. *Trevelyan, III*, p. 63.
12. Viotti, p. 112.

Chapter 46: Battle of Milazzo

1. Viotti, p. 124.
2. *Trevelyan, III*, p. 80.
3. *Trevelyan, III*, p. 86; Parris, p. 238.
4. Ridley, p. 467.
5. *Trevelyan, III*, pp. 92-95.
6. Parris, p. 96.
7. Viotti, p. 115.
8. *Trevelyan, III*, pp. 96-97.

Chapter 47: The Road to Naples

1. *Trevelyan, III*, pp. 103-109.
2. Parris, pp. 233-234; Ridley, pp. 463-464.
3. Parris, p. 234.
4. Parris, p. 235.
5. *Trevelyan, II*, pp. 57-58; Ridley, p. 465.
6. Parris, p. 236.
7. Ridley, p. 478.
8. Mack Smith, *Cavour*, p. 210.
9. Parris, p. 243.
10. Quoted in Ridley, p. 466.
11. Ridley, pp. 456-457.
12. *Trevelyan, III*, pp. 101-103.
13. For Garibaldi's invasion of the Italian mainland, see *Trevelyan, III*, pp. 126-138; Parris, pp. 246-247; Ridley, pp. 479-480; Viotti, pp. 116-117.
14. For Garibaldi's march on Naples, see *Trevelyan, III*, pp. 144- 149; Ridley, pp. 481-482.
15. *Trevelyan, III*, pp. 17-19, Ridley, p. 483.
16. *Trevelyan, III*, pp. 149-150.

Chapter 48: Defeat of the Bourbons

1. Quoted in *Trevelyan, III*, p. 177.
2. *Mack Smith, I*, p. 104.
3. *Trevelyan, III*, pp. 183-184.
4. Ridley, p. 485.
5. *Trevelyan III*, p. 184.
6. *Trevelyan III*, p. 195.
7. Parris, p. 251.
8. Ridley, p. 499.

Chapter 49: Battle of the Volturno: Autumn of 1860

1. Ridley, p. 489.
2. Mack Smith, *Cavour*, p. 226.
3. For Türr's defeat at Caiazzo, see *Trevelyan, III*, pp. 228-231; Viotti, p. 122.
4. Quoted from *Trevelyan, III*, p. 237.
5. *Trevelyan, III*, p. 241; Ridley, p. 498.
6. Ridley, p. 498.
7. Viotti, p. 128.
8. Quoted in Viotti, p. 129.
9. Parris, p. 259.
10. Mack Smith, *Cavour*, p. 227.

Chapter 50: End of the Dictatorship

1. Mack Smith, *Cavour*, p. 226.
2. Viotti, pp. 121-122.
3. Ridley, p. 503.
4. *Trevelyan III*, pp. 265-266.
5. Quoted in *Trevelyan, III*, p. 266.
6. Ridley, p. 505.
7. Parris, p. 259.
8. Quoted in *Trevelyan, III*, p. 271; Parris, p. 259; Ridley, p. 506.
9. Quoted in Parris, p. 260.
10. *Trevelyan, III*, pp. 274-275.
11. *Trevelyan, III*, p. 278; Parris, p. 260; Ridley, p. 507.
12. Ridley, p. 507.
13. Ridley, p. 506.
14. Ridley, pp. 506-507.
15. Ridley, p. 508.
16. Parris, p. 261.
17. Viotti, p. 129.

18. Viotti, p. 131.

Chapter 51: Garibaldi on Caprera: 1860–1861

1. *Mack Smith, I*, p. 112.
2. *Mack Smith, I*, p. 67.
3. *Mack Smith, I*, p. 66.
4. *Mack Smith, I*, p. 113.
5. *Mack Smith, I*, p. 112.
6. *Mack Smith, I*, p. 59.
7. Melena, *Recollections*, p. 43.
8. Ridley, pp. 511-512.
9. Ridley, p. 512.
10. Quoted in Viotti, p. 135.
11. Ridley, p. 522.
12. Parris, pp. 269-270.

Chapter 52: The Return of Garibaldi: Spring of 1861

1. Mack Smith, *Cavour*, pp. 229-231.
2. For a description of the melee in Parliament, see Parris, pp. 266-267; Ridley, pp. 518-519.
3. *Mack Smith, I*, p. 118.
4. Parris, p. 267.
5. Quoted in Ridley, p. 520.
6. Mack Smith, *Cavour*, p. 272.
7. For the reaction to Cavour's death, see Mack Smith, *Cavour*, pp. 272-273.
8. For British comments on Cavour, see Mack Smith, *Cavour*, p. 274.
9. Ridley, p. 529.
10. *Mack Smith, I*, p. 123.

Chapter 53: The March on Rome:

Summer of 1862

1. Quoted in *Mack Smith, I*, p. 129.
2. Parris, p. 277; Ridley, p. 534.
3. Quoted in Ridley, p. 535.
4. *Mack Smith, I*, p. 130.
5. *Mack Smith, I*, p. 131.
6. Parris, p. 278.
7. Quoted in Parris, p. 279; Ridley, p. 538.
8. Ridley, p. 540.
9. Parris, p. 280.
10. For a description of the surgery on Garibaldi's ankle, see Parris, pp. 282-283; *Mack Smith, II*, p. 137.
11. *Mack Smith, II*, p. 138.
12. *Mack Smith, I*, p. 136.

Chapter 54: Garibaldi Visits England: 1864

1. Ridley, pp. 562-563.
2. Ridley, pp. 376-377.
3. Quoted in Parris, p. 286.
4. *Trevelyan, III*, p. 289.
5. Parris, p. 288; Ridley, p. 549.
6. Viotti, p. 144.
7. Ridley, p. 560.
8. Quoted in *Mack Smith, I*, p. 141.
9. Quoted in Parris, p. 289.
10. Quoted in Ridley, p. 551.
11. Parris, p. 289.
12. Quoted in *Mack Smith, I*, p. 140-141.
13. Quoted in *Mack Smith, I*, p. 140.
14. Quoted in Ridley, p. 552.
15. *Mack Smith, II*, p. 75; Parris, p. 290.

16. Quoted in Parris, p. 290.

17. Quoted in Ridley, p. 559.

18. Ridley, p. 560.

19. Quoted in *Mack Smith, I,* pp. 145-146.

20. Parris, p. 291.

21. Ridley, p. 562.

Chapter 55: *Venetia Joins Italy: 1866*

1. Quoted in Viotti, p. 152.

2. Ridley, p. 570.

3. Quoted in Parris, p. 300.

4. Viotti, p. 153.

5. Quoted in Ridley, p. 574.

Chapter 56: *The Defeat at Mentana: 1867*

1. Viotti, *op. cit,* outlines Garibaldi's motion to the International Congress for Peace on p. 156.

2. Quoted in Viotti, p. 155.

3. *Ibid.*

4. For details of Garibaldi's daring escape from Caprera, see Ridley, pp. 583-585.

5. Viotti, p. 164.

6. *Mack Smith, I,* p. 166.

7. *Mack Smith, I,* p. 162.

8. Ridley, pp. 586-587.

9. Quoted in Ridley, p. 588.

10. *Ibid.*

11. Viotti, p. 167.

12. Quoted in Ridley, p. 589.

13. Ridley, p. 590.

Chapter 57: *The Army of the Vosges: 1870*

1. Quoted in Ridley, p. 624.

2. Quoted in Ridley, p. 605.

3. Quoted in Viotti, p. 177.

4. Quoted in Parris, p. 313.

5. Parris, p. 313.

6. Parris, p. 314.

7. Quoted in Viotti, p. 182.

8. Viotti, p. 183.

9. Garibaldi's appearance before the French National Assembly is described in Ridley, pp. 614-615.

10. Quoted in Viotti, p. 182.

Chapter 58: *Retirement on Caprera: 1871*

1. Parris, p. 322.

2. Viotti, p. 186.

3. Quoted in Parris, p. 322.

4. Viotti, pp. 186-187.

5. Parris, p. 323.

Chapter 59: *Death of Garibaldi*

1. Ridley, p. 631.

2. Ridley, p. 632.

3. Parris, p. 321.

4. Ridley, p. 633.

5. Quoted in Ridley, p. 634.

6. Viotti, p. 210.

7. Viotti, pp. 214-215.

Bibliography

Blanchard, Paula. *Margaret Fuller, From Transcendentalism to Revolution.* New York: Delacorte Press / Seymour Lawrence, 1978.

Crow, John A. "Juan Manual de Rosas: Tyrant of the Argentine" (In *The Epic of Latin America*). Garden City, New York: Doubleday & Co., Inc., 1946.

Dumas, Alexandre. *The Memoirs of Garibaldi*, trans. R. S. Garnett. London: Ernest Benn, Ltd., 1931 (cited as "Dumas").

Dwight, Theodore. (See Giuseppe Garibaldi, *The Life of General Garibaldi*.)

Garibaldi, Giuseppe. *The Life of General Garibaldi*, trans. Theodore Dwight. New York: Barnes and Burr, 1859 (cited as *Dwight*).

————. *My Life*, trans. Stephen Parkin. London: Hesperus Press, 2004.

Garnett, R. S. (See Dumas, *The Memoirs of Garibaldi*.)

Lewis, Daniel K. *The History of Argentina.* Westport, CT: Greenwood Press, 2001.

Library of Congress, Federal Research Division. *Uruguay, A Country Study* (2nd ed.). Washington, DC: n. p., 1992 (cited as "Uruguay, A Country Study").

Mack Smith, Denis. *Garibaldi: A Great Life in Brief.* New York: Alfred

A. Knopf, Inc., 1956 (cited as *Mack Smith, I*).

_____. *Garibaldi: Great Lives Observed.* Englewood Cliffs, NJ: Prentice Hall, Inc., 1969 (cited as *Mack Smith, II*).

_____. *Cavour.* New York: Alfred A. Knopf, Inc., 1985 (cited as Mack Smith, *Cavour*).

_____. *Modern Italy: A Political History.* Ann Arbor, MI: University of Michigan Press, 1997 (cited as *Mack Smith, Modern Italy*).

Mario, Jessie White. *Garibaldi e I suoi tempi* (3rd ed.). Milano: Fratelli Treves, 1887.

Maurois, Andre. *Alexandre Dumas: A Great Life in Brief.* New York: Alfred A. Knopf, Inc., 1966.

Melina, Elpis. *Garibaldi's Memoirs* (Anthony Campanella, Ed). Sarasota, FL: International Institute of Garibaldian Studies, 1981 (cited as "Melina.").

_____. *Garibaldi: Recollections of his Public and Private Life.* London: Trüber and Co., 1887 (cited as "Melena, Recollections").

Parris, John. *The Lion of Caprera.* New York: David McKay Company, Inc., 1962.

Ridley, Jasper. *G. Garibaldi.* New York: The Viking Press, Inc., 1976.

Schopp, Claude. *Alexandre Dumas: Genius of Life* (trans. A. J. Koch).

New York: Franklin Watts, 1988.

Scobie, James R. *Argentina, a City and a Nation* (2nd ed.). New York: Oxford University Press, 1971.

Trevelyan, George M. *Garibaldi's Defence of the Roman Republic*. London: Longmans, Green, 1907 (cited as "Trevelyan, I").

——————. *Garibaldi and the Thousand*. London: Longmans, Green, and Co., 1909 (cited as "Trevelyan, II").

——————. *Garibaldi and the Making of Italy*. London: Longmans, Green, and Co., 1909 (cited as "Trevelyan, III").

Trevelyan, Janet P. *A Short History of the Italian People* (rev. ed., with an epilogue by Denis Mack Smith). New York: Pitman Publishing Corp., 1959.

Valerio, Anthony. *Anita Garibaldi: A Biography*. Westport, CT: Praeger Publishers, 2001.

Viotti, Andrea. *Garibaldi, the Revolutionary and His Men*. London: Blandford Press, Ltd., 1979.

Watson, James. "A Woman Beyond Her Time." *Italy, Italy*, XX (December 2002-January 2003), 48-51.

Werner, A. (Trans.). *Autobiography of Giuseppe Garibaldi* (with a supplement by Jessie White Mario). London: Smith and Innes, 1889 (cited as "Werner").

Index